Natural Computing Series

Series Editors: G. Rozenberg
Th. Bäck A.E. Eiben J.N. Kok H.P. Spaink

Leiden Center for Natural Computing

Springer
Berlin
Heidelberg
New York
Hong Kong
London
Milan
Paris
Tokyo

A.E. Eiben • J.E. Smith

Introduction to Evolutionary Computing

With 73 Figures and 29 Tables

 Springer

Prof. Dr. A.E. Eiben
Faculty of Sciences
Vrije Universiteit Amsterdam
De Boelelaan 1081a
1081 HV Amsterdam
The Netherlands
gusz@cs.vu.nl

Dr. J.E. Smith
Faculty of Computing,
Engineering
and Mathematical Sciences
University of the West of England
Bristol, BS16 1QY
U.K.

Series Editors

G. Rozenberg (Managing Editor)
rozenber@liacs.nl
Th. Bäck, J.N. Kok, H.P. Spaink

Leiden Center for Natural Computing
Leiden University
Niels Bohrweg 1
2333 CA Leiden, The Netherlands

A.E. Eiben
Vrije Universiteit Amsterdam

Library of Congress Cataloging-in-Publication Data

Eiben, Agoston E.
    Introduction to evolutinary computing/A.E. Eiben, J.E. Smith.
        p. cm. - (Natural computing series)
    Includes bibliographical references and index.
    ISBN 3-540-40184-9 (alk. paper)
        1. Evolutionary programming (Computer science) 2. Evolutionary computation.
    I. Smith, J. E. (James E.), 1964- II. Title. III. Series.

QA76.618.E33 2003
006.3–dc22   2003057316

ACM Computing Classification (1998): I.2, I.2.8, I.2.6

ISBN 3-540-40184-9 Springer-Verlag Berlin Heidelberg New York

Springer-Verlag Berlin Heidelberg New York,
a member of BertelsmannSpringer Science+Business Media GmbH
http://www.springer.de

© Springer-Verlag Berlin Heidelberg 2003
Printed in Germany

Cover Design: KünkelLopka, Werbeagentur, Heidelberg
Typesetting: Camera ready by the authors
45/3142 – 5 4 3 2 1 0 – Printed on acid-free paper

GE: To my beloved wife Daphne

JS: To Cally and Jasper, constant sources of inspiration

Preface

This book is primarily a textbook for lecturers and graduate and undergraduate students. To this group the book offers a thorough introduction to evolutionary computing (EC), including the basics of all traditional variants (evolution strategies, evolutionary programming, genetic algorithms, and genetic programming); EC themes of general interest (such as algorithm parameter control, or constraint handling); a collection of particular EC techniques (e.g., niching, or coevolution); and an outlook to related areas (evolutionary art). This book is also meant for those who wish to apply EC to a particular problem or within a given application area. To this group the book is valuable because it presents EC as something to be *used*, rather than just being studied, and it contains an explicit treatment of guidelines for good experimentation. Last, but not least, this book contains information on the current state of the art in a wide range of subjects that are interesting to fellow researchers as quick reference on subjects outside of their own specialist field of evolutionary computing.

The motivation behind the book is education oriented. Both authors have many years of teaching experience, that is, have taught EC many times, not only within the context context of a university, but also at EC-related summer schools for doctoral students, and at commercial courses for practitioners from business and industry. The lack of one good textbook that covers all necessary aspects of EC, contains the factual knowledge but also paying attention to the skills needed to use this technology has been repeatedly experienced. This resulted in a joint effort to fill this gap and produce the textbook both authors felt was missing. The educative role of the book is emphasised by the following features:

1. There are example applications in each chapter, except the chapter on theory.
2. Each chapter closes with exercises and a list of recommended further reading.
3. The book has a supporting a Web site with identical copies at:

- `www.cs.vu.nl/~gusz/ecbook/ecbook.html`
- `www.cems.uwe.ac.uk/~jsmith/ecbook/ecbook.html`

4. On this Web site we outline a full academic course based on this material.
5. There are slides to each chapter on the Web in PowerPoint and in PDF format. These slides can be freely downloaded and used to teach the material covered in the book.
6. All illustrations used on the slides are available separately from the Web as source (editable), PostScript, and JPG files. These enable readers to use and reuse them and to create their own versions for their own slides.
7. Furthermore, the Web site offers more exercises, answers to the exercises, downloadables for easy experimentation, errata, and a discussion group.

Writing this book would not have been possible without the support of many. In the first place, we wish to express our gratitude to Daphne and Cally for their patience, understanding, and tolerance. Without their support this book could not have been written. Furthermore, we acknowledge the help of our colleagues within EvoNet and the EC community. We are especially grateful to Larry Bull, Maarten Keijzer, Nat Krasnogor, Ben Paechter, Günter Raidl, Rob Smith, and Dirk Thierens for their comments on earlier versions of this book. The people in our departments also deserve a word of thanks for their support. Finally, Gusz Eiben wishes to thank András Lörincz and the ELTE University in Budapest for providing the facilities needed to finalise the camera ready copy during his stay in Hungary.
We wish everybody a pleasant and fruitful time reading and using this book.

Amsterdam, Bristol, Budapest, July 2003

Gusz Eiben and Jim Smith

Contents

1

Introduction

1.1 Aims of this Chapter

This chapter provides the reader with the basics for studying evolutionary computing (EC) through this book. We give a brief history of the field of evolutionary computing, and an introduction to some of the biological processes that have served as inspiration and that have provided a rich source of ideas and metaphors to researchers. We pay a great deal of attention to motivations for working with and studying evolutionary computing methods. We suggest a division of the sorts of problems that one might wish to tackle with sophisticated search methods into three main classes, and give an example of where EC was successfully applied in each of these.

1.2 The Main Evolutionary Computing Metaphor

Evolutionary computing is a research area within computer science. As the name suggests, it is a special flavour of computing, which draws inspiration from the process of natural evolution. That some computer scientists have chosen natural evolution as a source of inspiration is not surprising, for the power of evolution in nature is evident in the diverse species that make up our world, with each tailored to survive well in its own niche. The fundamental metaphor of evolutionary computing relates this powerful natural evolution to a particular style of problem solving – that of trial-and-error.

Descriptions of relevant fragments of evolutionary theory and genetics are given later on. For the time being let us consider natural evolution simply as follows. A given environment is filled with a population of individuals that strive for survival and reproduction. The fitness of these individuals – determined by the environment – relates to how well they succeed in achieving their goals, i.e., it represents their chances of survival and multiplying. In the context of a stochastic trial-and-error (also known as generate-and-test) style problem solving process, we have a collection of candidate solutions. Their quality (that is, how well they solve the problem) determines the chance that they will be kept and used as seeds for constructing further candidate solutions (Table 1.1).

Evolution	Problem solving
Environment ⟷	Problem
Individual ⟷	Candidate solution
Fitness ⟷	Quality

Table 1.1. The basic evolutionary computing metaphor linking natural evolution to problem solving

1.3 Brief History

Surprisingly enough, this idea of applying Darwinian principles to automated problem solving dates back to the forties, long before the breakthrough of computers [146]. As early as 1948, Turing proposed "genetical or evolutionary search", and by 1962 Bremermann had actually executed computer experiments on "optimization through evolution and recombination". During the 1960s three different implementations of the basic idea were developed in different places. In the USA, Fogel, Owens, and Walsh introduced **evolutionary programming** [155, 156], while Holland called his method a **genetic algorithm** [98, 202, 204]. Meanwhile, in Germany, Rechenberg and Schwefel invented **evolution strategies** [317, 342]. For about 15 years these areas developed separately; but since the early 1990s they have been viewed as different representatives ("dialects") of one technology that has come to be known as **evolutionary computing** [22, 27, 28, 120, 271]. In the early 1990s a fourth stream following the general ideas emerged, **genetic programming**, championed by Koza [38, 229, 230]. The contemporary terminology denotes the whole field by evolutionary computing, the algorithms involved are termed **evolutionary algorithms**, and it considers evolutionary programming, evolution strategies, genetic algorithms, and genetic programming as subareas belonging to the corresponding algorithm variants.

The development of scientific forums devoted to EC gives an indication of the field's past and present. The first international conference specialising in the subject was the *International Conference on Genetic Algorithms* (ICGA), first held in 1985 [180] and repeated every second year until 1997 [182, 333, 43, 158, 137, 23].[1] In 1999 it merged with the *Annual Conference on Genetic Programming* [235, 234, 232] to become the annual *Genetic and Evolutionary*

---

[1] Please note that these and the other conferences are ordered historically rather than alphabetically by editor.

Computation Conference (GECCO) [37, 416, 381, 242]. At the same time the *Annual Conference on Evolutionary Programming*, held since 1992, [150, 151, 344, 268, 154, 12, 307] merged with the *IEEE Conference on Evolutionary Computation*, held since 1994, [210, 211, 212, 213, 214] to form the *Congress on Evolutionary Computation* (CEC) which has been held annually ever since [71, 72, 73, 74].

The first European event (explicitly set up to embrace all streams) was the *Parallel Problem Solving from Nature* (PPSN) in 1990 [343], which has became a biannual conference [259, 90, 410, 116, 337, 187]. It was in a panel discussion during the first PPSN that the name evolutionary computing was offered as an umbrella term for all existing "dialects". *Evolutionary Computation* (MIT Press), the first scientific journal devoted to this field, was launched in 1993. In 1997 the European Commission decided to fund a European research network in EC, called EvoNet, whose funds are guaranteed until 2003. At the time of writing (2003), there are three major EC conferences (CEC, GECCO, and PPSN) and many smaller ones, including one dedicated exclusively to theoretical analysis and development, *Foundations of Genetic Algorithms* (FOGA) – held biannually since 1990 [316, 420, 425, 44, 39, 261, 308]. By now there are three core scientific EC journals (*Evolutionary Computation, IEEE Transactions on Evolutionary Computation*, and *Genetic Programming and Evolvable Machines*) and many with a closely related profile, e.g., on natural computing, soft computing, or computational intelligence. We estimate the number of EC publications in 2003 at somewhere over 1500 – many of them in journals and proceedings of specific application areas.

1.4 The Inspiration from Biology

1.4.1 Darwinian Evolution

Darwin's theory of evolution [86] offers an explanation of the biological diversity and its underlying mechanisms. In what is sometimes called the macroscopic view of evolution, natural selection plays a central role. Given an environment that can host only a limited number of individuals, and the basic instinct of individuals to reproduce, selection becomes inevitable if the population size is not to grow exponentially. Natural selection favours those individuals that compete for the given resources most effectively, in other words, those that are adapted or fit to the environmental conditions best. This phenomenon is also known as **survival of the fittest**. Competition-based selection is one of the two cornerstones of evolutionary progress. The other primary force identified by Darwin results from phenotypic variations among members of the population. Phenotypic traits (see also Sect. 1.4.2) are those behavioural and physical features of an individual that directly affect its response to the environment (including other individuals), thus determining its fitness. Each individual represents a unique combination of phenotypic traits that is evaluated by the environment. If it evaluates favourably, then it is propagated via the individual's offspring, otherwise it is discarded by dying without offspring. Darwin's insight was that small, random variations – mutations – in phenotypic traits occur during reproduction from generation to generation. Through these variations, new combinations of traits occur and get evaluated. The best ones survive and reproduce, and so evolution progresses. To summarise this basic model, a population consists of a number of individuals. These individuals are the "units of selection", that is to say that their reproductive success depends on how well they are adapted to their environment relative to the rest of the population. As the more successful individuals reproduce, occasional mutations give rise to new individuals to be tested. Thus, as time passes, there is a change in the constitution of the population, i.e., the population is the "unit of evolution".

This process is well captured by the intuitive metaphor of an **adaptive landscape** or adaptive surface [431]. On this landscape the height dimension belongs to fitness: high altitude stands for high fitness. The other two (or more, in the general case) dimensions correspond to biological traits as shown in Fig. 1.1. The $x-y$-plane holds all possible trait combinations, the z-values

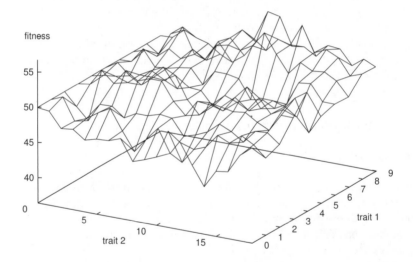

Fig. 1.1. Illustration of Wright's adaptive landscape with two traits

show their fitnesses. Hence, each peak represents a range of successful trait combinations, while troughs belong to less fit combinations. A given population can be plotted as a set of points on this landscape, where each dot is one individual realizing a possible trait combination. Evolution is then the process of gradual advances of the population to high-altitude areas, powered by variation and natural selection. Our familiarity with the physical landscape on which we exist naturally leads us to the concept of **multimodal problems**.

These are problems in which there are a number of points that are better than all their neighbouring solutions. We call each of these points a **local optimum** and denote the highest of these as the **global optimum**. A problem in which there is only one point that is fitter than all of its neighbours is known as **unimodal**.

The link with an optimisation process is as straightforward as misleading, because evolution is not a unidirectional uphill process [99]. Because the population has a finite size, and random choices are made in the selection and variation operators, it is common to observe the phenomenon of **genetic drift**, whereby highly fit individuals may be lost from the population, or the population may suffer from a loss of variety concerning some traits. One of the effects of this is that populations can "melt down" the hill, and enter low-fitness valleys. The combined global effects of drift and selection enable populations to move uphill as well as downhill, and of course there is no guarantee that the population will climb back up the same hill. Escaping from locally optimal regions is hereby possible, and according to Wright's "shifting balance" theory the maximum of a fixed landscape can be reached.

1.4.2 Genetics

The microscopic view of natural evolution is offered by the discipline of molecular genetics. It sheds light on the processes below the level of visible phenotypic features, in particular relating to heredity. The fundamental observation from genetics is that each individual is a dual entity: its phenotypic properties (outside) are represented at a low genotypic level (inside). In other words, an individual's **genotype** encodes its **phenotype**. **Genes** are the functional units of inheritance encoding phenotypic characteristics. In natural systems this encoding is not one-to-one: one gene might affect more phenotypic traits (**pleitropy**) and in turn, one phenotypic trait can be determined by more than one gene (**polygeny**). Phenotypic variations are always caused by genotypic variations, which in turn are the consequences of mutations of genes or recombination of genes by sexual reproduction.

Another way to think of this is that the genotype contains all the information necessary to build the particular phenotype. The term **genome** stands for the complete genetic information of a living being containing its total building plan. This genetic material, that is, all genes of an organism, is arranged in several chromosomes; there are 46 in humans. Higher life forms (many plants and animals) contain a double complement of chromosomes in most of their cells, and such cells – and the host organisms – are called **diploid**. Thus the chromosomes in human diploid cells are arranged into 23 pairs. **Gametes** (i.e., sperm and egg cells) contain only one single complement of chromosomes and are called **haploid**. The combination of paternal and maternal features in the offspring of diploid organisms is a consequence of fertilisation by a fusion of such gametes: the haploid sperm cell merges with the haploid egg cell and forms a diploid cell, the zygote. In the zygote, each chromosome pair is formed by a paternal and a maternal half. The new organism develops from this zygote by the process named **ontogenesis**, which does not change the genetic information of the cells. Consequently, all body cells of a diploid organism contain the same genetic information as the zygote it originates from.

In evolutionary computing, the combination of features from two individuals in offspring is often called crossover. It is important to note that this is not analogous to the working of diploid organisms, where **crossing-over** is not a process during mating and fertilisation, but rather happens during the formation of gametes, a process called meiosis.

Meiosis is a special type of cell division that ensures that gametes contain only one copy of each chromosome. As said above, a diploid body cell contains chromosome pairs, where one half of the pair is identical to the paternal chromosome from the sperm cell, and the other half is identical to the maternal chromosome from the egg cell. During meiosis a chromosome pair first aligns physically, that is, the copies of the paternal and maternal chromosomes, which form the pair, move together and stick to each other at a special position (the centromere, not indicated, see Fig. 1.2, left). In the second step the chromosomes double so that four strands (called chromatids) are aligned (Fig. 1.2, middle). The actual crossing-over takes place between the two inner strands that break at a random point and exchange parts (Fig. 1.2, right). The result is four different copies of the chromosome in question, of

Fig. 1.2. Three steps in the (simplified) meiosis procedure regarding one chromosome

which two are identical to the original parental chromosomes, and two are new recombinations of paternal and maternal material. This provides enough genetic material to form four haploid gametes, which is done via a random arrangement of one copy of each chromosome. Thus in the newly created gametes the genome is composed of chromosomes that are either identical to one of the parent chromosomes, or recombinants. It is clear that the resulting four haploid gametes are usually different from both original parent genomes, facilitating genotypic variation in offspring.

In the late 19th century Mendel first investigated and understood heredity in diploid organisms. Modern genetics has added many details to his early picture, but today we are still very far from understanding the whole genetic process. What we do know is that all life on Earth is based on DNA – the famous double helix of nucleotides encoding the whole organism be it a plant, animal, or *Homo Sapiens*. Triplets of nucleotides form so-called codons, each of which codes for a specific amino acid. The genetic code (the translation table from the $4^3 = 64$ possible codons to the 20 amino acids from which proteins are created) is universal, that is, it is the same for all life on Earth. This fact is generally acknowledged as strong evidence that the whole biosphere has the same origin. Genes are larger structures on the DNA, containing many codons, carrying the code of proteins. The path from DNA to protein consists of two main components. In the first step, called transcription, information from the DNA is written to RNA; the step from RNA to protein is called translation (Fig. 1.3).

Fig. 1.3. The pathway from DNA to protein via transcription and translation

It is one of the principal dogmas of molecular genetics that this information flow is only one-way. Speaking in terms of genotypes and phenotypes, this means that phenotypic features cannot influence genotypic information. This refutes earlier theories (for instance, that of Lamarck), which asserted that features acquired during an individual's lifetime could be passed on to its offspring via inheritance. A consequence of this view is that changes in the genetic material of a population can only arise from random variations and natural selection and definitely not from individual learning. It is important to understand that all variations (mutation and recombination) happen at the genotypic level, while selection is based on actual performance in a given environment, that is, at the phenotypic level.

1.5 Evolutionary Computing: Why?

Developing automated problem solvers (that is, algorithms) is one of the central themes of mathematics and computer science. Similarly to engineering, where looking at Nature's solutions has always been a source of inspiration, copying "natural problem solvers" is a stream within these disciplines. When looking for the most powerful natural problem solver, there are two rather straightforward candidates:

- The human brain (that created "the wheel, New York, wars and so on" [4][chapter 23])
- The evolutionary process (that created the human brain)

Trying to design problem solvers based on the first answer leads to the field of neurocomputing. The second answer forms a basis for evolutionary computing.

Another motivation can be identified from a technical perspective. Computerisation in the second half of the twentieth century has created a rapidly growing demand for problem-solving automation. The growth rate of the research and development capacity has not kept pace with these needs. Hence, the time available for thorough problem analysis and tailored algorithm design has been, and still is, decreasing. A parallel trend has been the increase in the complexity of problems to be solved. These two trends, and the constraint of limited capacity, imply an urgent need for robust algorithms with satisfactory performance. That is, there is a need for algorithms that are applicable to a wide range of problems, do not need much tailoring for specific problems, and deliver good (not necessarily optimal) solutions within acceptable time. Evolutionary algorithms do all this, and provide therefore an answer to the challenge of deploying automated solution methods for more and more problems, which are more and more complex, in less and less time.

A third motivation is one that can be found behind every science: human curiosity. Evolutionary processes are the subjects of scientific studies where the main objective is to understand how evolution works. From this perspective, evolutionary computing represents the possibility of performing experiments differently from traditional biology. Evolutionary processes can be simulated in a computer, where millions of generations can be executed in a matter of hours or days and repeated under various circumstances. These possibilities go far beyond studies based on excavations and fossils, or those possible *in vivo*. Naturally, the interpretation of such simulation experiments must be done very carefully. First, because we do not know whether the computer models represent the biological reality with sufficient fidelity. Second, it is unclear whether conclusions drawn in a digital medium, *in silico*, can be transferred to the carbon-based biological medium. These caveats and the lack of mutual awareness between biologists and computer scientists are probably the reason why there are few computer experimental studies about fundamental issues of biological evolution. Nevertheless, there is a strong tradition within evolutionary computing to "play around" with evolution for the sake of understanding how it works. Application issues do not play a role here, at least not in the short term. But of course, learning more about evolutionary algorithms in general can help in designing better algorithms later.

In the following we illustrate the power of the evolutionary approach to automated problem solving by a number of application examples from various areas. To position these and other applications, let us sketch a systems analysis perspective to problems. From this perspective we identify three main components of a working system: inputs, outputs, and the internal model connecting these two. Knowing the model means knowing how the system works. In this case it is possible to compute the systems response – the output – to any given input. Based on this view we can simply distinguish three types of problems, depending on which of the three system components is unknown.

- In an **optimisation** problem the model is known, together with the desired output, (or a description of the desired output) and the task is to find the input(s) leading to this output (Fig. 1.4). An example is the travelling salesman problem (in which we have to find the shortest tour around a number of cities), where we have a formula (the model) that for each given tour (the inputs) will compute the length of the tour (the output). The desired output property is optimality, that is, minimal length, and we are looking for inputs realising this.

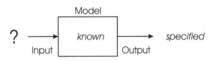

Fig. 1.4. Optimisation problems

- In a **modelling** or **system identification** problem, corresponding sets of inputs and outputs are known, and a model of the system is sought that delivers the correct output for each known input (Fig. 1.5). Let us take the stock exchange as an example, where the Dow-Jones index is seen as output, and some economic and societal indices (e.g., the unemployment rate, gold price, euro-dollar exchange rate, etc.) form the input. The task is now to find a formula that links the known inputs to the known outputs, thereby representing a model of this economic system. If one can find a correct model for the known data (from the past) and if we have good reasons to believe that the relationships enclosed in this model remain true, then we have a prediction tool for the value of the Dow-Jones index given new data.

Fig. 1.5. Modelling or system identification problems

- In a **simulation** problem we know the system model and some inputs, and need to compute the outputs corresponding to these inputs (Fig. 1.6). As an example, think of an electronic circuit for signal filtering, say a filter cutting low frequencies. Our model is a complex system of formulas (equations and inequalities) describing the working of the circuit. For any given input signal this model can compute the output signal. Using this model (for instance, to compare two circuit designs) is much cheaper than building the circuit and measuring its properties in the physical world.

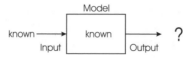

Fig. 1.6. Simulation problems

A good example of a challenging optimisation task that has successfully been carried out by evolutionary algorithms is the timetabling of university classes [70, 296]. Typically, some 2000–5000 events take place during a university week, and these must each be given a day, time, and room. The first optimisation task is to reduce the number of clashes, for example, a student needing to be in two places at once, or a room being used for two lectures at the same time. Producing feasible timetables (those with no clashes) is not an insignificant task, since the vast majority of the space of all timetables is filled with infeasible solutions. In addition to producing feasible timetables, we also want to produce timetables that are optimised as far as the users are concerned. This optimisation task involves considering a large number of objectives that compete with each other. For example, students may wish to have no more than two classes in a row, while their lecturers may be more concerned with having whole days free for conducting research. Meanwhile, the main goal of the university management might be to make room utilisation more efficient, or to cut down the amount of movement around or between the buildings.

EC applications in industrial design optimisation can be illustrated with the case of a satellite dish holder boom. This ladder-like construction connects the satellite's body with the dish needed for communication. It is essential that this boom is stable, in particular vibration resistant, as there is no air in space that would damp vibrations that could break the whole construction. Keane et al. [225] optimised this construction by an evolutionary algorithm. The resulting structure is by 20,000% (!) better than traditional shapes, but for humans it looks very strange: it exhibits no symmetry, and there is not any intuitive design logic visible (Fig. 1.7). The final design looks pretty much like a random drawing, and the crucial thing is this: it *is* a random drawing, drawn without intelligence, but evolving through a number of consecutive generations of improving solutions. This illustrates the power of evolution as a designer: it is not limited by conventions, aesthetic considerations, or ungrounded preferences for symmetry. On the contrary, it is purely driven by quality, and thereby it can come to solutions that lie outside of the scope of human thinking, with its implicit and unconscious limitations. It is worth mentioning that evolutionary design often goes hand-in-hand with reverse engineering. In particular, once a provably superior solution is evolved, it can be analysed and explained through the eyes of traditional engineering. This

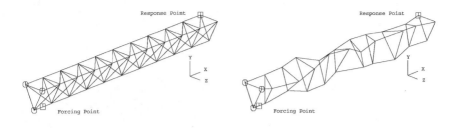

Fig. 1.7. The initial, regular design of the 3D boom (*left*) and the final design found by a genetic algorithm (*right*)

can lead to generalisable knowledge, i.e., the formulation of new laws, theories, or design principles applicable to a variety of other problems of similar type.[2]

Modelling tasks typically occur in data-rich environments. A frequently encountered situation is the presence of many examples of a certain event or phenomenon without a formal description. For instance, a bank may have one million client records (profiles) containing their socio–geographical data, financial overviews of their mortgages, loans, and insurances, details of their card usage, and so forth. Certainly, the bank also has information about client behaviour in terms of paying back loans, for instance. In this situation it is a reasonable assumption that the profile (facts and known data from the past) is related to behaviour (future events). In order to understand the repayment phenomenon, what is needed is a model relating the profile inputs to the behavioural patterns (outputs). Such a model would have predictive power, and thus would be very useful when deciding about new loan applicants. This situation forms a typical application context for the areas of machine learning and data mining. Evolutionary computing is a possible technology that could be used to solve such problems [160].

Another example of this type of modelling approach can be seen in [339], where Schulenberg and Ross use a learning classifier system to evolve sets of rules modelling the behaviour of stock market traders. As their inputs they used ten years of trading history, in the form of daily statistics such as volume of trade, current price, change in price over last few days, whether this price is a new high (or low), and so on for a given company's stock. The evolved traders consisted of sets of `condition`→`action` rules. Each day the current stock market conditions were presented to the trader, triggering a rule that decided whether stock was bought or sold. Periodically a genetic algorithm

---

[2] In case of the satellite dish boom, it is exactly the asymmetric character that works so well. Namely, vibrations are waves that traverse the boom along the rungs. If the rungs are of different lengths then these waves meet in a different phase and cancel each other. This small theory sounds trivial, but it took the asymmetric evolved solution to come to it.

is run on the set of (initially random) rules, so that well-performing ones are rewarded, and poorly performing ones are discarded. It was demonstrated that the system evolved trading agents that outperformed many well-known strategies, and varied according to the nature of the particular stock they were trading. Of particular interest, and benefit, compared to methods such as neural networks (which are also used for this kind of modelling problem in time-series forecasting), is the fact that the rule-base of the evolved traders are easily examinable, that is to say that the models that are evolved are particularly transparent to the user.

The simulation mode of using evolutionary computing can be applied to answer what-if questions in a context where the investigated subject matter is evolving, i.e., driven by variation and selection. Evolutionary economics is an established research area, roughly based on the perception that the game and the players in the socio–economical arena have much in common with the game of life. In common parlance, the survival of the fittest principle is also fundamental in the economic context. Evolving systems with a socio–economical interpretation can differ from biological ones in that the behavioural rules governing the individuals play a very strong role in the system. The term agent-based computational economy is often used to emphasise this aspect [395, 396]. Academic research into this direction is often based on a simple model called SugarScape world [135]. This features agent-like inhabitants in a grid space, and a commodity (the sugar) that can be consumed, owned, traded, and so on. by the inhabitants. There are many ways to set up system variants with an economical interpretation and conduct simulation experiments. For instance, Bäck et al. [32] investigate how artificially forced sugar redistribution (tax) and evolution interact under various circumstances. Clearly, the outcomes of such experiments must be done very carefully, avoiding ungrounded claims on transferability of results into a real socio–economic context.

Finally, we note that evolutionary computing experiments with a clear biological interpretation are also very interesting. Let us mention two approaches by way of illustration:

1. Trying existing biological features
2. Trying non-existing biological features

In the first approach, simulating a known natural phenomenon is a key issue. This may be motivated by an expectation that the natural trick will also work for algorithmic problem solving, or by simply willing to try whether the effects known in carbon would occur in silicon as well. Take incest as an example. A strong moral taboo against incest has existed for thousands of years, and for the last century or two there is also a scientific insight supporting this: incest leads to degeneration of the population. The results in [139] show that computer-simulated evolution also benefits from incest prevention. This confirms that the negative effects of incest are inherent for evolutionary processes, independently from the medium in which they take place. The other approach to simulations with a biological flavour is the opposite of this: it implements a feature that does not exist in biology, but can be implemented in a computer. As an illustration, let us take multiparent reproduction, where more than two parents are required for mating, and offspring inherit genetic material from each of them. Eiben et al. [111] have experimented a great deal with such mechanisms showing the beneficial effects under many different circumstances.

To summarise this necessarily brief introduction, evolutionary computing is a branch of computer science dedicated to the study of a class of algorithms that are broadly based on the Darwinian principles of natural selection, and draw inspiration from molecular genetics. Over the history of the world, many species have arisen and evolved to suit different environments, all using the same biological machinery. In the same way, if we provide an evolutionary algorithm with a new environment we hope to see adaptation of the initial population in a way that better suits the environment. Typically (but not always) this environment will take the form of a problem to be solved, with feedback to the individuals representing how well the solutions they represent solve the problem, and we have provided some examples of this. However, as we have indicated, the search for optimal solutions to some problem is not the only use of evolutionary algorithms; their nature as flexible adaptive systems gives rise to applications varying from economic modelling and simulation to the study of diverse biological processes during adaptation.

1.6 Exercises

1. Find out when hominids are first thought to have appeared, and estimate how many generations it has taken for you to evolve.

2. Find out the biological definition of evolution and give at least one example of how the term is frequently used in non-biological settings.

1.7 Recommended Reading for this Chapter

1. Charles Darwin. *The Origin of Species*. John Murray, 1859.
   The world-famous book introducing the theory of evolution, based on Darwin's observations from his trip in the Beagle.

2. R. Dawkins. *The Selfish Gene*. Oxford University Press, 1976.
   A "pop-science" classic, promoting "neo-Darwinism" as a synthesis of evolution with modern genetics. Its very "gene-centric" view of evolution, has been questioned by some.

3. J. Maynard-Smith. *The Evolution of Sex.* Cambridge University Press, 1978.
   A good, readable introduction to the biological basics of reproduction in haploid and diploid organisms.

4. S. Wright. The roles of mutation, inbreeding, cross-breeding, and selection in evolution. In: *Proc. of 6th Int. Congr. on Genetics*, vol. 1, pp. 356–366. Ithaca, NY, 1932.
   The paper introducing the idea of the adaptive landscapes.

5. D.B. Fogel, ed. *Evolutionary Computation: the Fossil Record.* IEEE Press, 1998.
   Fascinating collection of early works in the field, interesting not just for historical insight.

6. S.A. Kauffman. *Origins of Order: Self-Organization and Selection in Evolution.* Oxford University Press, New York, 1993.
   Offers a different perspective on the processes that lead to the origins of life.

2

What is an Evolutionary Algorithm?

2.1 Aims of this Chapter

The most important aim of this chapter is to describe what an evolutionary algorithm is. This description is deliberately based on a unifying view presenting a general scheme that forms the common basis of all evolutionary algorithm (EA) variants. The main components of EAs are discussed, explaining their role and related issues of terminology. This is immediately followed by two example applications (unlike other chapters, where example applications are typically given at the end) to make things more concrete. Further on we discuss general issues of the working of EAs. Finally, we put EAs into a broader context and explain their relation with other global optimisation techniques.

2.2 What is an Evolutionary Algorithm?

As the history of the field suggests there are many different variants of evolutionary algorithms. The common underlying idea behind all these techniques is the same: given a population of individuals, the environmental pressure causes natural selection (survival of the fittest), which causes a rise in the fitness of the population. Given a quality function to be maximised, we can randomly create a set of candidate solutions, i.e., elements of the function's domain, and apply the quality function as an abstract fitness measure – the higher the better. Based on this fitness, some of the better candidates are chosen to seed the next generation by applying recombination and/or mutation to them. Recombination is an operator applied to two or more selected candidates (the so-called parents) and results one or more new candidates (the children). Mutation is applied to one candidate and results in one new candidate. Executing recombination and mutation leads to a set of new candidates (the offspring) that compete – based on their fitness (and possibly age)– with the old ones for a place in the next generation. This process can be iterated until a candidate with sufficient quality (a solution) is found or a previously set computational limit is reached.

In this process there are two fundamental forces that form the basis of evolutionary systems:

- Variation operators (recombination and mutation) create the necessary diversity and thereby facilitate novelty.
- Selection acts as a force pushing quality.

The combined application of variation and selection generally leads to improving fitness values in consecutive populations. It is easy (although somewhat misleading) to see such a process as if the evolution is optimising, or at least "approximising", by approaching optimal values closer and closer over its course. Alternatively, evolution it is often seen as a process of adaptation. From this perspective, the fitness is not seen as an objective function to be optimised, but as an expression of environmental requirements. Matching these requirements more closely implies an increased viability, reflected in a higher number of offspring. The evolutionary process makes the population increasingly better at being adapted to the environment.

Let us note that many components of such an evolutionary process are stochastic. During selection fitter individuals have a higher chance to be selected than less fit ones, but typically even the weak individuals have a chance to become a parent or to survive. For recombination of individuals the choice of which pieces will be recombined is random. Similarly for mutation, the pieces that will be mutated within a candidate solution, and the new pieces replacing them, are chosen randomly. The general scheme of an evolutionary algorithm can is given in Fig. 2.1 in a pseudocode fashion; Fig. 2.2 shows a diagram.

```
BEGIN
    INITIALISE population with random candidate solutions;
    EVALUATE each candidate;
    REPEAT UNTIL ( TERMINATION CONDITION is satisfied ) DO
        1 SELECT parents;
        2 RECOMBINE pairs of parents;
        3 MUTATE the resulting offspring;
        4 EVALUATE new candidates;
        5 SELECT individuals for the next generation;
    OD
END
```

Fig. 2.1. The general scheme of an evolutionary algorithm in pseudocode

It is easy to see that this scheme falls in the category of generate-and-test algorithms. The evaluation (fitness) function represents a heuristic estimation of solution quality, and the search process is driven by the variation and the selection operators. Evolutionary algorithms possess a number of features that can help to position them within in the family of generate-and-test methods:

- EAs are population based, i.e., they process a whole collection of candidate solutions simultaneously.
- EAs mostly use recombination to mix information of more candidate solutions into a new one.
- EAs are stochastic.

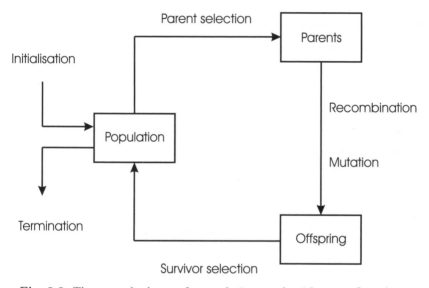

Fig. 2.2. The general scheme of an evolutionary algorithm as a flow-chart

The various dialects of evolutionary computing that we have mentioned previously all follow the above general outlines and differ only in technical details, as is shown in the overview table in Chap. 15. For instance, the representation of a candidate solution is often used to characterise different streams. Typically, the candidates are represented by (i.e., the data structure encoding a solution has the form of) strings over a finite alphabet in genetic algorithms (GA), real-valued vectors in evolution strategies (ES), finite state machines in classical evolutionary programming (EP), and trees in genetic programming (GP). These differences have a mainly historical origin. Technically, a given representation might be preferable over others if it matches the given problem better; that is, it makes the encoding of candidate solutions easier or more natural. For instance, for solving a satisfiability problem the straightforward choice is to use bit-strings of length n, where n is the number of logical variables, hence the appropriate EA would be a genetic algorithm. To evolve a computer program that can play checkers, trees are well-suited (namely, the parse trees of the syntactic expressions forming the programs), thus a GP approach is likely. It is important to note that the recombination and mutation operators working on candidates must match the given representation. Thus, for instance, in GP the recombination operator works on trees, while in GAs it operates on strings. As opposed to variation operators, selection takes only the fitness information into account; hence it works independently from the actual representation. Differences in the commonly applied selection mechanisms in each stream are therefore a tradition rather than a technical necessity.

2.3 Components of Evolutionary Algorithms

In this section we discuss evolutionary algorithms in detail. EAs have a number of components, procedures, or operators that must be specified in order to define a particular EA. The most important components, indicated by italics in Fig. 2.1, are:

- Representation (definition of individuals)
- Evaluation function (or fitness function)
- Population
- Parent selection mechanism
- Variation operators, recombination and mutation
- Survivor selection mechanism (replacement)

Each of these components must be specified in order to define a particular EA. Furthermore, to obtain a running algorithm the initialisation procedure and a termination condition must be also defined.

2.3.1 Representation (Definition of Individuals)

The first step in defining an EA is to link the "real world" to the "EA world", that is, to set up a bridge between the original problem context and the problem-solving space where evolution takes place. Objects forming possible solutions within the original problem context are referred to as **phenotypes**, while their encoding, that is, the individuals within the EA, are called **genotypes**. The first design step is commonly called **representation**, as it amounts to specifying a mapping from the phenotypes onto a set of genotypes that are said to represent these phenotypes. For instance, given an optimisation problem on integers, the given set of integers would form the set of phenotypes. Then one could decide to represent them by their binary code, hence 18 would be seen as a phenotype, and 10010 as a genotype representing it. It is important to understand that the phenotype space can be very different from the genotype space, and that the whole evolutionary search takes place in the genotype space. A solution – a good phenotype – is obtained by decoding the best genotype after termination. To this end, it should hold that the (optimal) solution to the problem at hand – a phenotype – is represented in the given genotype space.

The common EC terminology uses many synonyms for naming the elements of these two spaces. On the side of the original problem context, **candidate solution**, phenotype, and **individual** are used to denote points of the space of possible solutions. This space itself is commonly called the **phenotype space**. On the side of the EA, genotype, **chromosome**, and again individual can be used for points in the space where the evolutionary search actually takes place. This space is often termed the **genotype space**. There are also many synonymous terms for the elements of individuals. A place-holder is commonly called a variable, a **locus** (plural: loci), a position, or – in a biology-oriented terminology – a **gene**. An object on such a place can be called a value or an **allele**.

It should be noted that the word "representation" is used in two slightly different ways. Sometimes it stands for the mapping from the phenotype to the genotype space. In this sense it is synonymous with **encoding**, e.g., one could mention binary representation or binary encoding of candidate solutions. The inverse mapping from genotypes to phenotypes is usually called **decoding**, and it is required that the representation be invertible: to each genotype there has to be at most one corresponding phenotype. The word representation can also be used in a slightly different sense, where the emphasis is not on the mapping itself, but on the "data structure" of the genotype space. This interpretation is behind speaking about mutation operators for binary representation, for instance.

2.3.2 Evaluation Function (Fitness Function)

The role of the **evaluation function** is to represent the requirements to adapt to. It forms the basis for selection, and thereby it facilitates improvements. More accurately, it defines what improvement means. From the problem-solving perspective, it represents the task to solve in the evolutionary context. Technically, it is a function or procedure that assigns a quality measure to genotypes. Typically, this function is composed from a quality measure in the phenotype space and the inverse representation. To remain with the above example, if we were to maximise x^2 on integers, the fitness of the genotype 10010 could be defined as the square of its corresponding phenotype: $18^2 = 324$.

The evaluation function is commonly called the **fitness function** in EC. This might cause a counterintuitive terminology if the original problem requires minimisation for fitness is usually associated with maximisation. Mathematically, however, it is trivial to change minimisation into maximisation, and vice versa.

Quite often, the original problem to be solved by an EA is an optimisation problem (treated in more technical detail in Sect. 12.2.1). In this case the name **objective function** is often used in the original problem context, and the evaluation (fitness) function can be identical to, or a simple transformation of, the given objective function.

2.3.3 Population

The role of the **population** is to hold (the representation of) possible solutions. A population is a multiset[1] of genotypes. The population forms the unit of evolution. Individuals are static objects that do not change or adapt; it is the population that does. Given a representation, defining a population can be as simple as specifying how many individuals are in it, that is, setting the population size. In some sophisticated EAs a population has an additional spatial structure, with a distance measure or a neighbourhood relation. In such cases the additional structure has to be defined as well to fully specify a population. As opposed to variation operators that act on the one or two parent individuals, the selection operators (parent selection and survivor selection) work at population level. In general, they take the whole current population into account, and choices are always made relative to what we have. For instance, the best individual *of the given population* is chosen to seed the next generation, or the worst individual *of the given population* is chosen to be replaced by a new one. In almost all EA applications the population size is constant and does not change during the evolutionary search.

The **diversity** of a population is a measure of the number of *different* solutions present. No single measure for diversity exists. Typically people might refer to the number of different fitness values present, the number of different phenotypes present, or the number of different genotypes. Other statistical measures such as entropy are also used. Note that only one fitness value does not necessarily imply only one phenotype is present, and in turn only one phenotype does not necessarily imply only one genotype. The reverse is, however, not true: one genotype implies only one phenotype and fitness value.

2.3.4 Parent Selection Mechanism

The role of **parent selection** or **mating selection** is to distinguish among individuals based on their quality, in particular, to allow the better individuals to become parents of the next generation. An individual is a **parent** if it has been selected to undergo variation in order to create offspring. Together with the survivor selection mechanism, parent selection is responsible for pushing quality improvements. In EC, parent selection is typically probabilistic. Thus,

---

[1] A multiset is a set where multiple copies of an element are possible.

high-quality individuals get a higher chance to become parents than those with low quality. Nevertheless, low-quality individuals are often given a small, but positive chance; otherwise the whole search could become too greedy and get stuck in a local optimum.

2.3.5 Variation Operators

The role of **variation operators** is to create new individuals from old ones. In the corresponding phenotype space this amounts to generating new candidate solutions. From the generate-and-test search perspective, variation operators perform the "generate" step. Variation operators in EC are divided into two types based on their **arity**.[2]

Mutation

A unary[3] variation operator is commonly called **mutation**. It is applied to one genotype and delivers a (slightly) modified mutant, the **child** or **offspring** of it. A mutation operator is always stochastic: its output – the child – depends on the outcomes of a series of random choices.[4] It should be noted that an arbitrary unary operator is not necessarily seen as mutation. A problem-specific heuristic operator acting on one individual could be termed as mutation for being unary. However, in general mutation is supposed to cause a random, unbiased change. For this reason it might be more appropriate not to call heuristic unary operators mutation. The role of mutation in EC is different in various EC dialects; for instance, in genetic programming it is often not used at all, while in genetic algorithms it has traditionally been seen as a background operator to fill the gene pool with "fresh blood", and in evolutionary programming it is the one and only variation operator doing the whole search work.

It is worth noting that variation operators form the evolutionary implementation of the elementary steps within the search space. Generating a child amounts to stepping to a new point in this space. From this perspective, mutation has a theoretical role, too: it can guarantee that the space is connected. This is important since theorems stating that an EA will (given sufficient time) discover the global optimum of a given problem often rely on the property that each genotype representing a possible solution can be reached by the variation operators [114]. The simplest way to satisfy this condition is to allow the mutation operator to "jump" everywhere, for example, by allowing that any allele can be mutated into any other allele with a nonzero probability. However, it should also be noted that many researchers feel these proofs

---

[2] The arity of an operator is the number of objects that it takes as inputs.

[3] An operator is **unary** if it applies to one object as input.

[4] Usually these will consist of using a pseudorandom number generator to generate a series of values from some given probability distribution. We will refer to these as "random drawings".

have limited practical importance, and many implementations of EAs do not in fact possess this property.

Recombination

A binary variation operator[5] is called **recombination** or **crossover**. As the names indicate, such an operator merges information from two parent genotypes into one or two offspring genotypes. Similarly to mutation, recombination is a stochastic operator: the choice of what parts of each parent are combined, and the way these parts are combined, depend on random drawings. Again, the role of recombination is different in EC dialects: in genetic programming it is often the only variation operator, while in genetic algorithms it is seen as the main search operator, and in evolutionary programming it is never used. Recombination operators with a higher arity (using more than two parents) are mathematically possible and easy to implement, but have no biological equivalent. Perhaps this is why they are not commonly used, although several studies indicate that they have positive effects on the evolution [111].

The principle behind recombination is simple – by mating two individuals with different but desirable features, we can produce an offspring that combines both of those features. This principle has a strong supporting case: it is one which has been successfully applied for millennia by breeders of plants and livestock to produce species that give higher yields or have other desirable features. Evolutionary algorithms create a number of offspring by random recombination, and accept that some will have undesirable combinations of traits, most may be no better or worse than their parents, and hope that some have improved characteristics. Although the biology of the planet Earth (where with a *very* few exceptions lower organisms reproduce asexually, and higher organisms reproduce sexually [265, 266]), suggests that recombination is the superior form of reproduction, recombination operators in EAs are usually applied probabilistically, that is, with an existing chance of not being performed.

It is important to note that variation operators are representation dependent. That is, for different representations different variation operators have to be defined. For example, if genotypes are bit-strings, then inverting a 0 to a 1 (1 to a 0) can be used as a mutation operator. However, if we represent possible solutions by tree-like structures another mutation operator is required.

2.3.6 Survivor Selection Mechanism (Replacement)

The role of **survivor selection** or **environmental selection** is to distinguish among individuals based on their quality. In that it is similar to parent

---

[5] An operator is **binary** if it applies to two objects as input.

selection, but it is used in a different stage of the evolutionary cycle. The survivor selection mechanism is called after having having created the offspring of the selected parents. As mentioned in Sect. 2.3.3, in EC the population size is almost always constant, thus a choice has to to be made on which individuals will be allowed in the next generation. This decision is usually based on their fitness values, favouring those with higher quality, although the concept of age is also frequently used. As opposed to parent selection, which is typically stochastic, survivor selection is often deterministic, for instance, ranking the unified multiset of parents and offspring and selecting the top segment (fitness biased), or selecting only from the offspring (age biased).

Survivor selection is also often called **replacement** or replacement strategy. In many cases the two terms can be used interchangeably. The choice between the two is thus often arbitrary. A good reason to use the name survivor selection is to keep terminology consistent: steps 1 and 5 in Fig. 2.1 are both named selection, distinguished by an adjective. A preference for using replacement can be motivated by the skewed proportion of the number of individuals in the population and the number of newly created children. In particular, if the number of children is very small with respect to the population size, e.g., 2 children and a population of 100. In this case, the survivor selection step is as simple as to chose the two old individuals that are to be deleted to make places for the new ones. In other words, it is more efficient to declare that everybody survives unless deleted and to choose whom to replace. If the proportion is not skewed like this, e.g., 500 children made from a population of 100, then this is not an option, so using the term survivor selection is appropriate. In the rest of this book we will be pragmatic about this issue. We will use survivor selection in the section headers for reasons of generality and uniformity, while using replacement if it is commonly used in the literature for the given procedure we are discussing.

2.3.7 Initialisation

Initialisation is kept simple in most EA applications: The first population is seeded by randomly generated individuals. In principle, problem-specific heuristics can be used in this step aiming at an initial population with higher fitness. Whether this is worth the extra computational effort or not very much depends on the application at hand. There are, however, some general observations concerning this issue based on the so-called anytime behaviour of EAs. These are discussed in Sect. 2.5, and we also return to this issue in Chapt. 10.

2.3.8 Termination Condition

We can distinguish two cases of a suitable **termination condition**. If the problem has a known optimal fitness level, probably coming from a known optimum of the given objective function, then reaching this level (perhaps only with a given precision $\epsilon > 0$) should be used as stopping condition.

However, EAs are stochastic and mostly there are no guarantees to reach an optimum, hence this condition might never get satisfied and the algorithm may never stop. This requires that this condition be extended with one that certainly stops the algorithm. Commonly used options for this purpose are the following:

1. The maximally allowed CPU time elapses.
2. The total number of fitness evaluations reaches a given limit.
3. For a given period of time (i.e, for a number of generations or fitness evaluations), the fitness improvement remains under a threshold value.
4. The population diversity drops under a given threshold.

The actual termination criterion in such cases is a disjunction: optimum value hit *or* condition x satisfied. If the problem does not have a known optimum, then we need no disjunction. We simply need a condition from the above list or a similar one that is guaranteed to stop the algorithm. In Sect. 2.5 we return to the issue of when to terminate an EA.

In the coming chapters we describe various types of evolutionary algorithms by specifying how the EA components are implemented in the given type. That is, we give a treatment of the representation, variation, and selection operators specific for that EA variant and give an overview of the typical representatives in an EA tableau. However, we do not discuss the initialisation procedure and a termination condition, for they are usually not "dialect" specific, but are implemented along the general considerations outlined above.

2.4 Example Applications

2.4.1 The Eight-Queens Problem

In the eight-queens problem we are given a regular chessboard (8 by 8) and eight queens that must be placed on the board in such a way that no 2 queens can check each other. This problem can be naturally generalised, yielding the N-queens problem. Many classical artificial intelligence approaches to this problem work in a constructive, or incremental, fashion: one starts with placing one queen, and after having placed n queens, one attempts to place the $(n+1)$th on a feasible position, i.e., a position where the new queen does not check any others. Typically some sort of backtracking mechanism is applied; if there is no feasible position for the $(n+1)$th queen, the nth is moved to another position.

An evolutionary approach to this problem is drastically different in that it is not incremental. Our candidate solutions are complete, rather than partial, board configurations where all eight queens are placed. The phenotype space P is the set of all such configurations. Clearly, most elements of this space are infeasible, violating the condition of nonchecking queens. The quality $q(p)$ of any phenotype $p \in P$ can be simply quantified by the number of checking queen pairs. The lower this measure, the better a phenotype (board configuration), and a zero value, $q(p) = 0$, indicates a good solution. By this observation we can formulate a suitable objective function (to be minimised) with a known optimal value. Even though we have not defined genotypes at this point, we can state that the fitness (to be maximised) of a genotype g that represents phenotype p is some inverse of $q(p)$. There are many possibilities to specify what kind of inverse we wish to use here. For instance, $1/q(p)$ is an option, but it has the disadvantage that division by zero can deliver a problem. We could circumvent this by adding that when this occurs we have a solution, or by adding a small value ϵ i.e., $1/(q(p) + \epsilon)$. Another option is to use $-q(p)$ or $M - q(p)$, where M is a sufficiently large number to make all fitness values positive, e.g., $M = max\{ q(p) \mid p \in P \}$. This fitness function inherits the property of q that it has a known optimum M.

To design an EA to search the space P we need to define a representation of phenotypes from P. The most straightforward idea is to use elements of P represented as matrices directly as genotypes, meaning that we design variation operators acting such matrices. In this example, however, we define a more clever representation as follows. A genotype, or chromosome, is a permutation of the numbers $1, \ldots, 8$, and a given $g = \langle i_1, \ldots, i_8 \rangle$ denotes the (unique) board configuration, where the nth column contains exactly one queen placed on the i_nth row. For instance, the permutation $g = \langle 1, \ldots, 8 \rangle$ represents a board where the queens are placed along the main diagonal. The genotype space G is now the set of all permutations of $1, \ldots, 8$ and we also have defined a mapping $F : G \rightarrow P$.

It is easy to see that by using such chromosome we restrict the search to board configurations where horizontal constraint violations (two queens on the same row) and vertical constraint violations (two queens on the same column) do not occur. In other words, the representation guarantees "half" of the requirements against a solution – what remains to be minimised is the number of diagonal constraint violations. From a formal perspective we have chosen a representation that is not surjective, only part of P can be obtained by decoding elements of G. While in general this could carry the danger of missing solutions in P, in our present example this is not the case, since those phenotypes from $P \setminus F(G)$ can never be solutions.

The next step is to define suitable variation operators (mutation and crossover), fitting our representation, i.e., working on genotypes being permutations. The crucial feature of a suitable operator is that it does not lead out of the space G. In common parlance, offspring of a permutation must be permutations as well. Later in Sects. 3.4.4 and 3.5.4 we treat such operators in great detail. Here we only give one suitable mutation and one crossover operator for illustration purposes. As for mutation we can use an operator that selects two positions in a given chromosome randomly and swaps the values standing on those positions. A good crossover for permutations is less obvious, but the mechanism outlined in Fig. 2.3 will create two child permutations from two parents.

---

1. Select a random position, the crossover point, $i \in \{1, \ldots, 7\}$
2. Cut both parents in two segments after this position
3. Copy the first segment of parent 1 into child 1 and the first segment of parent 2 into child 2
4. Scan parent 2 from left to right and fill the second segment of child 1 with values from parent 2, skipping those that are already contained in it
5. Do the same for parent 1 and child 2

Fig. 2.3. "Cut-and-crossfill" crossover

The important thing about these variation operators is that mutation causes a small undirected change, and crossover creates children that inherit genetic material from both parents. It should be noted though that there can be large performance differences between operators, e.g., an EA using mutation A could find a solution quickly, while using mutation B can result in an algorithm never finding a solution. The operators we sketch here are not necessarily *efficient*; they merely serve as examples of operators that are *applicable* to the given representation.

The next step in setting up an EA is deciding about selection and the population update mechanism. As for managing the population we choose for a simple scheme. In each evolutionary cycle we select two parents delivering two children and the new population of size n will contain the best n of the resulting $n + 2$ individuals (the old population plus the two new ones).

Parent selection (step 1 in Fig. 2.1) will be done by choosing five individuals randomly from the population and taking the best two as parents that undergo crossover. This ensures a bias towards using parents with relatively high fitness. Survivor selection (step 5 in Fig. 2.1) checks which old individuals should be deleted to make place for the new ones – provided the new ones are better. Following the naming convention discussed from Sect. 2.3.6 we are to define a replacement strategy. The strategy we will use merges the population and offspring, then ranks them according to fitness, and deletes the worst two.

To obtain a full specification we can decide to fill the initial population with randomly generated permutations and terminate the search if we find a solution or 10,000 fitness evaluations have elapsed. We can furthermore decide to use a population size of 100, and using the variation operators with a certain frequency. For instance, we always apply crossover to the two selected parents and in 80% of the cases applying mutation to the offspring. Putting this all together, we obtain an EA as summarised in Table 2.1.

Representation	Permutations
Recombination	"Cut-and-crossfill" crossover
Recombination probability	100%
Mutation	Swap
Mutation probability	80%
Parent selection	Best 2 out of random 5
Survival selection	Replace worst
Population size	100
Number of Offspring	2
Initialisation	Random
Termination condition	Solution or 10,000 fitness evaluation

Table 2.1. Description of the EA for the eight-queens problem

2.4.2 The Knapsack Problem

The "0–1 knapsack" problem, a generalisation of many industrial problems, can be briefly described as follows: Given a set of n of items, each of which has some value v_i attached to it and some cost c_i, how do we select a subset of those items that maximises the value whilst keeping the summed cost within some capacity C_{max}? Thus, for example, when packing a backpack for a "round-the-world" trip, we must balance likely utility of the items we wish to take against the fact that we have a limited volume (the items chosen must fit in one bag) and weight (airlines impose fees for luggage over a given weight).

It is a natural idea to represent candidate solutions for this problem as binary strings of length n, where a 1 in a given position indicates that an item is included and a 0 that it is omitted. The corresponding genotype space G is the set of all such strings with size 2^n, which increases exponentially with the number of items considered. By this G we fix the representation in the sense of "data structure", and next we need to define the mapping from genotypes to phenotypes.

The first representation (in the sense of a mapping) that we consider takes the phenotype space P and the genotype space to be identical. The quality of a given solution p, represented by a binary genotype g, is thus determined by summing the values of the included items, i.e.: $Q_p = \sum_{i=1}^{n} v_i \cdot g_i$. However, this simple representation leads us to some immediate problems. By using a one-to-one mapping between the genotype space G and the phenotype space P, individual genotypes may correspond to invalid solutions that have an associated cost greater than the capacity, i.e., $\sum_{i=1}^{n} c_i \cdot g_i > C_{max}$. This issue is typical of a class of problems that we return to in Chapt. 12, and a number of mechanisms have been proposed for dealing with it.

The second representation that we outline here solves this problem by employing a "decoder" function that breaks the one-to-one correspondence between the genotype space G and the solution space P. In essence, our genotype representation remains the same, but when creating a solution we read from left to right along the binary string, and keep a running tally of the cost of included items. When we encounter a value 1, we first check to see if including the item would break our capacity constraint, i.e., rather than interpreting a value 1 as meaning *include this item*, we interpret it as meaning *include this item IF it does not take us over the cost constraint*. The effect of this scheme is to make the mapping from genotype to phenotype space many-to-one, since once the capacity has been reached, the values of all bits to the right of the current position are irrelevant as no more items will be added to the solution. Furthermore, this mapping ensures that all binary strings represent valid solutions with a unique fitness (to be maximised).

Having decided on a fixed-length binary representation, we can now choose off-the-shelf variation operators from the GA literature, because the bit-string representation is "standard" there. A suitable (but not necessarily optimal) recombination operator is one-point crossover, where we align two parents and pick a random point along their length. The two offspring are created by exchanging the tails of the parents at that point. We will apply this with 70% probability, i.e., for each pair of parents we will select a random value with uniform probability between 0 and 1. If it is below 0.7 then we will create two offspring by crossover, otherwise we will make copies of the parents. A suitable mutation operator is so-called bit-flipping: in each position we invert the value with a small probability $p_m \in [0, 1)$.

In this case we will create the same number of offspring as we have members our initial population. As noted above, we create two offspring from each two parents, so we will select that many parents and pair them randomly. We will use a tournament for selecting the parents, where each time we pick two members of the population at random (with replacement), and the one with the highest value Q_p wins the tournament and becomes a parent. We will institute a "generational" scheme for survivor selection, i.e., all of the population in each iteration are discarded and replaced by their offspring.

Finally we should consider initialisation (which we will do by random choice of 0 and 1 in each position of our initial population), and termination. In this case we do not know the maximum value that we can achieve, so we will run our algorithm until no improvement in the fitness of the best member of the population has been observed for 25 generations.

We have already defined our crossover probability as 0.7; we will work with a population size of 500 and a mutation rate of $p_m = 1/n$, i.e., that will *on average* change one value in every offspring. Our evolutionary algorithm to tackle this problem can be specified as below in Table 2.2.

Representation	Binary strings of length n
Recombination	One point crossover
Recombination probability	70%
Mutation	Each value inverted with independent probability p_m
Mutation probability p_m	$1/n$
Parent selection	Best out of random 2
Survival selection	Generational
Population size	500
Number of offspring	500
Initialisation	Random
Termination condition	No improvement in last 25 generations

Table 2.2. Description of the EA for the Knapsack Problem

2.5 Working of an Evolutionary Algorithm

Evolutionary algorithms have some rather general properties concerning how they work. To illuminate how an EA typically works we assume a one-dimensional objective function to be maximised. Fig. 2.4 shows three stages of the evolutionary search, exhibiting how the individuals are distributed in the beginning, somewhere halfway, and at the end of the evolution. In the first phase, directly after initialisation, the individuals are randomly spread over the whole search space (Fig. 2.4, left). Even after a few generations this distribution changes: because of selection and variation operators the population abandons low-fitness regions and starts to "climb" the hills (Fig. 2.4, middle). Yet later (close to the end of the search, if the termination condition is set appropriately), the whole population is concentrated around a few peaks, where some of these peaks can be suboptimal. In principle it is possible that the population "climbs the wrong hill" and all individuals are positioned around a local but not global optimum. Although there is no universally accepted definition of what the terms mean, these distinct phases of search are often categorised in terms of **exploration** (the generation of new individuals in as yet untested regions of the search space), and **exploitation** (the concentration of the search in the vicinity of known good solutions). Evolutionary search processes are often referred to in terms of a trade-off between exploration and exploitation, with too much of the former leading to inefficient search, and too much of the latter leading to a propensity to focus the search too quickly (see [128] for a good discussion of these issues). **Premature convergence** is the well-known effect of losing population diversity too quickly and getting trapped in a local optimum. This danger is generally present in evolutionary algorithms; techniques to prevent it are discussed in Chap. 9.

The other effect we want to illustrate is the **anytime behaviour** of EAs. We show this by plotting the development of the population's best fitness (objective function) value in time (Fig. 2.5). This curve is characteristic for evolutionary algorithms, showing rapid progress in the beginning and flatten-

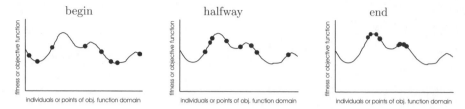

Fig. 2.4. Typical progress of an EA illustrated in terms of population distribution

ing out later on. This is typical for many algorithms that work by iterative improvements on the initial solution(s). The name "anytime" comes from the property that the search can be stopped at any time, and the algorithm will have some solution, even if it is suboptimal.

Fig. 2.5. Typical progress of an EA illustrated in terms of development of the best fitness (objective function to be maximised) value within population in time

Based on this anytime curve we can make some general observations concerning initialisation and the termination condition for EAs. As for initialisation, recall the question from Sect. 2.3.7 whether it is worth it to put extra computational effort into applying some intelligent heuristics to seed the initial populations with better-than-random individuals. In general, it could be said that that the typical progress curve of an evolutionary process makes it unnecessary. This is illustrated in Fig. 2.6. As the figure indicates, using heuristic initialisation can start the evolutionary search with a better population. However, typically a few (k in the figure) generations are enough to reach this level, making the worth of extra effort questionable. In Chap. 10 we will return to this issue.

The anytime behaviour also has some general indications regarding termination conditions of EAs. In Fig. 2.7 we divide the run into two equally long sections, the first and the second half. As the figure indicates, the progress in terms of fitness increase in the first half of the run (X) is significantly greater than the achievements in the second half (Y). This provides a general sug-

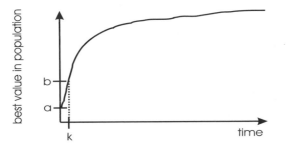

Fig. 2.6. Illustration of why heuristic initialisation might not be worth additional effort. Level *a* shows the best fitness in a randomly initialised population, level *b* belongs to heuristic initialisation

gestion that it might not be worthwhile to allow very long runs: because of the anytime behaviour of EAs, efforts spent after a certain time (number of fitness evaluations) may not result in better solution quality.

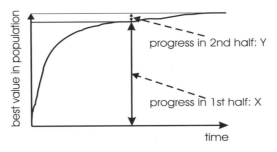

Fig. 2.7. Illustration of why long runs might not be worth performing. *X* shows the progress in terms of fitness increase in the first half of the run, while *Y* belongs to the second half

We close this review of EA behaviour by looking at EA performance from a global perspective. That is, rather than observing one run of the algorithm, we consider the performance of EAs for a wide range of problems. Fig. 2.8 shows the 1980s view after Goldberg [172]. What the figure indicates is that robust problem solvers –as EAs are claimed to be– show a roughly evenly good performance over a wide range of problems. This performance pattern can be compared to random search and to algorithms tailored to a specific problem type. EAs clearly outperform random search. A problem-tailored algorithm, however, performs much better than an EA, but only on that type of problem for which it was designed. As we move away from this problem type to different problems, the problem-specific algorithm quickly loses performance. In this sense, EAs and problem-specific algorithms form two antagonistic extremes. This perception has played an important role in positioning EAs and stressing the difference between evolutionary and random search, but it gradually changed in the 1990s based on new insights from practice as well as from theory. The contemporary view acknowledges the possibility to combine the two extremes into a hybrid algorithm. This issue is treated in detail in Chap. 10, where we also present the revised version of Fig. 2.8. As for theoretical considerations, the No Free Lunch theorem has shown that (under some conditions) no blackbox algorithm can outperform random walk when averaged over "all" problems [430]. That is, showing the EA line always above that of random search is fundamentally incorrect. This is discussed further in Chap. 11.

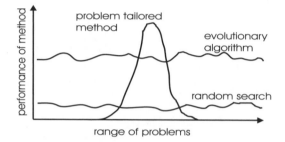

Fig. 2.8. 1980s view of EA performance after Goldberg [172]

2.6 Evolutionary Computing and Global Optimisation

In Chap. 1 we mentioned that there has been a steady increase in the complexity and size of problems that are desired to be solved by computing methods. We also noted that evolutionary algorithms are often used for problem optimisation. Of course, EAs are not the only optimisation technique known, and in this section we explain where EAs fall into the general class of optimisation methods, and why they are of increasing interest.

In an ideal world, we would possess the technology and algorithms that could provide a provably optimal solution to any problem that we could suitably pose to the system. In fact, such algorithms exist: an exhaustive enumeration of all of the possible solutions to our problem is clearly such an algorithm. For many problems that can be expressed in a suitably mathematical formulation, much faster, exact techniques such as branch and bound search are well known. However, despite the rapid progress in computing technology, and even if there is no halt to Moore's Law (which states that the available computing power doubles every one and a half years), it is a sad fact of life that all too often the types of problems posed by users exceed in their demands the capacity of technology to answer them.

Decades of computer science research have taught us that many "real-world" problems can be reduced in their essence to well-known abstract forms for which the number of potential solutions grows exponentially with the number of variables considered. For example, many problems in transportation can be reduced to the well-known "travelling sales person" problem, i.e., given a list of destinations, construct the shortest tour that visits each destination exactly once. If we have n destinations, with symmetric distances between them, the number of possible tours is given by $n!/2 = n \cdot (n-1) \cdot (n-2) \cdot \ldots \cdot 3$, which is exponential in n. Whilst exact methods whose time complexity scales linearly (or at least polynomially) with the number of variables exist for some of these problems (see [195] for an overview), it is widely accepted that for many types of problems often encountered, no such algorithms exist. Thus despite the increase in computing power, beyond a certain size of problem we must abandon the search for provably optimal solutions and look to other methods for finding good solutions.

We will use the term **global optimisation** to refer to the process of attempting to find the solution x^* out of a set of possible solutions S that has the optimal value for some fitness function f. In other words, if we are trying to find the solution x^* such that $x \neq x^* \Rightarrow f(x^*) \geq f(x)$ (here we have assumed a maximisation problem, and the inequality is simply reversed for minimisation).

As noted above, a number of *deterministic* algorithms exist that, if allowed to run to completion, are guaranteed to find x^*. The simplest example is, of course, complete enumeration of all the solutions in S, which can take an exponentially long time as the number of variables increases. A variety of other techniques exist (collectively known as box decomposition) that are based on ordering the elements of S into some kind of tree, and then reasoning about the quality of solutions in each branch in order to decide whether to investigate its elements. Although methods such as branch and bound can sometimes make very fast progress, in the worst case (caused by searching in a suboptimal order) the time complexity of the algorithms is still the same as complete enumeration.

After exact methods, we find a class of search methods known as *heuristics*, which may be thought of as sets of rules for deciding which potential solution out of S should next be generated and tested. For some *randomised* heuristics, such as **simulated annealing** [2, 227] and certain variants of EAs, convergence proofs do in fact exist, i.e., they are guaranteed to find x^*. Unfortunately these algorithms are fairly weak, in the sense that they will not identify x^* as being globally optimal, rather as simply the best solution seen so far.

An important class of heuristics is based on the idea of using operators that impose some kind of structure onto the elements of S, such that each point x has associated with it a set of neighbours $N(x)$. In Fig. 1.1 the variables (traits) x and y were taken to be real valued, which imposes a natural structure on S. The reader should note that for many types of problem where each variable takes one of a finite set of values (so-called **combinatorial optimisation**) there are many possible neighbourhood structures. As an example of how the landscape "seen" by a local search algorithm depends on its neighbourhood structure, the reader might wish to consider what a chessboard would look like if we reordered it so that squares that are possible next moves for a knight are adjacent to each other. Note that by its definition, the **global optimum** x^* will always be fitter than all of its neighbours *under any neighbourhood structure*.

So-called **local search** algorithms [2] and their many variants work by taking a starting solution x, and then searching the candidate solutions in $N(x)$ for one x' that performs better than x. If such a solution exists, then this is accepted as the new incumbent solution, and the search proceeds by examining the candidate solutions in $N(x')$. Eventually this process will lead to the identification of a **local optimum**: a solution that is superior to all those in its neighbourhood. Such algorithms (often referred to as **hill climbers** for maximisation problems) have been well studied over the decades, and have the advantage that they are often quick to identify a good solutions to the problem, which is in fact sometimes all that is required in practical applications. However, the downside is that frequently problems will exhibit numerous local optima, some of which may be significantly worse than the global optimum, and no guarantees can be offered in the quality of solution found.

A number of methods have been proposed to get around this problem by changing the search landscape, either by reordering it through a change of neighbourhood function (e.g., variable neighbourhood search [189]), or by temporally assigning low fitness to already seen good solutions (e.g., tabu search [169]). However the theoretical basis behind these algorithms is still very much in gestation.

There are a number of features of EAs that distinguish them from local search algorithms, relating principally to their use of a population. The population provides the algorithm with a means of defining a nonuniform probability distribution function (p.d.f.) governing the generation of new points from S. This p.d.f. reflects possible interactions between points in the population arising from the recombination of partial solutions from two or more members of the population (parents). This contrasts with the globally uniform distribution of blind random search, or the locally uniform distribution used by many other stochastic algorithms such as simulated annealing and various hill-climbing algorithms.

The ability of EAs to maintain a diverse set of points not only provides a means of escaping from one local optimum; it provides a means of coping with large and discontinuous search spaces. If several copies of a solution can be maintained, it provides a natural and robust way of dealing with problems where there is noise or uncertainty associated with the assignment of a fitness score to a candidate solution, as seen in later chapters.

2.7 Exercises

1. How big is the phenotype space for the eight-queens problem?
2. Try to design an incremental evolutionary algorithm for the eight-queens problem. That is, a solution must represent a way to place the queens on the chess board one by one. How big is the search space in your design?
3. Explain why the order in which items are listed in the representation is unimportant for the naive approach to the knapsack problem, but makes a big difference if we use the decoder approach.
4. Find a problem where EAs would certainly perform very poorly compared to alternative approaches. Explain why you expect this to be the case.

2.8 Recommended Reading for this Chapter

1. T. Bäck. *Evolutionary Algorithms in Theory and Practice.* Oxford University Press, New York, 1996

2. T. Bäck, H.-P. Schwefel. An overview of Evolutionary Algorithms for parameter optimisation. *Evolutionary Computation*, 1:1 pp. 1–23, 1993

3. A.E. Eiben. Evolutionary computing: the most powerful problem solver in the universe? *Dutch Mathematical Archive (Nederlands Archief voor Wiskunde)*, 5/3:2 pp.126–131, 2002
   Available at `http://www.cs.vu.nl/~gusz/papers/ec-intro-naw.ps`

4. D.B. Fogel. *Evolutionary Computation.* IEEE Press, 1995

5. M.S. Hillier, F.S. Hillier. Conventional optimization techniques. Chap. 1, pp. 3–25 in Sarker et. al., Eds. [331]

6. X. Yao. Evolutionary computation: A gentle introduction. Chap. 2, pp. 27–53 in Sarker et. al., Eds. [331]

3

Genetic Algorithms

3.1 Aims of this Chapter

In this chapter we describe the most widely known type of evolutionary algorithm: the genetic algorithm. After presenting a simple example to introduce the basic concepts, we begin with what is usually the most critical decision in any application, namely that of deciding how best to represent a candidate solution to the algorithm. We present four possible solutions, that is, four widely used representations. Following from this we then describe variation operators (mutation and crossover) suitable for different types of representation, before turning our attention to the selection and replacement mechanisms that are used to manage the populations of solutions.

As will be seen from this treatment, there is no single definitive genetic algorithm; rather we create algorithms from a suite of operators to suit our particular applications. Because of the richness of possible representations, variation, and selection operators, this chapter is necessarily quite long. In particular it is longer than the following chapters on other evolutionary algorithm dialects. This difference in length is not intended to indicate that one method is more or less important than any other, merely that we have happened to deal with genetic algorithms first, and so many of the issues that are also relevant to other paradigms occur for the first time, and are described, here. Finally, the chapter concludes with an example application, showing more details of the path from a problem to an evolutionary problem solver.

3.2 Introductory Example

The genetic algorithm was initially conceived by Holland as a means of studying adaptive behaviour, as suggested by the title of the book in which he drew together his early research: *Adaptation in natural and artificial systems*

[204]. However, they have largely[1] been considered as function optimisation methods, and we begin by sketching the application of what might be considered a classical genetic algorithm. This has a binary representation, fitness proportionate selection, a low probability of mutation, and an emphasis on genetically inspired recombination as a means of generating new candidate solutions. This is commonly referred to as the "simple GA" (SGA), or the "canonical GA" and is summarised in Table 3.1.

Representation	Bit-strings
Recombination	1-Point crossover
Mutation	Bit flip
Parent selection	Fitness proportional
Survival selection	Generational

Table 3.1. Sketch of the simple GA

To illustrate this, we show the details of one selection–reproduction cycle on a simple (thus traceable) problem after Goldberg [172], namely that of maximising the values of x^2 for x in the range 0–31. Using a simple 5-bit binary encoding, Table 3.2 shows a random initial population of four genotypes, the corresponding phenotypes, and their fitness values. The column $Prob_i$ shows the probability that an individual $i \in \{1, 2, 3, 4\}$ is chosen to be a parent, which for fitness proportionate selection is $Prob_i = f_i / \sum f_j$. The number of parents is the same as the size of our population, so the expected number of copies of each individual after selection is $f_i/\bar{f}$ (displayed values are rounded up). As can be seen, these numbers are not integers; rather they represent a probability distribution, and the mating pool is created by making number of random choices to sample from this distribution. The column "Actual count" stands for the number of copies in the mating pool, i.e., it shows *one* possible outcome.

The selected individuals are paired at random, and for each pair a random point along the string is chosen. Table 3.3 shows the results of crossover on the given mating pool for crossover points after the fourth and second genes, respectively, together with the corresponding fitness values.

In the SGA mutation works by generating a random number (from a distribution uniform over the range [0, 1]) in each bit position, and comparing it to a fixed low (e.g. 0.001 [98]) value, usually called the **mutation rate**. If the random number is below that rate, the value of the gene in the corresponding position is flipped. In our example we have $4 * 5 = 20$ genes, and Table 3.4 shows the outcome of mutation when the first and eighteenth values in our sequence of random numbers are below the bitwise mutation probability. In this case, the mutations shown happen to have caused positive changes in fitness,

---

[1] If perhaps mistakenly – see [99].

but we should emphasise that in later generations, as the number of "ones" in the population rises, mutation will be *on average* (but not always) deleterious. Although manually engineered, this example shows a typical progress: the average fitness grows from 293 to 588.5, and the best fitness in the population from 576 to 729 after crossover and mutation.

String no.	Initial population	x Value	Fitness $f(x) = x^2$	$Prob_i$	Expected count	Actual count
1	0 1 1 0 1	13	169	0.14	0.58	1
2	1 1 0 0 0	24	576	0.49	1.97	2
3	0 1 0 0 0	8	64	0.06	0.22	0
4	1 0 0 1 1	19	361	0.31	1.23	1
Sum			1170	1.00	4.00	4
Average			293	0.25	1.00	1
Max			576	0.49	1.97	2

Table 3.2. The x^2 example, 1: initialisation, evaluation, and parent selection

String no.	Mating pool	Crossover point	Offspring after xover	x Value	Fitness $f(x) = x^2$
1	0 1 1 0 | 1	4	0 1 1 0 0	12	144
2	1 1 0 0 | 0	4	1 1 0 0 1	25	625
2	1 1 | 0 0 0	2	1 1 0 1 1	27	729
4	1 0 | 0 1 1	2	1 0 0 0 0	16	256
Sum					1754
Average					439
Max					729

Table 3.3. The x^2 example, 2: crossover and offspring evaluation

String no.	Offspring after xover	Offspring after mutation	x Value	Fitness $f(x) = x^2$
1	0 1 1 0 0	1 1 1 0 0	26	676
2	1 1 0 0 1	1 1 0 0 1	25	625
2	1 1 0 1 1	1 1 0 1 1	27	729
4	1 0 0 0 0	1 0 1 0 0	18	324
Sum				2354
Average				588.5
Max				729

Table 3.4. The x^2 example, 3: mutation and offspring evaluation

3.3 Representation of Individuals

As explained in Chap. 2, the the first stage of building any evolutionary algorithm is to decide on a genetic **representation** of a candidate solution to the problem. This involves defining the genotype and the mapping from genotype to phenotype.

When choosing a representation, it is important to choose the "right" representation for the problem being solved. Getting the representation right is one of the most difficult parts of designing a good evolutionary algorithm. Often this only comes with practice and a good knowledge of the application domain. In the following sections, we look more closely at some commonly used representations and the genetic operators that might be applied to them. It is important to stress, however, that while the representations described here are commonly used, they might not the best representations for your application. Equally, although we present the representations and their associate operators separately, it frequently turns out in practice that using mixed representations is a more natural and suitable way of describing and manipulating a solution than trying to shoehorn different aspects of a problem into a common form.

3.3.1 Binary Representations

The first representation we look at is one of the simplest – the binary one used in the example above. This is one of the earliest representations, and historically many GAs have mistakenly used this representation almost independently of the problem they were trying to solve. Here the genotype consists simply of a string of binary digits – a bit-string.

For a particular application we have to decide how long the string should be, and how we will interpret it to produce a phenotype. In choosing the genotype–phenotype mapping for a specific problem, one has to make sure that the encoding allows that all possible bit strings denote a valid solution to the given problem[2] and that, vice versa, all possible solutions can be represented.

For some problems, particularly those concerning Boolean decision variables, the genotype–phenotype mapping is natural, but frequently (as in our example) bit-strings are used to encode other nonbinary information. For example, we might interpret a bit-string of length 80 as ten 8-bit integers, or five 16-bit real numbers. Usually this is a mistake, and better results can be obtained by using the integer or real-valued representations directly.

One of the problems of coding numbers in binary is that different bits have different significance. This can be helped by using **Gray coding**, which is a variation on the way that integers are mapped on bit strings. The standard method has the disadvantage that the Hamming distance between two consecutive integers is often not equal to one. If the goal is to evolve an integer

---

[2] In practice this restriction to validity in not always possible; see Chap. 12 for a more complete discussion of this issue.

number, you would like to have the chance of changing a 7 into a 8 equal to that of changing it to a 6. The chance of changing 0111 to 1000 by independent bit-flips is not the same, however, as that of changing it to 0110. Gray coding is a representation that ensures that consecutive integers always have Hamming distance one. Further details can be seen in Appendix A.

3.3.2 Integer Representations

As we hinted in the previous section, binary representations are not always the most suitable if our problem more naturally maps onto a representation where different genes can take one of a set of values. One obvious example of when this might occur is the problem of finding the optimal values for a set of variables that all take integer values. These values might be unrestricted (i.e., any integer value is permissible), or might be restricted to a finite set: for example, if we are trying to evolve a path on a square grid, we might restrict the values to the set {0,1,2,3} representing {*North, East, South, West*}. In either case an integer encoding is probably more suitable than a binary encoding. When designing the encoding and variation operators, it is worth considering whether there are any natural relations between the possible values that an attribute can take. This might be obvious for **ordinal attributes** such as integers (2 is more like 3 than it is 389), but for **cardinal attributes** such as the compass points above, there may not be a natural ordering.

3.3.3 Real-Valued or Floating-Point Representation

Often the most sensible way to represent a candidate solution to a problem is to have a string of real values. This occurs when the values that we want to represent as genes come from a continuous rather than a discrete distribution. Of course, on a computer the precision of these real values is actually limited by the implementation, so we will refer to them as floating-point numbers. The genotype for a solution with k genes is now a vector $\langle x_1, \ldots, x_k \rangle$ with (almost) $x_i \in \mathbb{R}$.

3.3.4 Permutation Representations

Many problems naturally take the form of deciding on the order in which a sequence of events should occur. While other forms do occur (for example decoder functions based on unrestricted integer representations [28, 186] or "floating keys" based on real-valued representations [27, 41]), the most natural representation of such problems is as a permutation of a set of integers. One immediate consequence is that while an ordinary GA string allows numbers to occur more than once, such sequences of integers will not represent valid permutations. It is clear that we need new variation operators to preserve the permutation property that each possible allele value occurs exactly once in the solution.

When choosing appropriate variation operators it is also worth bearing in mind that there are actually two classes of problems that are represented by permutations. In the first of these, the *order* in which events occur is important. This might happen when the events use limited resources or time, and a typical example of this sort of problem is the "job shop scheduling" problem described in Sect. 3.9. As an example, it might be better for widget 1 to be produced before widgets 2 and 3, which in turn might be preferably produced before widget 4, no matter how far in advance this is done. In this case it might well be that the sequences [1,2,3,4] and [1,3,2,4] have similar fitness , and are much better than, for example, [4,3,2,1].

An alternative type of order-based problems depends on *adjacency*, and is typified by the travelling sales person problem (TSP). The problem is to find a complete tour of n given cities of minimal length. The search space for this problem is very big: there are $(n-1)!$ different routes possible for n given cities (for the asymmetric case counting back and forth as two routes).[3] For $n = 30$ there are approximately 10^{32} different tours. We label the cities $1, 2, \ldots, n$. One complete tour is a permutation of the cities, so that for $n = 4$, the routes [1,2,3,4] and [3,4,2,1] are both valid. The difference from order-based problems can clearly be seen if we consider that the starting point of the tour is not important, thus [1,2,3,4] , [2,3,4,1], [3,4,1,2], and [4,1,2,3] are all equivalent. Many examples of this class are also symmetric, so that [4,3,2,1] and so on are also equivalent.

Finally, we should mention that there are two possible ways to encode a permutation. In the first (most commonly used) of these the ith element of the representation denotes the event that happens in that place in the sequence (or the ith destination visited). In the second, the value of the ith element denotes the position in the sequence in which the ith event happens. Thus for the four cities [A,B,C,D], and the permutation [3,1,2,4], the first encoding denotes the tour [C,A,B,D] and the second [B,C,A,D].

3.4 Mutation

Mutation is the generic name given to those variation operators that use only one parent and create one child by applying some kind of randomised change to the representation (genotype). The form taken depends on the choice of encoding used, as does the meaning of the associated parameter, which is often referred to as the mutation rate. In the descriptions below we concentrate on the choice of operators rather than of parameters. However, the latter can make a significant difference in the behaviour of the genetic algorithm, and is discussed in more depth in Chap. 8.

---

[3] These comments about the size of the search space apply to all permutation problems.

3.4.1 Mutation for Binary Representations

Although a few other schemes have been occasionally used, the most common mutation operator used for binary encodings considers each gene separately and allows each bit to flip (i.e., from 1 to 0 or 0 to 1) with a small probability p_m. The actual number of values changed is thus not fixed, but depends on the sequence of random numbers drawn, so for an encoding of length L, on average $L \cdot p_m$ values will be changed. In Fig. 3.1 this is illustrated for the case where the third, fourth, and eighth random values generated are less than the bitwise mutation rate p_m.

Fig. 3.1. Bitwise mutation for binary encodings

A number of studies and recommendations have been made for the choice of suitable values for the bitwise mutation rate p_m, and it is worth noting at the outset that the most suitable choice to use depends on the desired outcome. For example, does the application require a population in which *all* members have high fitness, or simply that *one* highly fit individual is found? However, most binary coded GAs use mutation rates in a range such that on average between one gene per generation and one gene per offspring is mutated.

3.4.2 Mutation Operators for Integer Representations

For integer encodings there are two principal forms of mutation used, both of which mutate each gene independently with user-defined probability p_m.

Random Resetting

Here the "bit-flipping" mutation of binary encodings is extended to "random resetting", so that with probability p_m a new value is chosen at random from the set of permissible values in each position. This the most suitable operator to use when the genes encode for cardinal attributes, since all other gene values are equally likely to be chosen.

Creep Mutation

This scheme was designed for ordinal attributes and works by adding a small (positive or negative) value to each gene with probability p. Usually these values are sampled randomly for each position, from a distribution that is symmetric about zero, and is more likely to generate small changes than large ones. It should be noted that creep mutation requires a number of parameters controlling the distribution from which the random numbers are drawn, and hence the size of the *steps* that mutation takes in the search space. Finding appropriate settings for these parameters may not be easy, and it is sometimes common to use more than one mutation operator in tandem from integer-based problems. For example, in [92] both a "big creep" and a "little creep" operator are used. Alternatively, random resetting might be used with low probability, in conjunction with a creep operator that tended to make small changes relative to the range of permissible values.

3.4.3 Mutation Operators for Floating-Point Representations

For floating-point representations, it is normal to ignore the discretisation imposed by hardware and consider the allele values as coming from a continuous rather than a discrete distribution, so the forms of mutation described above are no longer applicable. Instead it is common to change the allele value of each gene randomly within its domain given by a lower L_i and upper U_i bound,[4] resulting in the following transformation:

$$\langle x_1, \ldots, x_n \rangle \to \langle x'_1, \ldots, x'_n \rangle, \quad \text{where} \quad x_i, x'_i \in [L_i, U_i].$$

Two types can be distinguished according to the probability distribution from which the new gene values are drawn: uniform and nonuniform mutation.

Uniform Mutation

For this operator the values of x'_i are drawn uniformly randomly from $[L_i, U_i]$. This is the most straightforward option, analogous to bit-flipping for binary encodings and the random resetting sketched above for integer encodings. It is normally used with a positionwise mutation probability.

Nonuniform Mutation with a Fixed Distribution

Perhaps the most common form of nonuniform mutation used with floating-point representations takes a form analogous to the creep mutation for integers. It is designed so that usually, but not always, the amount of change introduced is small. This is achieved by adding to the current gene value an amount drawn randomly from a Gaussian distribution with mean zero and user-specified standard deviation, and then curtailing the resulting value to the range $[L_i, U_i]$ if necessary. The Gaussian (or normal) distribution has the

---

[4] We assume here that the domain of each variable is a single interval $[L_i, U_i] \subseteq \mathbb{R}$. The generalisation to a union of disjoint intervals is straightforward.

property that approximately two thirds of the samples drawn lie within one standard deviation. This means that most of the changes made will be small, but there is nonzero probability of generating very large changes since the tail of the distribution never reaches zero. It is normal practice to apply this operator with probability one per gene, and instead the mutation parameter is used to control the standard deviation of the Gaussian and hence the probability distribution of the step sizes taken.

An alternative to the Gaussian distribution is the use of a Cauchy distribution, which has a "fatter" tail. That is, the probabilities of generating larger values are slightly higher than for a Gaussian with the same standard deviation [434].

3.4.4 Mutation Operators for Permutation Representations

For permutation representations, it is no longer possible to consider each gene independently, rather finding legal mutations is a matter of moving alleles around in the genome. This has the immediate consequence that the mutation parameter is interpreted as the probability that the *string* undergoes mutation, rather than that a single gene in the string is altered. The three most common forms of mutation used for order-based problems were first described in [390]. Whereas the first three operators below (in particular insertion mutation) work by making small changes to the order in which allele values occur, for adjacency-based problems these can cause huge numbers of links to be broken, and so inversion is more commonly used.

Swap Mutation

This operator works by randomly picking two positions (genes) in the string and swapping their allele values. This is illustrated in Fig. 3.2, where the values in positions two and five have been swapped.

Fig. 3.2. Swap mutation

Insert Mutation

This operator works by picking two alleles at random and moving one so that it is next to the other, shuffling along the others to make room.This is illustrated in Fig. 3.3, where the values two and five have been chosen.

Fig. 3.3. Insert mutation

Scramble Mutation

Here the entire string, or some randomly chosen subset of values within it, have their positions scrambled. This is illustrated in Fig. 3.4, where the values from two to five have been chosen.

Fig. 3.4. Scramble mutation

Inversion Mutation

Inversion mutation works by randomly selecting two positions in the string and reversing the order in which the values appear between those positions. It effectively breaks the string into three parts with all links inside a part being preserved, and only the two links between the parts being broken. The inversion of a randomly chosen substring is the thus smallest change that can be made to an adjacency-based problem The ordering of the search space induced by this operator thus forms a natural basis for considering this class of problems, equivalent to the Hamming space for binary problem representations. It is the basic move behind the 2-opt search heuristic for TSP [249], and by extension k-opt. This operator is illustrated in Fig. 3.5, where the substring between positions two and five was chosen for inversion.

3.5 Recombination

Recombination, the process whereby a new individual solution is created from the information contained within two (or more) parent solutions, is considered by many to be one of the most important features in genetic algorithms.

Fig. 3.5. Inversion mutation

Much research activity has focused on it as the primary mechanism for creating diversity, with mutation considered as a background search operator. Regardless of the merits (or otherwise) of this viewpoint, it is certainly one of the features that most distinguishes GAs – and other EAs using recombination – from other global optimisation algorithms.

Although the term recombination has come to be used for the more general case, early authors used the term **crossover** (also from a biological analogy to meiosis, Sect. 1.4.2), and we will occasionally use the terms interchangeably, although crossover tends to refer to the most common two-parent case. Recombination operators are usually applied probabilistically according to a **crossover rate** p_c, which is typically in the range [0.5,1.0]. Usually two parents are selected and then a random variable is drawn from [0,1) and compared to p_c. If the value is lower, two offspring are created via recombination of the two parents; otherwise they are created **asexually**, i.e., by copying the parents. The net effect is that in general the resulting set of offspring consists of some copies of the parents, and other individuals that represent previously unseen solutions. Thus, in contrast to the mutation probability p_m, which controls how parts of the chromosome are perturbed independently, the crossover probability determines the chance that a chosen pair of parents undergoes this operator.

3.5.1 Recombination Operators for Binary Representations

Three standard forms of recombination are generally used for binary representations. They all start from two parents and create two children, although all of these have been extended to the more general case where a number of parents may be used [133], and there are also situations in which only one of the offspring might be considered (Sect. 3.6).

One-Point Crossover

One-point crossover was the original recombination operator proposed in [204] and examined in [98]. It works by choosing a random number in the range $[0, l-1]$ (with l the length of the encoding), and then splitting both parents at this point and creating the two children by exchanging the tails (Fig. 3.6).

Fig. 3.6. One-point crossover

N-Point Crossover

One-point crossover can easily be generalised to *n*-point crossover, where the representation is broken into more than two segments of contiguous genes, and then the offspring are created by taking alternative segments from the two parents. In practice this means choosing *n* random crossover points in $[0, l-1]$, which is illustrated in Fig. 3.7 for $n = 2$.

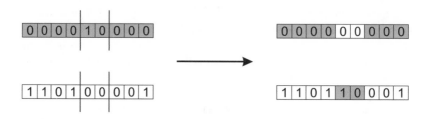

Fig. 3.7. *n*-point crossover: $n = 2$

Uniform Crossover

The previous two operators worked by dividing the parents into a number of sections of contiguous genes and reassembling them to produce offspring. In contrast to this, uniform crossover [389] works by treating each gene independently and making a random choice as to which parent it should be inherited from. This is implemented by generating a string of L random variables from a uniform distribution over [0,1]. In each position, if the value is below a parameter p (usually 0.5), the gene is inherited from the first parent; otherwise from the second. The second offspring is created using the inverse mapping. This is illustrated in Fig. 3.8.

Fig. 3.8. Uniform crossover. In this example the array [0.35, 0.62, 0.18, 0.42, 0.83, 0.76, 0.39, 0.51, 0.36] of random variables drawn uniformly from [0,1) was used to decide inheritance

From Figs. 3.6 and 3.7 it should be immediately apparent that whereas in our discussion we suggested that in the absence of prior information, recombination worked by randomly mixing parts of the parents, n-point crossover has an inherent bias in that it tends to keep together genes that are located close to each other in the representation. Furthermore, when n is odd (e.g., one-point crossover), there is a strong bias against keeping together combinations of genes that are located at opposite ends of the representation. These effects are known as **positional bias** and have been extensively studied from both a theoretical and experimental perspective [138, 378] (see Sect. 11.2.3 for more details). In contrast, uniform crossover does not exhibit any positional bias, but does have a strong tendency towards transmitting 50% of the genes from each parent and against transmitting an offspring a large number of coadapted genes from one parent. This is known as **distributional bias**.

The general nature of these algorithms (and the No Free Lunch theorem [430], Sect. 11.8) make it impossible to state that one or the other of these operators performs best on any given problem. However, an understanding of the types of bias exhibited by different recombination operators can be invaluable when designing an algorithm for a particular problem, particularly if there are known patterns or dependencies in the chosen representation that can be exploited.

3.5.2 Recombination Operators for Integer Representations

For representations where each gene has a higher number of possible allele values (such as integers) it is normal to use the same set of operators as for binary representations. This is because usually it does not make any sense to consider "blending" allele values of this sort. For example, even if genes represent integer values, averaging an even and an odd integer yields a nonintegral result.

3.5.3 Recombination Operators for Floating-Point Representations

We have two options for recombining two floating-point strings:

- Using an analogous operator to those used for bit-strings, but now split between floats. In other words, an allele is one floating-point value instead of one bit. This has the disadvantage (shared with all of the recombination operators described above) that only mutation can insert new values into the population, since recombination only gives us new combinations of existing floats. Recombination operators of this type for floating-point representations are known as **discrete recombination** and have the property that if we are creating an offspring z from parents x and y, then the allele value for gene i is given by $z_i = x_i$ or y_i with equal likelihood.
- Using an operator that, in each gene position, creates a new allele value in the offspring that lies between those of the parents. Using the terminology above, we have $z_i = \alpha x_i + (1 - \alpha)y_i$ for some α in [0,1]. In this way, recombination is now able to create new gene material, but it has the disadvantage that as a result of the averaging process the range of the allele values in the population for each gene is reduced. Operators of this type are known as **intermediate** or **arithmetic recombination**.

Arithmetic Recombination

Three types of arithmetic recombination are described in [271]. In all of these, the choice of the parameter α is sometimes made at random over [0,1], but in practice it is common to use a constant value, often 0.5 (in which case we have **uniform arithmetic recombination**).

Simple Recombination

First pick a recombination point k. Then, for child 1, take the first k floats of parent 1 and put them into the child. The rest is the arithmetic average of parent 1 and 2:

Child 1: $\langle x_1, \ldots, x_k, \alpha \cdot y_{k+1} + (1 - \alpha) \cdot x_{k+1}, \ldots, \alpha \cdot y_n + (1 - \alpha) \cdot x_n \rangle$.

Child 2 is analogous, with x and y reversed (Fig. 3.9).

Single Arithmetic Recombination

Pick a random allele k. At that position, take the arithmetic average of the two parents. The other points are the points from the parents, i.e.:

Child 1: $\langle x_1, \ldots, x_{k-1}, \alpha \cdot y_k + (1 - \alpha) \cdot x_k, x_{k+1}, \ldots, x_n \rangle$.

The second child is created in the same way with x and y reversed (Fig. 3.10).

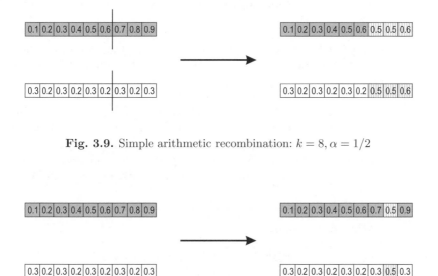

Fig. 3.9. Simple arithmetic recombination: $k = 8, \alpha = 1/2$

Fig. 3.10. Single arithmetic recombination: $k = 3, \alpha = 1/2$

Whole Arithmetic Recombination

This is the most commonly used operator and works by taking the weighted sum of the two parental alleles for each gene, i.e.:

$$\text{Child 1} = \alpha \cdot \bar{x} + (1 - \alpha) \cdot \bar{y}, \qquad \text{Child 2} = \alpha \cdot \bar{y} + (1 - \alpha) \cdot \bar{x}.$$

This is illustrated in Fig. 3.11. As the example shows, if $\alpha = 1/2$ the two offspring will be identical for this operator.

Fig. 3.11. Whole arithmetic recombination: $\alpha = 1/2$

3.5.4 Recombination Operators for Permutation Representations

At first sight, permutation-based representations present particular difficulties for the design of recombination operators, since it is not generally possible simply to exchange substrings between parents and still maintain the permutation property. However, this situation is alleviated when we consider what it is that the solutions actually represent, i.e., either an order in which elements occur, or a set of moves linking pairs of elements. A number of specialised recombination operators have been designed for permutations, which aim at transmitting as much as possible of the information contained in the parents, especially that held in common. We shall concentrate here on describing two of the best known and most commonly used operators for each subclass of permutation problems.

Partially Mapped Crossover

Partially mapped crossover (PMX) was first proposed by Goldberg and Lingle as a recombination operator for the TSP in [175], and has become one of the most widely used operators for adjacency-type problems. During the years many slight variations of the definition of PMX occurred in the literature; here we use that of Whitley from [415] that works as follows (Figs. 3.12 – 3.14).

1. Choose two crossover points at random, and copy the segment between them from the first parent (P1) into the first offspring.
2. Starting from the first crossover point look for elements in that segment of the second parent (P2) that have not been copied.
3. For each of these (say i), look in the offspring to see what element (say j) has been copied in its place from P1.
4. Place i into the position occupied j in P2, since we know that we will not be putting j there (as we already have it in our string).
5. If the place occupied by j in P2 has already been filled in the offspring by an element k, put i in the position occupied by k in P2.
6. Having dealt with the elements from the crossover segment, the rest of the offspring can be filled from P2, and the second child is created analogously with the parental roles reversed.

Inspection of the offspring created shows that in this case six of the nine links present in the offspring are present in one or more of the parents. However, of the two edges {5–6} and {7–8} common to both parents, only the first is present in the offspring. Radcliffe [315] suggests that a desirable property of any recombination operator is that of *respect*, i.e., that any information carried in both parents should also be present in the offspring. A moment's reflection tells us that this is clearly true for all of the recombination operators described above for binary and integer representations, and for discrete recombination for floating-point representations, but as the example above

Fig. 3.12. PMX, step 1: copy randomly selected segment from first parent into offspring

Fig. 3.13. PMX, step 2: consider in turn the placement of the elements that occur in the middle segment of parent 2 but not parent 1. The position that 8 takes in P2 is occupied by 4 in the offspring, so we can put the 8 into the position vacated by the 4 in P2. The position of the 2 in P2 is occupied by the 5 in the offspring, so we look first to the place occupied by the 5 in P2, which is position 7. This is already occupied by the value 7, so we look to where this occurs in P2 and finally find a slot in the offspring that is vacant – the third. Finally, note that the values 6 and 5 occur in the middle segments of both parents.

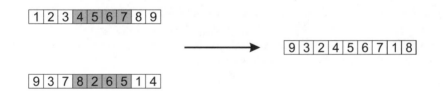

Fig. 3.14. PMX, step 3: copy remaining elements from second parent into same positions in offspring

shows, is not necessarily true of PMX. With this issue in mind, several other operators have been designed for adjacency-based permutation problems, of which the best known is described next.

Edge Crossover

Edge crossover is based on the idea that an offspring should be created as far as possible using only edges that are present in one or more parent. It has undergone a number of revisions over the years. Here we describe the most commonly used version: edge-3 crossover after Whitley [415], which is designed to ensure that common edges are preserved.

In order to achieve this, an edge table (also known as adjacency lists) is constructed, which for each element, lists the other elements that are linked to it in the two parents. A "+" in the table indicates that the edge is present in both parents. The operator works as follows:

1. Construct edge table
2. Pick an initial element at random and put it in the offspring
3. Set the variable $current\_element = entry$
4. Remove all references to $current\_element$ from the table
5. Examine list for $current\_element$
   - If there is a common edge, pick that to be next element
   - Otherwise pick the entry in the list which itself has the shortest list
   - Ties are split at random
6. In the case of reaching an empty list, the other end of the offspring is examined for extension; otherwise a new element is chosen at random

Clearly only in the last case will so-called foreign edges be introduced.

Edge-3 recombination is illustrated by the following example where the parents are the same two permutations used in the PMX example [*1 2 3 4 5 6 7 8 9*] and [*9 3 7 8 2 6 5 1 4*], giving the edge table seen in Table 3.5 and the construction illustrated in Table 3.6. Note that only one child per recombination is created by this operator.

Element	Edges	Element	Edges
1	2,5,4,9	6	2,5+,7
2	1,3,6,8	7	3,6,8+
3	2,4,7,9	8	2,7+, 9
4	1,3,5,9	9	1,3,4,8
5	1,4,6+		

Table 3.5. Edge crossover: example edge table

Choices	Element selected	Reason	Partial result
All	1	Random	[1]
2,5,4,9	5	Shortest list	[1 5]
4,6	6	Common edge	[1 5 6]
2,7	2	Random choice (both have two items in list)	[1 5 6 2]
3,8	8	Shortest list	[1 5 6 2 8]
7,9	7	Common edge	[1 5 6 2 8 7]
3	3	Only item in list	[1 5 6 2 8 7 3]
4,9	9	Random choice	[1 5 6 2 8 7 3 9]
4	4	Last element	[1 5 6 2 8 7 3 9 4]

Table 3.6. Edge crossover: example of permutation construction

Order Crossover

The order crossover operator [92] was designed by Davis for order-based permutation problems. It begins in a similar fashion to PMX, by copying a randomly chosen segment of the first parent into the offspring. However, it proceeds differently because the intention is to transmit information about *relative order* from the second parent.

1. Choose two crossover points at random, and copy the segment between them from the first parent (P1) into the first offspring.
2. Starting from the second crossover point in the second parent, copy the remaining unused numbers into the first child in the order that they appear in the second parent, wrapping around at the end of the list.
3. Create the second offspring in an analogous manner, with the parent roles reversed.

This is illustrated in Figs. 3.15 and 3.16.

Fig. 3.15. Order crossover, step 1: copy randomly selected segment from first parent into offspring

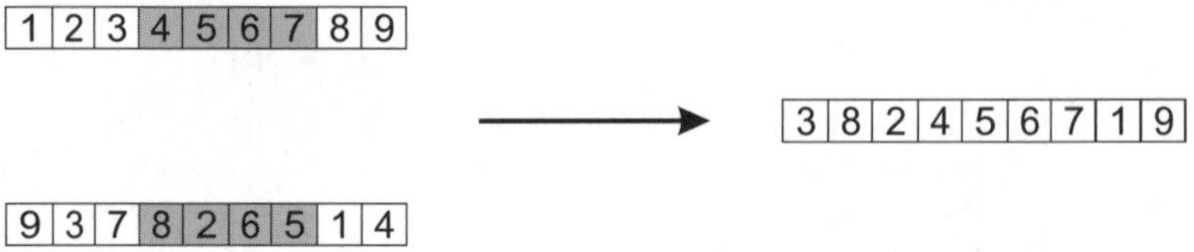

1 2 3 4 5 6 7 8 9
9 3 7 8 2 6 5 1 4
3 8 2 4 5 6 7 1 9

Fig. 3.16. Order crossover, step 2: copy rest of alleles in order they appear in second parent, treating string as toroidal

Cycle Crossover

The final operator that we will consider in this section is cycle crossover [295], which is concerned with preserving as much information as possible about the *absolute* position in which elements occur. The operator works by dividing the elements into *cycles*. A cycle is a subset of elements that has the property that each element always occurs paired with another element of the same cycle when the two parents are aligned. Having divided the permutation into cycles, the offspring are created by selecting alternate cycles from each parent. The procedure for constructing cycles is as follows:

1. Start with the first unused position and allele of P1
2. Look at the allele in the *same position* in P2
3. Go to the position with the *same allele* in P1
4. Add this allele to the cycle
5. Repeat steps 2 through 4 until you arrive at the first allele of P1

The complete operation of the operator is illustrated by an example in Figs. 3.17 and 3.18.

1 2 3 4 5 6 7 8 9
9 3 7 8 2 6 5 1 4
1 2 3 4 5 6 7 8 9
9 3 7 8 2 6 5 1 4
1 3 7 4 2 6 5 8 9
9 3 7 8 2 6 5 1 4

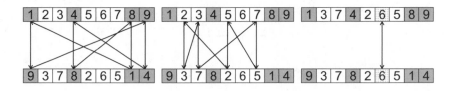

Fig. 3.17. Cycle crossover, step 1: identification of cycles

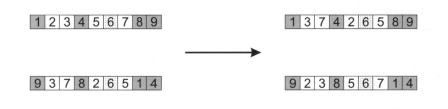

Fig. 3.18. Cycle crossover, step 2: construction of offspring

3.5.5 Multiparent Recombination

Looking at variation operators from the perspective of their arity a makes it a straightforward idea to go beyond the usual $a = 1$ (mutation) and $a = 2$ (crossover). The resulting **multiparent recombination** operators for $a = 3, 4, \ldots$ are simple to define and implement. This provides the opportunity to experiment with evolutionary processes using reproduction schemes that do not exist in biology. From the technical point of view this offers a tool for amplifying the effects of recombination. Although such operators are not widely used in EC, there are many examples that have been proposed during the development of the field, even as early as 1966 [64], see [113] for an overview. These operators can be categorised by the basic mechanism used for combining the information of the parent individuals. This mechanism can be:

- Based on allele frequencies, e.g., p-sexual voting [288] generalising uniform crossover
- Based on segmentation and recombination of the parents, e.g., the diagonal crossover in [122], generalising n-point crossover
- Based on numerical operations on real-valued alleles, e.g., the center of mass crossover [399], generalising arithmetic recombination operators

In general, it cannot be claimed that increasing the arity of recombination has a positive effect on the peformance of an EA – this depends very much on the type of recombination and the problem at hand. However, systematic studies on landscapes with tunable ruggedness [127] and a large number of experimental investigations on various problems clearly show that using more than two parents is advantageous in many cases.

3.6 Population Models

So far in our discussion of genetic algorithms, we have focused on the way that potential solutions are represented to give a population of diverse individuals, and on the way that variation (recombination and mutation) operators work on those individuals to yield offspring. These offspring will generally inherit some of their parents' properties but also differ slightly from them, providing new potential solutions to be evaluated. We now turn our attention to the second important element of the evolutionary process – that of the differential survival of individuals to compete for resources and take part in reproduction, based on their relative fitness.

Two different GA models are discerned in literature: the **generational model** and the **steady-state model**. The generational model is described in the example in Sect. 3.2. In each generation we begin with a population of size μ, from which a **mating pool** of μ parents is selected. Next, λ $(= \mu)$ offspring are created from the mating pool by the application of variation operators, and evaluated. After each generation, the whole population is replaced by its offspring, which is called the "next generation".[5]

In the steady state model, the entire population is not changed at once, but rather a part of it. In this case, λ $(< \mu)$ old individuals are replaced by λ new ones, the offspring. The percentage of the population that is replaced is called the **generational gap**, and is equal to λ/μ. Since its introduction in Whitley's GENITOR algorithm [423], the steady-state model has been widely studied and applied [101, 320, 407], usually with $\lambda = 1$ and a corresponding generation gap of $1/\mu$.

At this stage it is worth making the point that the operators, selection and replacement, which are responsible for this competitive element of population management, work on the basis of an individual's fitness (evaluated or estimated). This means that our emphasis is now shifting from partial solutions, to whole solutions. A direct consequence of this is that these operators work independently of the problem representation chosen.

As was seen in the general description of an evolutionary algorithm at the start of Chapter 2, there are two points in the evolutionary cycle at which fitness-based competition can occur: during selection to take part in mating, and during the selection of individuals to survive into the next generation. We begin by describing the most commonly used methods for parent selection, but note that many of these can also be applied during the survival selection phase. As a final preliminary, please note that we will adopt a convention that we are trying to maximise fitness, and that fitness values are non-negative. Often problems are expressed in terms of an objective function to be minimised, and sometimes negative fitness values occur. However, in all cases these can be mapped into the desired form by using an appropriate transformation.

---

[5] Let us note that there are other frequently used symbols in the literature for denoting the population size and the number of children, although without any real standard. By using μ and λ we adopt the notation of evolution strategies, wherein these symbols do form a standard, even providing the names of selection mechanisms, cf. Sects. 4.6 and 4.7.

3.7 Parent Selection

3.7.1 Fitness Proportional Selection

The principles of **fitness proportional selection** (FPS) were described in the simple example in Section 3.2. Recall that for each choice, the probability that an individual f_i is selected for mating is $f_i / \sum_{j=1}^{\mu} f_j$, that is to say that the selection probability depends on the *absolute* fitness value of the individual compared to the *absolute* fitness values of the rest of the population.

This selection mechanism was introduced in [204] and was much studied thereafter. However, it has been recognised that there are some problems with this selection mechanism:

- Outstanding individuals, i.e., individuals that are a lot better than the rest, take over the entire population very quickly. This is known as **premature convergence**.
- When fitness values are all very close together, there is almost no **selection pressure**, since the parts of the roulette wheel assigned to the individuals are more or less the same size, so selection is almost uniformly random, and having a slightly better fitness is not very "useful" to an individual. Therefore, later in a run, when some convergence has taken place and the worst individuals are gone, the performance only increases very slowly.
- The mechanism behaves differently on transposed versions of the same fitness function.

This last point is illustrated in Fig. 3.19, which shows the changes in selection probabilities for three points that arise when a random fitness function $y = f(x)$ is transposed by adding 10.0 to all fitness values. As can be seen the selective advantage of the fittest point (B) is reduced.

To avoid the second two problems with FPS, a procedure known as windowing is often used. Under this scheme, fitness differentials are maintained by subtracted from the raw fitness $f(x)$ a value β^t, which depends in some way on the recent search history. The simplest approach is just to set $\beta = min_{y \in P^t} f(y)$, i.e., to subtract the value of the least-fit member of the current population P^t. This value may fluctuate quite rapidly, so one alternative is to use a running average over the last few generations.

Another well-known approach is Goldberg's **sigma scaling** [172], which incorporates information about the mean $\bar{f}$ and standard deviation σ_f of fitnesses in the population:

$$f'(x) = max(f(x) - (\bar{f} - c \cdot \sigma_f), 0.0),$$

where c is a constant value, usually set to 2.

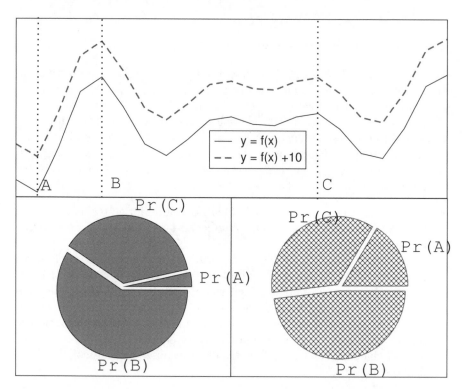

Fig. 3.19. Example of the susceptibility of fitness proportionate selection to function transposition. *Top*: the fitness of three points for fitness functions $f(x)$ and $f' = f(x) + 10$. *Bottom left*: selection probabilities of the three points under $f(x)$. *Bottom right*: selection probabilities of the three points under $f'(x)$

3.7.2 Ranking Selection

Rank-based selection is another method that was inspired by the observed drawbacks of fitness proportionate selection [33]. It preserves a constant selection pressure by sorting the population on the basis of fitness, and then allocating selection probabilities to individuals according to their rank, rather than according to their actual fitness values. The mapping from rank number to selection probability is arbitrary and can be done in many ways, for example, linearly or exponentially decreasing, of course with the proviso that the sum over the population of the probabilities must be unity.

The usual formula for calculating the selection probability for linear ranking schemes is parameterised by a value s ($1.0 < s \leq 2.0$). In the case of a generational GA, where $\mu = \lambda$, this is the expected number of offspring allotted to the fittest individual. If this individual has rank μ, and the worst has rank 1, then the selection probability for an individual of rank i is:

$$P_{lin-rank}(i) = \frac{(2-s)}{\mu} + \frac{2i(s-1)}{\mu(\mu-1)}.$$

In Table 3.7 we show an example of how the selection probabilities differ for a population of three different individuals with fitness proportionate and rank-based selection with different values of s.

	Fitness	Rank	P_{selFP}	P_{selLR} $(s=2)$	P_{selLR} $(s=1.5)$
A	1	1	0.1	0	0.167
B	5	2	0.5	0.67	0.5
C	4	2	0.4	0.33	0.33
Sum	10		1.0	1.0	1.0

Table 3.7. Fitness proportionate (FP) versus linear ranking (LR) selection

When a linear mapping is used from rank to selection probabilities, the amount of selection pressure that can be applied is limited. This arises from the assumption that, on average, an individual of median fitness should have one chance to be reproduced, which in turn imposes a maximum value of $s = 2.0$. If a higher selection pressure is required, i.e., more emphasis on selecting individuals of above-average fitness, an *exponential ranking* scheme is often used, of the form:

$$P_{exp-rank}(i) = \frac{1 - e^{-i}}{c}.$$

The normalisation factor c is chosen so that the sum of the probabilities is unity, i.e., it is a function of the population size.

3.7.3 Implementing Selection Probabilities

In the discussion above we described two alternative schemes for deciding a probability distribution that defines the likelihood of each individual in the population being selected for reproduction. In an ideal world, the mating pool of parents taking part in recombination would have exactly the same proportions as this selection probability distribution. However, in practice this is not possible because of the finite size of the population, i.e., when we multiply the selection probability by the total number of parents in the mating pool, we typically find that individuals have an expected number of copies which is noninteger. In other words, the mating pool of parents is *sampled* from the selection probability distribution, but will not in general accurately reflect it, as seen in the example in Sect. 3.2.

The simplest way of achieving this sampling is known as the **roulette wheel** algorithm. Conceptually this is the same as spinning a one-armed roulette wheel, where the sizes of the holes reflect the selection probabilities. If we assume that the algorithm is being applied to select λ members from the set of μ parents into a mating pool, it is usually implemented as follows. Assuming some order over the population (ranking or random) from 1 to μ, we calculate a list of values $[a_1, a_2, \ldots, a_\mu]$ such that $a_i = \sum_1^i P_{sel}(i)$, where $P_{sel}(i)$ is defined by the selection distribution — fitness proportionate or ranking. Note that this implies $a_\mu = 1.0$. The outlines of the algorithm are given in Fig. 3.20.

```
BEGIN
  set current_member = 1;
  WHILE ( current_member ≤ μ ) DO
    Pick a random value r uniformly from [0, 1];
    set i = 1;
    WHILE ( aᵢ < r ) DO
      set i = i + 1;
    OD
    set mating_pool[current_member] = parents[i];
    set current_member = current_member + 1;
  OD
END
```

Fig. 3.20. Pseudocode for the roulette wheel algorithm

Despite its inherent simplicity, it has been recognised that the roulette wheel algorithm does not in fact give a particularly good sample of the required distribution. Whenever more than one sample is to be drawn from the distribution, the use of the **stochastic universal sampling** (SUS) algorithm [33] is preferred. Conceptually, this is equivalent to making one spin of a wheel with μ equally spaced arms, rather than μ spins of a one-armed wheel, and calculates the list of cumulative selection probabilities $[a_1, a_2, \ldots, a_\mu]$ as described in Fig. 3.21.

Since the value of the variable r is initialised in the range $[0, 1/\mu]$ and increases by an amount $1/\mu$ every time a selection is made, it is guaranteed that the number of copies made of each parent i is at least the integer part of $\mu \cdot P_{sel}(i)$ and is no more than one greater. Finally, we should note that with minor changes to the code, SUS can be used to make any number of selections from the parents, and in the case of making just one selection, it is the same as the roulette wheel.

```
BEGIN
  set current_member = i = 1;
  Pick a random value r uniformly from [0, 1/μ];
  WHILE ( current_member ≤ μ ) DO
    WHILE ( r ≤ a[i] ) DO
      set mating_pool[current_member] = parents[i];
      set r = r + 1/μ;
      set current_member = current_member + 1;
    OD
    set i = i + 1;
  OD
END
```

Fig. 3.21. Pseudocode for the stochastic universal sampling algorithm

3.7.4 Tournament Selection

The previous two selection methods and the algorithms used to sample from their probability distributions relied on a knowledge of the entire population. In certain situations, for example, if the population size is very large, or if the population is distributed in some way (perhaps on a parallel system), obtaining this knowledge is either highly time consuming or at worst impossible. In yet other cases there might not be a universal fitness definition at all. Think, for instance, of an application evolving game playing strategies. In this case we might not be able to quantify the strength of a given individual, that is, a particular strategy, but we can compare any two of them by simulating a game played by these strategies as opponents. Similar situations occur also in evolutionary design and evolutionary art applications [46, 47]. In such applications it is common that the user subjectively selects among the individuals representing designs or pieces of art by comparing them, without using a quantitative measure that assigns a fitness value to each member of the population, cf. Sect. 13.3.

Tournament selection is an operator with the useful property that it does not require any global knowledge of the population. Instead it only relies on an ordering relation that can rank any two individuals. It is therefore conceptually simple and fast to implement and apply. The application of tournament selection to select μ parents works according to the procedure shown in Fig. 3.22.

Because tournament selection looks at relative rather than absolute fitness, it has the same properties as ranking schemes in terms of invariance to translation and transposition of the fitness function. The probability that an individual will be selected as the result of a tournament depends on four factors, namely:

```
BEGIN
  set current_member = 1;
  WHILE ( current_member ≤ μ ) DO
    Pick k individuals randomly, with or without replacement;
    Select the best of these k comparing their fitness values;
    Denote this individual as i;
    set mating_pool[current_member] = i;
    set current_member = current_member + 1;
  OD
END
```

Fig. 3.22. Pseudocode for the tournament selection algorithm

- Its rank in the population. Effectively this is estimated without the need for sorting the whole population.
- The **tournament size** k. The larger the tournament, the more chance that it will contain members of above-average fitness, and the less that it will consist entirely of low-fitness members.
- The probability p that the most fit member of the tournament is selected. Usually this is 1.0 (*deterministic tournaments*), but stochastic versions are also used with $p < 1.0$. Clearly in this case there is lower selection pressure.
- Whether individuals are chosen with or without replacement. In the second case, with deterministic tournaments, the $k - 1$ least-fit members of the population can never be selected, whereas if the tournament candidates are picked with replacement, it is always possible for even the least-fit member of the population to be selected as a result of a lucky draw.

These properties of tournament selection were characterised in [20, 54], and it was shown [173] that for binary ($k = 2$) tournaments with parameter p the expected time for a single individual of high fitness to take over the population is the same as that for linear ranking with $s = 2p$. However, since λ tournaments are required to produce λ selections, it suffers from the same problems as the roulette wheel algorithm, in that the outcomes can show a high variance from the theoretical probability distribution. Despite this drawback, tournament selection is perhaps the most widely used selection operator in modern applications of GAs, due to its extreme simplicity and the fact that the selection pressure is easy to control by varying the tournament size k.

3.8 Survivor Selection

The survivor selection mechanism is responsible for managing the process whereby the working memory of the GA is reduced from a set of μ parents and λ offspring to produce the set of μ individuals for the next generation. As explained in Section 2.3.6, this step in the main evolutionary cycle is also called replacement. In the present section we often use this latter term to be consistent with the literature. Over the history of GAs a number of replacement strategies have been suggested and are widely used, which can be categorised according to whether they discriminate on the basis of the fitness or by the age of individuals.

3.8.1 Age-Based Replacement

The basis of these schemes is that the fitness of individuals is not taken into account during the selection of which individuals to replace in the population, rather they are designed so that each individual exists in the population for the same number of GA iterations. This does not preclude the persistent presence of highly fit solutions in the population, but this is dependent on their being chosen at least once in the selection phase and then surviving the recombination and mutation stages.

This is the strategy used in the simple GA. Since the number of offspring produced is the same as the number of parents ($\mu = \lambda$), each individual exists for just one cycle, and the parents are simply discarded and replaced by the entire set of offspring. This replacement strategy can be implemented simply in a GA with overlapping populations ($\lambda < \mu$), and at the other extreme where a single offspring is created and inserted in the population in each cycle. In this case the strategy takes the form of a first-in-first-out (FIFO) queue.

An alternative method of age-based replacement for steady-state GAs is to randomly select a parent for replacement, which has the same mean effect. DeJong and Sarma [101] investigated this strategy experimentally, and found that the algorithm showed higher variance in performance than a comparable generational GA, and Smith and Vavak [364] showed that this was because the random strategy is far more likely to lose the best member of the population than a delete-oldest (FIFO) strategy. For these reasons the random replacement strategy is not recommended.

3.8.2 Fitness-Based Replacement

A wide number of strategies have been proposed for choosing which μ of the $\mu + \lambda$ parents and offspring should go forward to the next GA iteration. Many of these also include some element of age, so that all of the offspring go forward, e.g., they use fitness to decide which λ of the $\mu > \lambda$ parents should be replaced by the offspring.

We have already discussed fitness proportionate and tournament selection, and the stochastic version of rank-based selection above. Therefore we will restrict this discussion to mentioning that these are also possible replacement schemes (based on inverse fitness or rank), and briefly describe two other common mechanisms.

Replace Worst (GENITOR)

In this scheme the worst λ members of the population are selected for replacement. Although this can lead to very rapid improvements in the mean population fitness, it can also lead to premature convergence as the population tends to rapidly focus on the fittest member currently present. For this reason it is commonly used in conjunction with large populations and/or a "no duplicates" policy.

Elitism

This scheme is commonly used in conjunction with age-based and stochastic fitness-based replacement schemes, in an attempt to prevent the loss of the current fittest member of the population. In essence a trace is kept of the current fittest member, and it is always kept in the population. Thus if it is chosen in the group to be replaced, and none of the offspring being inserted into the population has equal or better fitness, then it is kept and one of the offspring is discarded.

3.9 Example Application: Solving a Job Shop Scheduling Problem

Two examples of applications of genetic algorithms were given in Sections 2.4.1 and 2.4.2. These examples used *direct* representations, where the genotype and phenotype have a fairly simple mapping. Another (sometimes very useful) method is to use an *indirect* representation. Here there is some **growth function** that builds the phenotype and uses the genotype as an input parameter. In the following example, the job shop scheduling problem is solved by having a heuristic schedule builder and an order-based representation that specifies in which order to attempt to place the jobs into the schedule.

We define our problem by:

- J, a set of jobs
- O, a set of operations
- M, a set of machines
- $Able : O \rightarrow M$, a function defining which machine can perform a given operation
- $Pre \subseteq O \times O$, a relation defining which operation should precede other operations
- $d : O \times M \rightarrow \mathbb{R}$, a function defining the duration of $o \in O$ on $m \in M$

In general, there could be more machines that are able to perform a given operation. In this case $Able \subseteq O \times M$ is a relation, rather than a function. To keep things simple for this example, we eliminate this dimension and assume that for each operation there is exactly one machine $Able(o) \in M$ it can be performed on. Scheduling an operation means to assign a starting time to it (on the only machine that can perform it), and a schedule is a collection of such assignments containing an operation at most once. The goal now is to find a schedule that is:

- Complete: all jobs are scheduled
- Correct: all conditions defined by *Pre* are satisfied
- Optimal: the total duration of the schedule is minimal

We can set up a GA for this problem by having a population of individuals that are all permutations of the set of possible operations. Such a permutation stands for an ordering of all operations, and we are to use a schedule builder that creates a schedule for any ordering by scheduling each operation in the order of occurrence in the given permutation. The schedule builder works in the following way:

- Take the next (staring with the first) operation as specified in the permutation.
- Look up its machine.
- Assign the earliest possible starting time on this machine, subject to the occupation of the machine and to the precedence relations that hold for this operation in the schedule so far.

By now we have defined the representation, that is, we defined what are our genotypes (permutations), phenotypes (schedules), and we specified how a genotype is mapped onto a phenotype (by the schedule builder). It is important to note that our design guarantees the completeness and the correctness requirements. Completeness is simply a consequence of using permutations that contain all operations in O. The correctness condition is satisfied by the schedule builder that assigns starting times, taking the precedence constraints into account. As for the optimality requirement, the schedule builder uses a locally optimal heuristic, always assigning the earliest possible starting time to the given operation. This, however, does not imply that the schedule as a whole will be optimal. To achieve this goal we define the fitness of an individual, that is, a genotype, as the duration of the corresponding phenotype (schedule). Obviously, this fitness must be minimised. To complete the design of a GA for this problem we have to specify the remaining algorithm components: selection operators (for parent and survivor selection) and variation operators (mutation and recombination). Finally, we have to define an initialisation procedure and a termination condition. A very attractive feature of evolutionary algorithms is that there are many widely applicable operators that can be simply taken "off the shelf". Variation operators are strongly related to the representation, that is, to the used from of genotypes. In our case we can draw from the collection of order-based mutation and crossover operators. Formally any of them will do, in the sense that they will be applicable: syntactically correct parents (permutations) will always result in syntactically correct children. The difference between them can be their performance in terms of the end

solution delivered by the GA using them. As for selection operators, the issue
is even more simple as they do not depend on any particular representation,
so they do not have to be matched to the genotypes. Here we can use any of
the mechanisms discussed in this chapter. The only thing we must be aware of
is that we are minimising the durations of the schedules. Concerning the last
two components, initialisation and termination condition, it usually suffices
to use random initialisation and, for instance, allow a maximum number of
fitness evaluations.

3.10 Exercises

1. Given a function $f(x) : [0,1] \rightarrow \mathbb{R}$. We want to find an optimal x value
   with a required precision of 0.001 of the solution. That is, we want to be
   sure that the distance between the found optimum and the real optimum is
   at most 0.001. How many bits are needed at least to achieve this precision
   when using a bit-string GA?
2. Given the fitness function $f(x) = x^2$, calculate target sampling rates for
   RWS for the individuals $x = 1$, $x = 2$, $x = 3$. Calculate the target sampling
   rates for a transposed fitness function $f + 10$.
3. Discuss whether there is survival of the fittest in a generational GA.
4. Calculate the probability that a binary chromosome with length L will
   not be changed by applying the usual bit-flip mutation with $p_m = 1/L$.
5. A generational GA has a population size of 100, uses fitness proportionate
   selection without elitism, and after t generations has a mean population
   fitness of 76.0. There is one copy of the current best member, which has
   fitness 157.0.
   • What is the expectation for the number of copies of the best individual
     present in the mating pool?
   • What is the probability that there will be *no* copies of that individual
     in the mating pool, if selection is implemented using the roulette wheel
     algorithm?
   • What is the probability if the implementation uses SUS?
6. Given a population of μ individuals, which are bit-strings of length L. Let
   the frequency of allele 1 be 0.3 at position i, that is, 30% of all individuals
   contains a 1, and 70% a 0. How does this allele frequency change after
   performing k crossover operations with one-point crossover? How does it
   change if uniform crossover is performed?
7. Write a computer program to implement a generational GA for the One-
   Max problem $f(x) = \sum_{i=1}^{L} x_i$ (see Appendix B) with the following
   parameters:
   • Representation: binary strings of length $L = 25$
   • Initialisation: random
   • Parent selection: fitness proportionate, implemented via roulette wheel
     or SUS.

- Recombination: one-point crossover with probability $p_c = 0.7$
- Mutation: bit-flip with probability $p_m = 1/L$
- Replacement: strict generational (no elitism)
- Population size $= 100$
- Termination criterion: 100 generations or optimum found (whichever quickest)

After every generation find the best, worst, and mean fitness in the population, and plot these on a graph with time as the x-axis. Now do ten runs and find the mean and standard deviation of the time taken to find the optimum.

8. Repeat the exercise above for a bigger problem, e.g., $L = 75$. How do your results change?
9. Now repeat the exercises 8 and 9 using tournament selection with $k = 2$. What difference do you see?

3.11 Recommended Reading for this Chapter

1. Kenneth De Jong. Genetic algorithms are NOT function optimizers. In Whitley [420], pages 5–18. [99]

2. D.E. Goldberg. *Genetic Algorithms in Search, Optimization and Machine Learning.* Addison-Wesley, 1989. [172]
   A classic book that had a great impact in promoting the field. On page 6, Figure 1.4 it suggests that GAs are robust methods working well across a broad spectrum of problems.

3. J.H. Holland. *Adaption in natural and artificial systems.* MIT Press, 1992. [204] First edition: 1975, The University of Michigan.

4. Z. Michalewicz. *Genetic Algorithms + Data structures = Evolution programs.* Springer, Berlin, 3rd edition, 1996. [271]
   This book put the EC field into a new perspective, emphasising the usefulness of problem specific heuristic knowledge within an EA. Compare Figure 14.3 on page 293 with Goldberg's view.

5. M. Mitchell. *An Introduction to Genetic Algorithms.* MIT Press, 1996. [280]

4

Evolution Strategies

4.1 Aims of this Chapter

In this chapter we introduce evolution strategies (ES), another member of the evolutionary algorithm family. We also use these algorithms to illustrate a very useful feature in evolutionary computing: **self-adaptation** of strategy parameters. In general, self-adaptivity means that some parameters of the EA are varied during a run in a specific manner: the parameters are included in the chromosomes and coevolve with the solutions. This feature is inherent in modern evolution strategies. That is, since the procedure was detailed in 1977 [340] most ESs have been self-adaptive, and over the last ten years other EAs have increasingly adopted self-adaptivity. A summary of ES is given in Table 4.1.

Representation	Real-valued vectors
Recombination	Discrete or intermediary
Mutation	Gaussian perturbation
Parent selection	Uniform random
Survivor selection	(μ, λ) or $(\mu + \lambda)$
Speciality	Self-adaptation of mutation step sizes

Table 4.1. Sketch of ES

4.2 Introductory Example

Evolution strategies were invented in the early 1960s by Rechenberg and Schwefel, who were working at the Technical University of Berlin on an application concerning shape optimisation (see [52] for a brief history). Here we describe the basic algorithm, termed the two-membered evolution strategy, for the abstract problem of minimising an n-dimensional function $\mathbb{R}^n \to \mathbb{R}$ [342]. An outline of a simple two-membered evolution strategy is given in Fig. 4.1.

```
BEGIN
   set t = 0;
   Create an initial point ⟨x₁ᵗ,...,xₙᵗ⟩ ∈ ℝⁿ;
   REPEAT UNTIL ( TERMINATION CONDITION is satisfied ) DO
      draw zᵢ from a normal distr. for all i ∈ {1,...,n} independently;
      yᵢᵗ = xᵢᵗ + zᵢ for all i ∈ {1,...,n};
      IF (f(x̄ᵗ) ≤ f(ȳᵗ)) THEN
         x̄ᵗ⁺¹ = x̄ᵗ;
      ELSE
         x̄ᵗ⁺¹ = ȳᵗ;
      FI
      set t = t + 1;
   OD
END
```

Fig. 4.1. Outline of simple two-membered evolution strategy

Given a current solution $\bar{x}^t$ in the form of a vector of length n, a new candidate $\bar{x}^{t+1}$ is created by adding a random number z_i for $i \in \{1, \ldots, n\}$ to each of the n components. A Gaussian, or normal, distribution is used with zero mean and standard deviation σ for drawing the random numbers. This distribution is symmetric about zero and has the feature that the probability of drawing a random number with any given magnitude is a rapidly decreasing function of the standard deviation σ. Thus the σ value is a parameter of the algorithm that determines the extent to which given values x_i are perturbed by the mutation operator. For this reason σ is often called the **mutation step size**. Theoretical studies motivated an on-line adjustment of step sizes by the famous **1/5 success rule** of Rechenberg [317]. This rule states that the ratio of successful mutations (those in which the child is fitter than the parent) to all mutations should be 1/5. Hence if the ratio is greater than 1/5 the step size should be increased to make a wider search of the space, and if the ratio is less than 1/5 then it should be decreased to concentrate the search more around the current solution. The rule is executed at periodic intervals, for instance, after k iterations each σ is reset by

$$\sigma = \begin{cases} \sigma/c & \text{if } p_s > 1/5, \\ \sigma \cdot c & \text{if } p_s < 1/5, \\ \sigma & \text{if } p_s = 1/5, \end{cases}$$

where p_s is the relative frequency of successful mutations measured over a number of trials, and the parameter c is in the range $0.817 \leq c \leq 1$ [340]. As is apparent, using this mechanism the step sizes change based on feedback from the search process.

This example illuminates some essential characteristics of evolution strategies:

1. Evolution strategies are typically used for continuous parameter optimisation.
2. There is a strong emphasis on mutation for creating offspring.
3. Mutation is implemented by adding some random noise drawn from a Gaussian distribution.
4. Mutation parameters are changed during a run of the algorithm.

4.3 Representation

Evolution strategies are typically used for continuous parameter optimisation, meaning that the problem at hand can be given as an objective function $\mathbb{R}^n \to \mathbb{R}$. Standard representation of the object variables $x_1, \ldots, x_n$ is very straightforward, where each x_i is represented by a floating-point variable. Disregarding self-adaptivity for the time being, this implies that the genotype space is identical to the phenotype space $\mathbb{R}^n$, hence no special encoding step is needed. However, since nowadays evolution strategies almost always use self-adaptation (rather than the $1/5$ success rule adaptation), the vector $\bar{x} = \langle x_1, \ldots, x_n \rangle$ forms only part of a typical ES genotype. Individuals contain some strategy parameters, in particular, parameters of the mutation operator. Details of mutation are treated in the next section; here we only discuss the structure of individuals, and specify the meaning of the special genes there.

Strategy parameters can be divided into two sets, the σ values and the α values. The σ values represent the mutation step sizes, and their number n_σ is usually either 1 or n, as seen in Sects. 4.4.1 and 4.4.2. For any reasonable self-adaptation mechanism at least one σ must be present. The α values, which represent interactions between the step sizes used for different variables (Sect. 4.4.3), are not always used. In the most general case their number $n_\alpha = (n - \frac{n_\sigma}{2})(n_\sigma - 1)$. Putting this all together, we obtain

$$\langle \underbrace{x_1, \ldots, x_n}_{\bar{x}}, \underbrace{\sigma_1, \ldots, \sigma_{n_\sigma}}_{\bar{\sigma}}, \underbrace{\alpha_1, \ldots, \alpha_{n_\alpha}}_{\bar{\alpha}} \rangle$$

as the general form of individuals in ES.

4.4 Mutation

The mutation operator in ES is based on a normal (Gaussian) distribution requiring two parameters: the mean ξ and the standard deviation σ. Mutations then are realized by adding some Δx_i to each x_i, where the Δx_i values are randomly drawn using the given Gaussian $N(\xi, \sigma)$, with the corresponding probability density function (p.d.f.)

$$p(\Delta x_i) = \frac{1}{\sigma\sqrt{2\pi}} \cdot e^{-\frac{(\Delta x_i - \xi)^2}{2\sigma^2}}. \tag{4.1}$$

In practice, the mean ξ is always set to zero, and the vector $\bar{x}$ is mutated by replacing x_i values by

$$x_i' = x_i + N(0, \sigma),$$

where $N(0, \sigma)$ denotes a random number drawn from a Gaussian distribution with zero mean and standard deviation σ. By using a Gaussian distribution here, small mutations are more likely than large ones. The particular feature of mutation – and the very basis of self-adaptation – in ES is that the step sizes are also included in the chromosomes and they themselves undergo variation and selection. In the simplest case we would have one step size that applied to all the components x_i and candidate solutions of the form $\langle x_1, \ldots, x_n, \sigma \rangle$. Mutations are then realized by replacing $\langle x_1, \ldots, x_n, \sigma \rangle$ by $\langle x_1', \ldots, x_n', \sigma' \rangle$, where σ' is the mutated value of σ and

$$x_i' = x_i + N(0, \sigma').$$

Details on how to mutate the value of σ are given in Sects. 4.4.1, 4.4.2, and 4.4.3. What is important here is that the mutation step sizes are not set by the user; rather the σ is coevolving with the solutions (the $\bar{x}$ part). In order to achieve this behaviour it is essential to modify the value of σ first, and then mutate the x_i values with the new σ value. The rationale behind this is that a new individual $\langle \bar{x}', \sigma' \rangle$ is effectively evaluated twice. Primarily, it is evaluated directly for its viability during survivor selection based on $f(\bar{x}')$. Second, it is evaluated for its ability to create good offspring. This happens indirectly: a given step size evaluates favourably if the offspring generated by using it prove viable (in the first sense). Thus, an individual $\langle \bar{x}', \sigma' \rangle$ represents both a good $\bar{x}'$ that survived selection and a good σ' that proved successful in generating this good $\bar{x}'$ from $\bar{x}$.

The alert reader may have noticed that there is an important underlying assumption behind the idea of using varying mutation step sizes. Namely, we assume that under different circumstances different step sizes will behave differently: some will be better than others. These "circumstances" can be given various interpretations. For instance, we might consider "time" and distinguish different stages within the evolutionary search process and expect that different mutation strategies would be appropriate in different stages. Self-adaptation can then be a mechanism adjusting the mutation strategy as the search is proceeding. Alternatively, we can consider "space" and observe that the local vicinity of an individual, i.e., the shape of the fitness landscape in its neighbourhood, determines what good mutations are: those that jump into the direction of fitness increase. Assigning a separate mutation strategy to each individual, which coevolves with it, opens the possibility to learn and use a mutation operator suited for the local topology. Issues related to this considerations are treated extensively in the chapter on parameter control, Chap. 8. In the following we describe three special cases of mutation in evolution strategies in more detail.

4.4.1 Uncorrelated Mutation with One Step Size

In the case of uncorrelated mutation with one step size, the same distribution is used to mutate each x_i, therefore we only have one strategy parameter σ in each individual. This σ is mutated each time step by multiplying it by a term e^{Γ}, with Γ a random variable drawn each time from a normal distribution with mean 0 and standard deviation τ. Since $N(0,\tau) = \tau \cdot N(0,1)$, the mutation mechanism is thus specified by the following formulas:

$$\sigma' = \sigma \cdot e^{\tau \cdot N(0,1)}, \tag{4.2}$$

$$x_i' = x_i + \sigma' \cdot N_i(0,1). \tag{4.3}$$

Furthermore, since standard deviations very close to zero are unwanted (they will have on average a negligible effect), the following boundary rule is used to force step sizes to be no smaller than a threshold:

$$\sigma' < \varepsilon_0 \Rightarrow \sigma' = \varepsilon_0.$$

In these formulas $N(0,1)$ denotes a draw from the standard normal distribution, while $N_i(0,1)$ denotes a separate draw from the standard normal distribution for each variable i. The proportionality constant τ is an external parameter to be set by the user. It is usually inversely proportional to the square root of the problem size:

$$\tau \propto 1/\sqrt{n}.$$

The parameter τ can be interpreted as a kind of **learning rate**, as in neural networks. Bäck [22] explains the reasons for mutating σ by multiplying with a variable with a lognormal distribution as follows:

- Smaller modifications should occur more often than large ones.
- Standard deviations have to be greater than 0.
- The median (0.5-quantile) should be 1, since we want to multiply the σ.
- Mutation should be neutral on average. This requires equal likelihood of drawing a certain value and its reciprocal value, for all values.

The lognormal distribution satisfies all these requirements.

In Fig. 4.2 the effects of mutation are shown in two dimensions. That is, we have an objective function $\mathbb{R}^2 \to \mathbb{R}$, and individuals are of the form $\langle x, y, \sigma \rangle$. Since there is only one σ, the mutation step size is the same in each direction (x and y), and the points in the search space where the offspring can be placed with a given probability form a circle around the individual to be mutated.

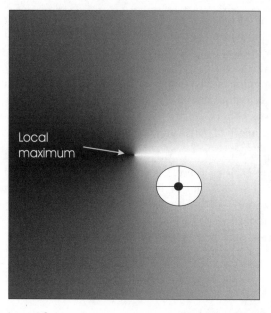

Fig. 4.2. Mutation with $n = 2, n_\sigma = 1, n_\alpha = 0$. Part of a fitness landscape with a *conical shape* is shown. The *black dot* indicates an individual. Points where the offspring can be placed with a given probability form a *circle*. The probability of moving along the y-axis (little effect on fitness) is the same as that of moving along the x-axis (large effect on fitness)

4.4.2 Uncorrelated Mutation with n Step Sizes

The motivation behind using n step sizes is the wish to treat dimensions differently. In particular, we want to be able to use different step sizes for different dimensions $i \in \{1, \ldots, n\}$. The reason for this is the trivial observation that the fitness landscape can have a different slope in one direction (along axis i) than in another direction (along axis j). The solution is straightforward: each basic chromosome $\langle x_1, \ldots, x_n \rangle$ is extended with n step sizes, one for each dimension, resulting in $\langle x_1, \ldots, x_n, \sigma_1, \ldots, \sigma_n \rangle$. The mutation mechanism is now specified as follows:

$$\sigma_i' = \sigma_i \cdot e^{\tau' \cdot N(0,1) + \tau \cdot N_i(0,1)}, \tag{4.4}$$

$$x_i' = x_i + \sigma_i \cdot N_i(0,1),. \tag{4.5}$$

where $\tau' \propto 1/\sqrt{2n}$, and $\tau \propto 1/\sqrt{2\sqrt{n}}$. Once again a boundary rule is applied to prevent standard deviations very close to zero.

$$\sigma_i' < \varepsilon_0 \Rightarrow \sigma_i' = \varepsilon_0.$$

Notice that the mutation formula for σ is different from that in Eq. (4.2). The present mutation mechanism is based on a finer granularity. Instead of the individual level (each individual $\bar{x}$ having its own σ) it works on the coordinate level (one σ_i for each x_i in $\bar{x}$). The corresponding straightforward modification of Eq. (4.2) is

$$\sigma_i' = \sigma_i \cdot e^{\tau \cdot N_i(0,1)},$$

but ES use Eq. (4.4). Technically, this is correct since the sum of two normally distributed variables is also normally distributed, hence the resulting distribution is still lognormal. The conceptual motivation is that the common base mutation $e^{\tau' \cdot N(0,1)}$ allows for an overall change of the mutability, guaranteeing the preservation of all degrees of freedom, while the coordinate-specific $e^{\tau \cdot N_i(0,1)}$ provides the flexibility to use different mutation strategies in different directions.

Fig. 4.3. Mutation with $n = 2, n_\sigma = 2, n_\alpha = 0$. Part of a fitness landscape with a *conical shape* is shown. The *black dot* indicates an individual. Points where the offspring can be placed with a given probability form an *ellipse*. The probability of moving along the x-axis (large effect on fitness) is larger than that of moving along the y-axis (little effect on fitness)

In Fig. 4.3 the effects of mutation are shown in two dimensions. Again, we have an objective function $\mathbb{R}^2 \to \mathbb{R}$, but the individuals now have the form $\langle x, y, \sigma_x, \sigma_y \rangle$. Since the mutation step sizes can differ in each direction (x and

y), the points in the search space where the offspring can be placed with a given probability form an ellipse around the individual to be mutated. The axes of such an ellipse are parallel to the coordinate axes, with the length along axis i proportional to the value of σ_i.

4.4.3 Correlated Mutations

The second version of mutation discussed in the previous section introduced different standard deviations for each axis, but this only allows ellipses orthogonal to the axes. The rationale behind correlated mutations is to allow the ellipses to have any orientation by rotating them with a rotation (covariance) matrix C.

The probability density function for $\overline{\Delta x}$ replacing Eq. (4.1) now becomes

$$p(\overline{\Delta x}) = \frac{e^{-\frac{1}{2}\overline{\Delta x}^T \cdot C^{-1} \cdot \overline{\Delta x}}}{(\det C \cdot (2\pi)^n)^{1/2}},$$

with C the covariance matrix with entries

$$c_{ii} = \sigma_i^2, \tag{4.6}$$

$$c_{ij,i\neq j} = \begin{cases} 0 & \text{no correlations,} \\ \frac{1}{2}(\sigma_i^2 - \sigma_j^2)\tan(2\alpha_{ij}) & \text{correlations.} \end{cases} \tag{4.7}$$

The relation between covariance and rotation angle is as follows:

$$\tan(2\alpha_{ij}) = \frac{2c_{ij}}{\sigma_i^2 - \sigma_j^2},$$

which explains Eq. (4.7). This formula is derived from the trigonometric properties of rotations. A rotation in two dimensions is a multiplication with the matrix

$$\begin{pmatrix} \cos(\alpha_{ij}) & -\sin(\alpha_{ij}) \\ \sin(\alpha_{ij}) & \cos(\alpha_{ij}) \end{pmatrix}.$$

A rotation in more dimensions can be performed by a successive series of 2D rotations, i.e., matrix multiplications.

The complete mutation mechanism is described by the following equations:

$$\sigma_i' = \sigma_i \cdot e^{\tau' \cdot N(0,1) + \tau \cdot N(0,1)},$$
$$\alpha_j' = \alpha_j + \beta \cdot N(0,1),$$
$$\overline{x}' = \overline{x} + \overline{N}(\overline{0}, C'),$$

where $n_\alpha = \frac{n \cdot (n-1)}{2}$, $j \in 1, \ldots, n_\alpha$. The other constants are usually taken as: $\tau \propto 1/\sqrt{2\sqrt{n}}$, $\tau' \propto 1/\sqrt{2n}$, and $\beta \approx 5°$.

The object variables $\bar{x}$ are now mutated by adding $\overline{\Delta x}$ drawn from an n-dimensional normal distribution with covariance matrix C'. The C' in the formula is the old C after mutation of the α values (and re-calculation of covariances). The σ_i are mutated in the same way as before: with a multiplication by a log-normal variable, which consists of a global and an individual part. The α_j are mutated with an additive, normally distributed variation, similar to mutation of object variables.

We also have a boundary rule for the α_j values. The rotation angles should lie in the range $[-\pi, \pi]$, so the new value is simply mapped circularly into the feasible range:

$$|\alpha'_j| > \pi \Rightarrow \alpha'_j = \alpha'_j - 2\pi \, \text{sign}(\alpha'_j).$$

Fig. 4.4 shows the effects of correlated mutations in two dimensions. The individuals now have the form $\langle x, y, \sigma_x, \sigma_y, \alpha_{x,y} \rangle$, and the points in the search space where the offspring can be placed with a given probability form a rotated ellipse around the individual to be mutated, where again the axis lengths are proportional to the σ values.

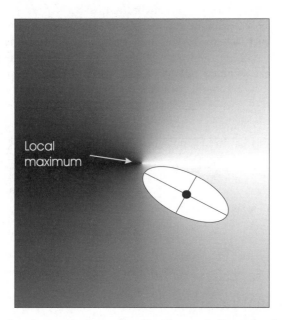

Fig. 4.4. Correlated mutation: $n = 2, n_\sigma = 2, n_\alpha = 1$. Part of a fitness landscape with a *conical shape* is shown. The *black dot* indicates an individual. Points where the offspring can be placed with a given probability form a *rotated ellipse*. The probability of generating a move in the direction of the steepest ascent (largest effect on fitness) is now larger than that for other directions

Table 4.2 summarises three possible common settings for mutation in evolution strategies regarding the length and structure of the individuals. Simply considering the size of the representation of the individuals in each scheme, i.e., the number of values that need to be learned by the algorithm as it evolves (let alone their complex interrelationships) brings home an important point: we can get nothing for free! In other words, what we must consider is that as the ability of the algorithm to adapt the nature of its search according to the local topology increases, so too does the scale of the learning task. To simplify matters a little, as we increase the precision with which we can specify the shape of the lines of equiprobable mutations, so we increase the number of different options which should be tried. Since the merits of these different possibilities are evaluated indirectly, i.e., by applying them and gauging the relative fitness of the individuals created, it is reasonable to conclude that an increased number of function evaluations will be needed to learn good search strategies as the complexity of the mutation operator increases.

Whilst this may sound a little pessimistic, it is also worth noting that it is easy to imagine a situation where the extra complexity is required, for example, if the landscape contains a "ridge" of increasing fitness, perhaps running at an angle to the co-ordinate axis. In short, there are no fixed recommendations about which scheme to use, but a common approach is to start with uncorrelated mutation with n σ values and then try moving to a simpler model if good results are obtained but too slowly (or if the σ_i all evolve to similar values), or to the more complex model if the results are not of good enough quality.

n_σ	n_α	Structure of individuals	Remark
1	0	$\langle x_1, \ldots, x_n, \sigma \rangle$	Standard mutation
n	0	$\langle x_1, \ldots, x_n, \sigma_1, \ldots, \sigma_n \rangle$	Standard mutations
n	$n \cdot (n-1)/2$	$\langle x_1, \ldots, x_n, \sigma_1, \ldots, \sigma_n, \alpha_1, \ldots, \alpha_{n \cdot (n-1)/2} \rangle$	Correlated mutations

Table 4.2. Some possible settings of n_σ and n_α for different mutation operators

4.5 Recombination

The basic recombination scheme in evolution strategies involves two parents that create one child. To obtain λ offspring recombination is performed λ times. There are two recombination variants distinguished by the manner of recombining parent alleles. Using **discrete recombination** one of the parent alleles is randomly chosen with equal chance for either parents. In **intermediate recombination** the values of the parent alleles are averaged. Formally, given two parent vectors $\bar{x}$ and $\bar{y}$, one child $\bar{z}$ is created, where

$$z_i = \begin{cases} (x_i + y_i)/2 & \text{intermediary recombination} \\ x_i \text{ or } y_i \text{ chosen randomly} & \text{discrete recombination} \end{cases}$$

for all $i \in \{1, \ldots, n\}$.

An extension of this scheme allows the use of more than two recombinants, because the two parents $\bar{x}$ and $\bar{y}$ are drawn randomly for each position $i \in \{1, \ldots, n\}$ in the offspring anew. These drawings take the whole population of μ individuals into consideration, and the result is a recombination operator with possibly more than two individuals contributing to the offspring. The exact number of parents, however, cannot be defined in advance. This multiparent variant is called **global recombination**. To make terminology unambiguous, the original variant is called **local recombination**.

Evolution strategies typically use global recombination. Interestingly, different recombination is used for the object variable part (discrete is recommended) and the strategy parameters part (intermediary is recommended). This scheme preserves diversity within the phenotype (solution) space, allowing the trial of very different combinations of values, whilst the averaging effect of intermediate recombination assures a more cautious adaptation of strategy parameters.

4.6 Parent Selection

Parent selection in evolution strategies is not biased by fitness values. Whenever a recombination operator requires a parent, it is drawn randomly with uniform distribution from the population of μ individuals. It should be noted that the ES terminology deviates from the GA terminology in its use of the word "parent". In ES the whole population is seen as parent – often called the **parent population**. In contrast, in GAs the term "parent" denotes a member of the population that has actually been selected to undergo variation (crossover or mutation). The reason for this particular terminology in ES lies in the selection mechanism as described here.

4.7 Survivor Selection

After creating λ offspring and calculating their fitness, the best μ of them are chosen *deterministically*, either from the offspring only, called (μ, λ) **selection**, or from the union of parents and offspring, called $(\mu + \lambda)$ **selection**. Both the (μ, λ) and the $(\mu + \lambda)$ selection schemes are strictly deterministic and are based on rank rather than an absolute fitness value.

The selection scheme that is generally used in evolution strategies is (μ, λ) selection, which is preferred over $(\mu + \lambda)$ selection for the following reasons:

- The (μ, λ) discards all parents and is therefore in principle able to leave (small) local optima, so it is advantageous in the case of multimodal topologies.

- If the fitness function is not fixed, but changes in time, the $(\mu+\lambda)$ selection preserves outdated solutions, so it is not able to follow the moving optimum well.
- $(\mu + \lambda)$ selection hinders the self-adaptation mechanism with respect to strategy parameters to work effectively, because misadapted strategy parameters may survive for a relatively large number of generations when an individual has relatively good object variables and bad strategy parameters. In that case often all its children will be bad, so with elitism, the bad strategy parameters may survive.

The selective pressure in evolution strategies is very high because λ is typically much higher than μ (a 1/7 ratio is recommended). The **takeover time** τ^* of a given selection mechanism is defined as the number of generations it takes until the application of selection completely fills the population with copies of the best individual, given one copy initially. Goldberg and Deb [173] showed that

$$\tau^* = \frac{\ln \lambda}{\ln(\lambda/\mu)}.$$

For a typical evolution strategy with $\mu = 15$ and $\lambda = 100$, this results in $\tau^* \approx 2$. For proportional selection in a genetic algorithm it is

$$\tau^* = \lambda \ln \lambda,$$

resulting in $\tau^* = 460$ for population size $\lambda = 100$.

4.8 Self-Adaptation

One of the main contributions of evolution strategies to the field of EC is self-adaptation. That is, this feature was introduced first in ES, and its benefits have been clearly shown by ES research, not only for real-valued, but also for binary and integer search spaces [24]. This has had an inspiring effect on other EC branches that started incorporate self-adaptive features in other style EAs. In this section we have a closer look at this phenomenon.

The central claim within ES is that self-adaptation works. Besides experimental evidence, showing that an ES with self-adaptation outperforms the same ES without self-adaptation, there are also theoretical results backing up this claim [50]. Theoretical and experimental results can neatly complement each other in this area if for a (simple) objective function $f : \mathbb{R}^n \to \mathbb{R}$ theoretically optimal mutation step sizes can be calculated.[1] If experimentally obtained data show a good match with the theoretically derived values, then

---

[1] The problem and the algorithm must be simple to make the system tractable, since for a complex problem and/or algorithm a theoretical analysis is infeasible. Optimal mutation step sizes need to be defined in light of some performance criteria, e.g., progress rate during a run.

we can conclude that self-adaptation works in the sense that it is able to find the near-optimal step sizes.

Theoretical and experimental results agree on the fact that for a successful run the σ values must decrease over time. The intuitive explanation for this is that in the beginning of a search process a large part of the search space has to be sampled in an explorative fashion to locate promising regions (with good fitness values). Therefore, large mutations are appropriate in this phase. As the search proceeds and optimal values are approached, only fine tuning of the given individuals is needed; thus smaller mutations are required.

Another kind of convincing evidence for the power of self-adaptation is provided in the context of changing fitness landscapes. In this case, where the objective function is changing, the evolutionary process is aiming at a moving target. When the objective function changes, the present population needs to be reevaluated, and quite naturally the given individuals may have a low fitness, since they have been adapted to the old objective function. Often the mutation step sizes will prove ill-adapted: they are too low for the new exploration phase required. The experiment presented in [201] illustrates how self-adaptation is able to reset the step sizes after each change in the objective function (Fig. 4.5).

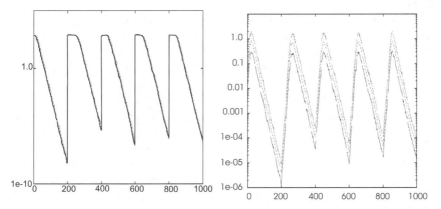

Fig. 4.5. Moving optimum ES experiment on the sphere function with $n = 30$, $n_\sigma = 1$. The location of the optimum is changed after every 200 generations (*x-axes*) with a clear effect on the average best objective function values (*y-axis, left*) in the given population. Self-adaptation is adjusting the step sizes (*y-axes, right*) with a small delay to larger values appropriate for exploring the new fitness landscape, whereafter the values of σ start decreasing again once the population is closing in on the new optimum

Over the last decades much experience has been gained over self-adaptation in ES. The accumulated knowledge has identified necessary conditions for self-adaptation:

1. $\mu > 1$ so that different strategies are present
2. Generation of an offspring surplus: $\lambda > \mu$
3. A not too strong selective pressure (heuristic: $\lambda/\mu = 7$, e.g., (15,100))
4. (μ, λ)-selection (to guarantee extinction of misadapted individuals
5. Recombination also on strategy parameters (especially intermediate recombination)

4.9 Example Applications

4.9.1 The Ackley Function

The first example we discuss is a typical ES application that concerns the optimisation of a multidimensional real-valued function. To illustrate how an ES is applied to such problems we use the Ackley function with $n = 30$ dimensions (Appendix B). This function is highly multimodal, with a large number of local minima, but with one global minimum at the origin $\bar{x} = \bar{0}$ with value 0.0.

To design an ES for this problem one need not consider the representation issue that is so prominent in GAs. To be more specific, representation of the object variables is straightforward, therefore one only needs to decide about the strategy parameters. This is closely related to choosing the mutation operator. For instance, we can decide to use uncorrelated mutations, thus omitting the α values from the representation. We can also use a separate mutation step size for each dimension, implying chromosomes consisting of sixty real-valued numbers, that is, thirty for $\bar{x}$ and thirty for $\bar{\sigma}$.

Hereafter, the definition of the variation operators boils down to deciding what recombination to use, if at all. A possible choice here is to use discrete recombination on the object variables and global intermediate recombination on the strategy parameters – an option that is frequently used in ES.

As for selection, the decision concerns "comma" or "plus", and following the general recommendations from Sect. 4.7 we could choose for (μ, λ). Furthermore, we can set $\mu = 30$ and $\lambda = 200$ and decide to terminate a run after 200,000 function evaluations, or when the optimum is found. This pretty much completes the specification of our ES, leaving only initialisation open. This can be performed as simply as creating the initial population of vectors whose components are chosen uniformly randomly in the range $-30.0 \leq x_i \leq 30.0$.

In [30] results are given for the optimisation of this function using an ES as specified above. The algorithm was run ten times, and in each run the global optimum was located, i.e., an individual was found that was on the globally optimal peak, if not at its very top. The average of the best solution in the final generation had a function value of just $7.48 \cdot 10^{-8}$.

4.9.2 Subjective Evolution of Colour Mixes

In a classic experiment to illustrate the fact that human beings can sometimes have a role to play within the evolution of good solutions, Herdy [193] describes how a group of students is used to act as a subjective evaluation function for an ES. The aim of the evolution is to discover appropriate quantities of clear water, red, yellow, and blue dye, that when put in a test tube and mixed will create 30 ml of liquid with the same colour as a well-known brand of cherry brandy. The representation chosen is a simple vector of length 4 (one component representing the quantity of each ingredient used), and during the genotype to phenotype mapping the values are scaled to yield the 30-ml final volume.

When humans are included "in the loop" of an evaluation process, a common finding is that they tend to get bored quickly and do not deliver consistent judgements. For this reason the algorithm is carefully designed to deliver fast convergence, and the students are just required to pick the single best offspring for survival. In this way, a relatively high selection pressure is used: a $(1, 8)$ strategy (the students are grouped into eights). Because of the short run lengths, self-adaptation of step sizes is not used (it would take too long), and only a single step size is used for each offspring. These are chosen so that one third have $\sigma = 1$, one third have a lower value, and one third a higher value.

The experiment then proceeds as follows:

- Starting from a blue mixture of known proportions, eight offspring recipes are created by mutation.
- Each student makes up a test tube according to the specifications for their offspring.
- The eight mixtures are put up against a light source, and the students decide which among them is closest to the desired mixture.
- This is repeated until the students are satisfied that the desired colour has been matched.

Typically the cherry brandy colour is found in less than 20 generations. Fig. 4.6 shows the evolution of a typical run.

It is worth noting that since the mixtures are made up by hand, there are some inevitable experimental errors arising from mismeasurements and so on, which introduce a source of noise into the evaluation. In order to investigate this effect, the experiment is then run backwards, i.e., the goal colour is changed to be the original blue for which the correct solution is known. Herdy reports that typically the blue colour is discovered with a maximum error of 1.3 ml. Given an estimated error of $\pm$ 1 ml in the pipette for filling the test tubes, this is an impressive result and illustrates the robustness of the ES approach.

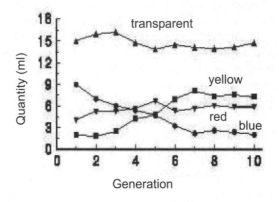

Fig. 4.6. Evolution of a mixture of dyes to produce a cherry brandy colour using subjective evaluation

4.10 Exercises

1. Recall Exercise 1 from Chapter 3. How many variables are needed (what is the length of individuals) to have the same precision with an evolution strategy using: a) one σ; b) n σ's; and c) n σ's and all α's? How many variables are needed if the objective function is n-dimensional?
2. Discuss why generational GAs and ES form opposites regarding where the fitness information influences the search.
3. Discuss why steady-state GAs and ES form two extremes regarding off-spring size.
4. The formula $x_i' = x_i + N(0, \sigma)$ may suggest that we can only add a (positive) number to x_i during mutation. Discuss whether this interpretation is correct.
5. Create an Evolutionary Strategy for the Ackley function with $n=30$, using the set-up in Sect. 4.9.1 and a comma selection strategy. Make 100 independent runs, store the best value of each run and calculate the mean and standard deviation of these values.
6. Repeat this experiment with the plus selection strategy, and compare the results.

4.11 Recommended Reading for this Chapter

1. T. Bäck. *Evolutionary Algorithms in Theory and Practice.* Oxford University Press, New York, 1996.

2. T. Bäck, D.B. Fogel, and Z. Michalewicz, editors. *Evolutionary Computation 1: Basic Algorithms and Operators.* Institute of Physics Publishing, 2000.

3. T. Bäck, D.B. Fogel, and Z. Michalewicz, editors. *Evolutionary Computation 2: Advanced Algorithms and Operators.* Institute of Physics Publishing, 2000.

4. Hans-Georg Beyer. *The theory of Evolution Strategies.* Springer, Berlin, 2001.

5. H.-G. Beyer and H.-P. Schwefel. Evolution strategies: A comprehensive introduction. *Natural Computing,* 1(1):3–52, 2002.

6. H.-P. Schwefel. *Evolution and Optimum Seeking.* Wiley, New York, 1995.

5

Evolutionary Programming

5.1 Aims of this Chapter

In this chapter we present evolutionary programming (EP), another historical member of the EC family. Other EC streams have an algorithm variant that can be identified as being the "standard", or typical, version of genetic algorithms, evolution strategies, or genetic programming. For EP such a standard version is hard to define for reasons discussed later in this chapter. The summary of EP in Table 5.1 is therefore a representative rather than a standard algorithm variant.

Representation	Real-valued vectors
Parent selection	Deterministic (each parent creates one offspring via mutation)
Recombination	None
Mutation	Gaussian perturbation
Survivor selection	Probabilistic ($\mu + \mu$)
Speciality	Self-adaptation of mutation step sizes (in meta-EP)

Table 5.1. Sketch of EP

5.2 Introductory Example

Evolutionary programming was originally developed to simulate evolution as a learning process with the aim of generating artificial intelligence [145, 156]. Intelligence, in turn, was viewed as the capability of a system to adapt its behaviour in order to meet some specified goals in a range of environments. Adaptive behaviour is the key term in this definition, and the capability to predict the environment was considered to be a prerequisite for adaptivity, and hence for intelligent behaviour.

In the classical example of EP, predictors were evolved in the form of finite
state machines. A finite state machine (FSM) is a transducer that can be
stimulated by a finite alphabet of input symbols and can respond in a finite
alphabet of output symbols. It consists of a number of states S and a number
of state transitions. The state transitions define the working of the FSM:
depending on the current state and the current input symbol, they define an
output symbol and the next state to go to. An example three-state FSM is
shown in Fig. 5.1.

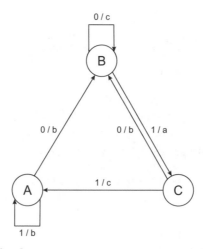

Fig. 5.1. Example of a finite state machine consisting of three states: A, B, and
C. The input alphabet is $I = \{0, 1\}$, and the output alphabet is $O = \{a, b, c\}$. The
FSM's transition function $\delta : S \times I \rightarrow S \times O$ that transforms the input stream to the
output stream is specified by the arrows and their labels indicating the input/output
of the given transition

A simple prediction task to be learned by an FSM is to guess the following
input symbol in an input stream. That is, considering n inputs, predict the
$(n+1)$th one, and articulate this prediction by the nth output symbol. In this
case, the performance of an FSM is measured by the percentage of inputs
where $input_{n+1} = output_n$. Clearly, this requires the input alphabet and the
output alphabet to be the same. An example is given in Fig. 5.2.

Fogel et al. [156] describe an experiment where predictors were evolved to
tell whether the next input (being an integer) in a sequence is a prime or not.
For this task FSMs were used as individuals with the input alphabet $I = \mathrm{IN}$
and output alphabet $O = \{0, 1\}$. The fitness of an FSM was defined as its
prediction accuracy on the input sequence of consecutive integers $1, 2, 3, \ldots$
(minus some penalty for containing too many states). Many technical details
of this application are hardly traceable today, but [145] and personal communication give some details. Parent selection does not take place, but each FSM

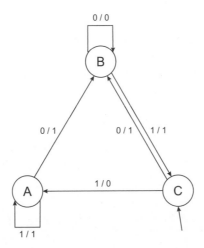

Fig. 5.2. Finite state machine as a predictor. The initial state of this FSM is C, and the given input string is 011101. The FSM's response is the output string 110111. On this string, its prediction performance is 60% (inputs 2, 3, and 6 correctly predicted)

in the given population is mutated once to generate one offspring. There are five generally usable mutation operators to generate new FSMs:

- Changing an output symbol
- Changing a state transition (i.e. change the next state)
- Adding a state
- Deleting a state
- Changing the initial state

A choice from these mutation operators is made randomly with a uniform distribution. Recombination (crossover) is not used, and after having created μ offspring from a population of μ FSMs, the top 50% of their union is saved as the next generation.

The results obtained with this system show that after 202 input symbols the best FSM is a very opportunistic one, having only one state and always guessing "no" (output 0). Given the sparcity of primes this strategy is good enough for accuracies above 81%. Using more sophisticated setups these outcomes could be improved. However, the main point was not perfect accuracy (which is theoretically impossible), but the empirical proof that a simulated evolutionary process is able to create good solutions for an intelligent task.

For historical reasons EP has been long associated with prediction tasks and the use of finite state machines as their representation. However, since the 1990s EP variants for optimisation of real valued parameter vectors have become more frequent and even positioned as "standard" EP [22, 31]. In the remaining of this chapter we adopt this viewpoint modified by the following remark. Today the EP community typically considers EP as a very open framework in terms of representation and mutation operators. The fundamental attitude is that the representation should not be fixed in advance and in general, but derived from the problem to be solved. Likewise, the mutation operators should be designed to match the representation at hand. This is a very pragmatic approach indeed, but for a textbook it makes it hard to treat EP in a way similar to the treatment of the other EC dialects. Therefore we adhere to the view summarised in Table 5.1.

5.2.1 Representation

As noted above, EP is used for many different applications, and takes a very pragmatic approach of choosing the representation based on the problem's features. However, it is most frequently used for optimising functions of the form $f : \mathbb{R}^n \to \mathbb{R}$, and in this case evolutionary programming uses a straightforward floating-point representation where $\langle x_1, \ldots, x_n \rangle \in \mathbb{R}^n$ form the individuals. Although formerly self-adaptation of mutation parameters was identified as an extra feature of the so-called meta-EP, nowadays it is a frequently used option. Therefore, we include it as a "standard" feature, amounting to adding strategy parameters to the individuals. Similarly to ES, this leads to

$$\underbrace{\langle x_1, \ldots, x_n,}_{\bar{x}} \underbrace{\sigma_1, \ldots, \sigma_n \rangle}_{\bar{\sigma}}$$

as the general form of individuals in EP.

5.2.2 Mutation

Given the observation that the EP community tends to put an emphasis on the choice of the most natural representation for the problem at hand, the obvious follow-on from this is that there is no single EP mutation operator; rather the choice is determined by the representation as we saw for GAs in Sect. 3.4.

Here we restrict ourselves to illustrating the mutation operator most widely associated with what came to become known as "meta-EP" – the variant with self-adaptation of strategy parameters and a real-valued representation.

Mutation transforms a chromosome $\langle x_1, \ldots, x_n, \sigma_1, \ldots, \sigma_n \rangle$ into $\langle x_1', \ldots, x_n', \sigma_1', \ldots, \sigma_n' \rangle$, where

$$\sigma_i' = \sigma_i \cdot (1 + \alpha \cdot N(0,1)), \tag{5.1}$$
$$x_i' = x_i + \sigma_i' \cdot N_i(0,1).$$

Here $N(0,1)$ denotes the outcome of a random drawing from a Gaussian distribution with zero mean and standard deviation 1, and with $\alpha \approx 0.2$. A boundary rule to prevent standard deviations very close to zero, and thereby allow effective mutations, is also applicable:

$$\sigma_i' < \varepsilon_0 \Rightarrow \sigma_i' := \varepsilon_0. \qquad (5.2)$$

Let us remark that during the history of EP a number of mutation schemes, such as one in which the step size is inversely related to the fitness of the solutions, have been proposed. Since the proposal of **meta-EP** [144, 145], self-adaptation of step sizes has become the norm, however, various formulas different from that in Eq. (5.1) have also been proposed. These differences concern

- The formula for modifying the step sizes, e.g., using the lognormal scheme, as in evolution strategies rather than this additive scheme
- The incorporation of *variances* rather than *standard deviations* as strategy parameters
- The order in which the the σ and the x values are mutated.

Of these, the first and second led to problems whereby the scheme frequently generated negative and therefore invalid values for the offspring variance. For this reason the boundary condition rule of Eq. (5.2) is frequently called into play. By comparison, especially since the Gaussian distribution is symmetric about its mean, the signs of negative standard deviations can simply be reversed.

The third item is the most remarkable, since mutating the σ and the x values in a reversed order would violate the rationale explained in Sect. 4.4 after Eqs. (4.2) and (4.4). Tracing the literature on this issue, the paper by Gehlhaar and Fogel [165] seems to be a turning point. Here the authors explicitly compare the "sigma first" and "sigma last" strategies and conclude that the first one – the standard ES manner – offers a consistent general advantage over the second one. Notably in a recent paper and book [78, 147], Fogel uses the lognormal adaptation of n standard deviations σ_i, *followed* by the mutation of the object variables x_i themselves, suggesting that EP is practically merging with ES regarding this aspect.

Other ideas from ES have also informed the development of EP algorithms, and a version with self-adaptation of covariance matrices, called **R-meta-EP** is also in use. As was discussed in Section 4.8, the self-adaptation of strategy parameters relies on the association between good strategies and good solutions in order to evolve suitable operator parameters. One perspective used to explain this effect with (μ, λ) selection, where $\lambda >> \mu$, is that effectively λ/μ search strategies are being tried starting from each parent. Several recent research papers experimented with making this more explicit, with good results. Thus in Yao's improved fast evolutionary programming algorithm (IFEP) [436], two offspring are created from each parent, one using a Gaussian distribution to generate the random mutations, and the other using the Cauchy distribution. The latter has a fatter tail (i.e., more chance of generating a large mutation), which the authors suggest gives the overall algorithm greater chance of escaping from local minima, whilst the Gaussian distribution (if small step sizes evolve) gives greater ability to fine-tune the current parents.

5.3 Recombination

The issue of recombination in EP can be handled very briefly since it is not used. In the beginning recombination of FSMs was proposed, based on a majority vote mechanism, but this was never incorporated into the EP algorithm [145]. As of today, the EP arguments against recombination are conceptual rather than technical. In particular, a point in the search space is not viewed as an individual of some species, but as the abstraction of a species itself. As a consequence, recombination does not make sense as it cannot be applied to different species. Technically, of course, it is possible to design and apply variation operators merging information from two or more individuals.

The issue of the advantage of using a mutation-only algorithm versus a recombination and mutation variant has been intensively discussed since the 1990s. Fogel and Atmar [149] compared the results of EP algorithms with and without recombination on a series of linear functions with parameterisable interactions between genes. They concluded that improved performance was obtained from the version without recombination. This led to intensive periods of research in both the EP and the GA communities to try and establish the circumstances under which the availability of a recombination operator yielded improved performance [140, 153, 205, 374].

As befits a mature research field, the current state of thinking has moved on to a stable middle ground. The latest results [216] confirm that the ability of both crossover or Gaussian mutation to produce new offspring of superior fitness to their parents depends greatly on the state of the search process, with mutation better initially but crossover gaining in ability as evolution progresses. These conclusions agree with theoretical results developed elsewhere and discussed in more depth in Chap. 8. In particular it is stated that: "the traditional practice of setting operator probabilities at constant values, ... is quite limiting and may even prevent the successful discovery of suitable solutions." However, it is perhaps worth noting that even in these latest studies the authors did not detect a difference between the performance of different crossover operators, which they claim casts significant doubt on the "building block hypothesis" (Sect. 11.2), so we are not entirely without healthy scientific debate!

5.4 Parent Selection

The question of selecting parents to create offspring is almost nonissue for EP, and this distinguishes it from the other EA dialects. In EP every member of the population creates exactly one offspring via mutation. In this way it differs from GAs and GP, where selective pressure based on fitness is applied at this stage. It also differs from ES, since the choice of parents in EP is deterministic, whereas in ES it is stochastic, i.e., in ES each parent takes part in, *on average*, λ/μ offspring creation events, but possibly in none.

5.5 Survivor Selection

The selection operator is generally $(\mu + \mu)$ selection. Typically, the following stochastic variant is used. Pairwise tournament competitions are held in round-robin format involving both parent and offspring populations. Each solution $\bar{a} \in P(t) \cup P'(t)$ is evaluated against q other randomly chosen solutions. For each comparison, a "win" is assigned if $\bar{a}$ is better than its opponent. The μ solutions with the greatest number of wins are retained to be the parents of the next generation. Typically, $q = 10$ is recommended.

It is worth noting that this variant of selection allows for less-fit solutions to survive into the generation if they had a lucky draw of opponents. As the value of q increases this chance becomes more and unlikely, until in the limit the mechanism becomes deterministic $\mu + \mu$ as in the case of evolution strategies.

5.6 Example Application

5.6.1 The Ackley Function

As described in Section 4.9.1, Bäck et al. evaluated the behaviour of a typical evolution strategy on a thirty-dimensional version of Ackley's function [30]. They also evaluated the behaviour of an early version on meta-EP on the same problem. Since the function is one with continuous variables, a floating-point representation is natural, with one gene per variable (dimension). They used the "standard" version of meta-EP at that time, with $\mu = 200$, $q = 10$, and featuring the self-adaptation of thirty variances, with a lower limit of 0.02 and initial values of $\eta = 6.0$, where η denotes the step sizes). The mutation of the function variables occurred **before** the mutation of the strategy parameters. They reported that the globally optimal basin was located in all ten runs, but that the mean final best solution had fitness of $1.39 \cdot 10^{-2}$ as opposed to $7.48 \cdot 10^{-8}$ for the ES.

Yao et al. [436] examined the effects of changing the probability distribution used to generate mutations. They compared algorithms using two mutation mechanisms. The first was a version of what they called "classical" EP (CEP):

$$x'_i = x_i + \eta_i \cdot N_i(0,1), \tag{5.3}$$

$$\eta'_i = \eta_i \cdot exp(\tau' N(0,1) + \tau N_i(0,1)), \tag{5.4}$$

where $N(0,1)$ represents a random variable drawn for each offspring, $N_i(0,1)$ is a similar variable drawn afresh for each variable, and $\tau = (\sqrt{2\sqrt{n}})^{-1}$ and $\tau' = (\sqrt{2n})^{-1}$ are the **learning rates**.

The second variant they called "fast-EP" (FEP), which differed from Eq. (5.3) in that the first line was replaced by

$$x'_i = x_i + \eta_i \cdot \delta_i,$$

where δ_i is a drawn from a Cauchy distribution $f_t(x) = \frac{1}{\pi} \frac{t}{t^2+x^2}$ with the scale parameter $t = 1$.

Their algorithm used a population size of $\mu = 100$, round-robin tournaments with $q = 10$, and initial step sizes set to 3.0. They compared performance on a number of different functions, but we concentrate here on their results for the Ackley function. For self-adapted Gaussian mutations their results verified those of Bäck et al., but they observed improved results when they used the Cauchy distribution (fast EP), and the mean final score was reduced to $4.83 \cdot 10^{-3}$ when they tried the IFEP algorithm described in Sect. 5.2.2. Note that they still performed mutation of the object variables **before** the strategy parameters, so it is possible that these results could be improved still further. A recent follow-up on this study with much experimental data and a large test suite can be found in [435].

5.6.2 Evolving Checkers Players

In [78], which is expanded into a highly readable book [147] and further summarised in [148], Fogel charts the development of a program for playing the game of checkers (a.k.a. "draughts"), a board game for children that is also highly popular on the Internet. In this two-player game a standard 8×8 squared board is used, and each player has an (initially fixed) number of pieces (checkers), which move diagonally on the board. A checker can "take" an opponent's piece if it is adjacent, and the checker jumps over it into an empty square (both players use the same-coloured squares on the board). If a checker reaches the opponent's home side, it becomes a "king" in which case it can move forwards as well as backwards. Human checker players regularly compete against each other in a variety of tournaments (often Internet-hosted), and there is a standard scheme for rating a player according to their results.

In order to play the game, the program evaluates the future value of possible moves. It does this by calculating the likely board state if that move is made, using an iterative approach that looks a given distance ("ply") into the future. A board state is assigned a value by a neural network, whose output is taken as the "worth" of the board position from the perspective of the player who had just moved.

The board state is presented to the neural network as a vector of length 32, since there are 32 possible board sites. Each component comes from the set $\{-K, -1, 0, 1, K\}$, where the minus sign presents an opponent's king or piece, and K takes a value in the range [1.0,3.0].

The neural network thus defines a "strategy" for playing the game, and it is this strategy that is evolved with EP. A fixed structure is used for the neural networks, which has a total of 5046 weights and bias terms that are evolved, along with the importance given to the kings K. An individual solution is thus a vector of dimension 5047.

The authors used a population size of 15, with a tournament size $q = 5$. When programs played against each other they scored +1, 0, -2 points for a win, draw, and loss respectively. The 30 solutions were ranked according to their scores over the 5 games, then the best 15 became the next generation.

The mutation operator used took two forms: the weights/biases were mutated using the addition of Gaussian noise, with lognormal adaptation of the step sizes *before* mutation of the variables, i.e., using standard ES-style self-adaptation with $n = 5046$ strategy parameters. The offspring king weightings were mutated accorded to $K' = K + \delta$, where δ is sampled uniformly from [-0.1,0.1], and the resulting values of K' are constrained to the range [1.0,3.0]. Weights and biases were initialised randomly over the range [-0.2,0.2]. The K values were initially set to 2.0, and the strategy parameters were initialised with value 0.05.

The authors proceeded by having the neural networks compete against each other for 840 generations (6 months) before taking the best evolved strategy and testing it against human opponents on the Internet. The results were highly impressive: over a series of trials the program earned an average ranking, which put it in the "expert" class, and better than 99.61% of all rated players on the Web site. This work is particularly interesting in the context of artificial intelligence research for the following reasons:

- There is no input of human expertise about good short-term strategies or endgames.
- There is no input to tell the evolving programs that in evaluating board positions, a negative vector sum (that is, the opponent has a higher piece-count) is worse than a positive vector sum.
- There is no explicit "credit assignment" mechanism to reward moves that lead to wins; rather a "top-down" approach is taken that gives a single reward for an entire game.
- The selection function averages over five games, so the effects of strategies that lead to wins or losses are blurred.
- The strategies evolve by playing against themselves, with no need for human intervention!

5.7 Exercises

1. Recall Figure 5.2. What is the last state of the given FSM after the input string 011101?
2. Discuss the similarities and differences between ES and (modern) EP.
3. Discuss the EP convention on crossover.
4. Why could it be expected that the original order of first mutating the object variable (x) and then mutating the mutation parameter (σ) is inferior to the reversed order?
5. Assuming that μ parents produce μ offspring, of which one has a new best fitness value for a q value of ten, how many copies of the best solution would you expect to see in the next set of parents?

6. Now assume that there are n copies of the best solution and one copy of the next best in the union of parents and offspring. What is the probability that in the next generation of parents there will be *no* copies of this second-best solution?

7. Implement an EP for the Ackley function with $n=30$. Make 100 runs, storing the best value found in each, and then calculate the mean and standard deviation of these values. Compare your results with those from exercises 5 and 6 in Chap. 4.

5.8 Recommended Reading for this Chapter

1. L.J. Fogel, A.J. Owens, M.J. Walsh. *Artificial Intelligence through Simulated Evolution.* John Wiley, 1966

2. D.B. Fogel. *Evolutionary Computation.* IEEE Press, Piscataway, NJ, 1995

3. T. Bäck. *Evolutionary Algorithms in Theory and Practice.* Oxford University Press, New York, 1996

4. T. Bäck, D.B. Fogel, Z. Michalewicz, Eds. *Evolutionary Computation 1: Basic Algorithms and Operators.* Institute of Physics Publishing, Bristol, 2000

5. T. Bäck, D.B. Fogel, Z. Michalewicz, Eds. *Evolutionary Computation 2: Advanced Algorithms and Operators.* Institute of Physics Publishing, Bristol, 2000

6. T. Bäck, G. Rudolph, H.-P. Schwefel. Evolutionary programming and evolution strategies: Similarities and differences. In Fogel, Atmar Eds. [151], pp. 11–22

7. D.K. Gehlhaar, D.B. Fogel. Tuning evolutionary programming for conformationally flexible molecular docking. In Fogel et al. [154], pp. 419–429. Seminal paper comparing different EP variants and different approaches to self-adaptation

8. D.B. Fogel. *Blondie24: Playing at the Edge of AI.* Morgan Kaufmann, San Francisco, 2002

The following papers form a good starting point for readers interested in the crossover versus mutation debate.

9. David B. Fogel and J. W. Atmar. Comparing genetic operators with Gaussian mutations in simulated evolutionary processes using linear

systems. *Biological Cybernetics*, 63(2):111–114, 1990

10. W.M. Spears. Crossover or mutation. In Whitley [420], pp. 220–237

11. Larry J. Eshelman and J. David Schaffer. Crossover's niche. In Forrest [158], pp. 9–14

6

Genetic Programming

6.1 Aims of this Chapter

In this chapter we present genetic programming, the youngest member of the evolutionary algorithm family. Besides the particular representation (using trees as chromosomes), it differs from other EA strands in its application area. While the EAs discussed so far are typically applied to optimisation problems, GP could instead be positioned in machine learning. In terms of the different problem types as discussed in Chapter 1, most other EAs are for finding some input realising maximum payoff (Fig. 1.4), whereas GP is used to seek models with maximum fit (Fig. 1.5). Clearly, once maximisation is introduced, modelling problems can be seen as special cases of optimisation. This, in fact, is the basis of using evolution for such tasks: models are treated as individuals, and their fitness is the model quality to be maximised. The summary of GP is given in Table 6.1.

Representation	Tree structures
Recombination	Exchange of subtrees
Mutation	Random change in trees
Parent selection	Fitness proportional
Survivor selection	Generational replacement

Table 6.1. Sketch of GP

6.2 Introductory Example

As an example we consider a credit scoring problem within a bank that lends money and keeps a track of how its customers pay back their loans. This information about the clients can be used to develop a model describing good versus bad customers. Later on, this model can be used to predict customers' behaviour and thereby assist in evaluating future loan applicants. Technically, the classification model is developed based on (historical) data using personal information along with a creditworthiness index (good or bad) of customers. The model uses personal data as input, and produces a binary output, standing for the predicted creditworthiness of the corresponding person. For instance, the annual salary, the marriage status, and the number of children can be used as input. Table 6.2 shows a small data set. A possible

Customer Id	No. of children	Salary	Marital status	Creditworthiness
Id-1	2	45.000	Married	0
Id-2	0	30.000	Single	1
Id-3	1	40.000	Married	1
Id-4	2	60.000	Divorced	1
...	...	...	...	...
Id-10000	2	50.000	Married	1

Table 6.2. Data for the credit scoring problem

classification model using these data might be the following:

$$\text{IF } (No.\ children = 2) \text{ AND } (Salary > 80000) \text{ THEN } good \text{ ELSE } bad \qquad (6.1)$$

In general, the model will look like this:

$$\text{IF } formula \text{ THEN } good \text{ ELSE } bad$$

Notice, that *formula* is the only unknown in this rule, and all other elements are fixed. Our goal is thus to find the optimal formula that forms an optimal rule classifying a maximum number of known clients correctly.

At this point we have formulated our problem as a search problem in the space of possible formulas,[1] where the quality of a formula Φ can be defined as the percentage of customers correctly classified by the model IF Φ THEN *good* ELSE *bad*. In evolutionary terms we have defined the phenotypes (formulas) and the fitness (classification accuracy). In accordance with the typical GP approach we use parse trees as genotypes representing formulas. Fig. 6.1 shows the parse tree of the formula in Eq. (6.1).

This representation differs from those used in GAs or ES in two important aspects:

---

[1] Notice that we have not defined the syntax, thus the space of possible formulas, exactly. For the present treatment this is not needed and Sect. 6.3 treats this issue in general.

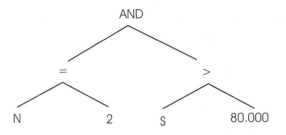

Fig. 6.1. Parse tree

- The chromosomes are nonlinear structures, while in GAs and ES they are typically linear vectors of the type $\bar{v} \in D_1 \times \ldots \times D_n$, where D_i is the domain of v_i.
- The chromosomes can differ in size, measured by the number of nodes of the tree, while in GAs and ES their size, that is, the chromosome length n, is usually fixed.

This new type of chromosomes necessitates new variation operators suitable for trees. Such crossover and mutation operators are discussed in Sects. 6.4 and 6.5. As for selection, notice that it only relies on fitness information and therefore it is independent from the chromosome structure. Hence, any selection scheme known in other EAs, e.g., (μ, λ) selection, or fitness proportional with generational replacement, can be simply applied.

6.3 Representation

As the introductory example has shown, the general idea in GP is to use parse trees as chromosomes. Such parse trees capture expressions in a given formal syntax. Depending on the problem at hand, and the users' perceptions on what the solutions must look like, this can be the syntax of arithmetic expressions, formulas in first-order predicate logic, or code written in a programming language. To illustrate the matter, let us consider one of each of these types of expressions.

- An arithmetic formula:

$$2 \cdot \pi + ((x + 3) - \frac{y}{5 + 1}), \tag{6.2}$$

- A logical formula:

$$(x \wedge true) \rightarrow ((x \vee y) \vee (z \leftrightarrow (x \wedge y))), \tag{6.3}$$

- The following program:

$$i = 1;$$
$$\text{while } (i < 20)$$
$$\{$$
$$\qquad i = i+1$$
$$\}$$

Figs. 6.2 and 6.3 show the parse trees belonging to these expressions.

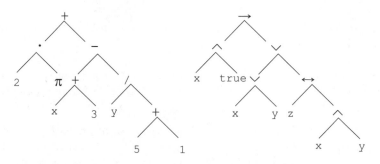

Fig. 6.2. Parse trees belonging to Eqs. (6.2) (*left*) and (6.3) (*right*)

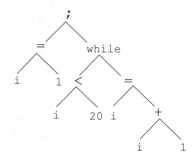

Fig. 6.3. Parse tree belonging to the above program

These examples illustrate generally how parse trees can be used and interpreted. Depending on the interpretation GP can be positioned in different ways. From a strictly technical point of view, GP is simply a variant of GAs working with a different data structure: the chromosomes are trees. This view disregards application-dependent interpretation issues. Nevertheless, such parse trees are often given an interpretation. In particular, they can be envisioned as executable codes, that is, programs. The syntax of functional programming, e.g., the language LISP, very closely matches the so-called Polish notation of expressions. For instance, the formula in Eq. (6.2) can be rewritten in this Polish notation as

$$+(\cdot(2,\pi),-(+(x,3),/(y,+(5,1))))),$$

while the executable LISP code[2] looks like:

$$(+\ (\cdot\ 2\ \pi)\ (-\ (+\ x\ 3)\ (/\ y\ (+\ 5\ 1))))).$$

Adopting this perception, GP can be positioned as the "programming of computers by means of natural selection" [229], or the "automatic evolution of computer programs" [38]. In the following we describe genetic programming with a rather technical flavour, that is, we emphasise the mechanisms, rather than the interpretation and context-specific issues.

Technically speaking, the specification of how to represent individuals in GA boils down to defining the syntax of the trees, or equivalently the syntax of the symbolic expressions (**s-expressions**) they represent. This is commonly done by defining a **function set** and a **terminal set**. Elements of the terminal set are allowed as leaves, while symbols from the function set are internal nodes. For example, a suitable function and terminal set that allow the expression in Eq. (6.2) as syntactically correct is given in Table 6.3.

Function set	$\{+,-,\cdot,/\}$
Terminal set	$\mathbb{R} \cup \{x,y\}$

Table 6.3. Function and terminal set that allow the expression in Eq. (6.2) as syntactically correct

Strictly speaking, a function symbol from the function set also must be given an arity, that is, the number of attributes it takes must be specified. For standard arithmetic or logical functions this is often omitted. Furthermore, for the complete specification of the syntax a definition of correct expressions (thus trees) based on the function and terminal set must be given. This definition follows the general way of defining terms in formal languages and therefore is also often omitted. For the sake of completeness we provide it below:

- All elements of the terminal set T are correct expressions.
- If $f \in F$ is a function symbol with arity n and $e_1,\ldots,e_n$ are correct expressions, then so is $f(e_1,\ldots,e_n)$.
- There are no other forms of correct expressions.

Note that in this definition we do not distinguish different types of expressions; each function symbol can take any expression as argument. This feature is known as the **closure property** in GP.

---

[2] To be precise we should use PLUS, etc., for the operators, but for the sake of an easy comparison with Eq. (6.3) we keep the arithmetical symbols.

In general, it can happen that function symbols and terminal symbols are typed and there are syntactic requirements excluding wrongly typed expressions. For instance, one might need both arithmetic and logical function symbols, e.g., to allow $(N = 2) \wedge (S > 80.000))$ as a correct expression. In this case it must be enforced that an arithmetic (logical) function symbol only has arithmetic (logical) arguments, e.g., to exclude $N \wedge 80.000$ as a correct expression. This issue is addressed in strongly typed genetic programming [281].

Before we go into the details of variation operators in GP, let us note that very often GP uses mutation *or* crossover in one step. This is in contrast to GA and ES, where crossover (recombination) *and* mutation are used in two consecutive steps. This subtle difference is visible on the GP flowchart given in Fig. 6.4 after Koza [229]. This chart compares the loop for filling the next generation in a generational GA with that of GP.

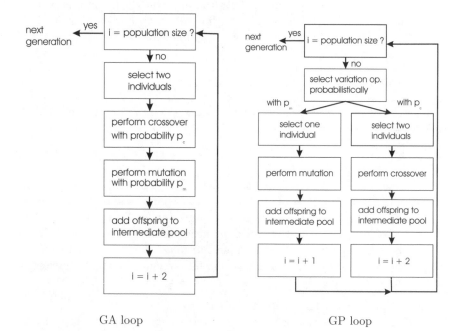

GA loop   GP loop

Fig. 6.4. GP flowchart

6.4 Mutation

In theory, the task of **mutation** in GP is the same as in all other EC branches, that is, creating a new individual from an old one through some small random variation. The most common implementation works by replacing the subtree starting at a randomly selected node by a randomly generated tree. The newly created tree is usually generated the same way as in the initial population, (Sect. 6.8). Fig. 6.5 illustrates how the parse tree belonging to Eq. (6.2) (left) is mutated into a parse tree standing for $2 \cdot \pi + ((x + 3) - y)$. Note that the size (tree depth) of the child can exceed that of the parent tree.

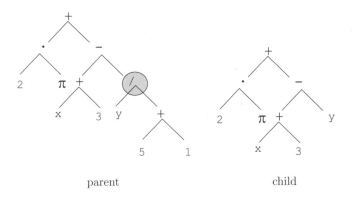

parent   child

Fig. 6.5. GP mutation illustrated: the node designated by a *circle* in the tree *on the left* is selected for mutation. The subtree staring at that node is replaced by a randomly generated tree, which is a leaf here

Mutation in GP has two parameters:

- The probability of choosing mutation at the junction with recombination
- The probability of choosing an internal point within the parent as the root of the subtree to be replaced

It is remarkable that Koza's classic book on GP from 1992 [229] advises users to set the mutation rate at 0, i.e., it suggests that GP works *without* mutation. More recently Banzhaf et al. recommended 5% [38]. In giving mutation such a limited role, GP differs from other EA streams. The reason for this is the generally shared view that crossover has a large shuffling effect, acting in some sense as a macromutation operator [10]. The current GP practice uses low, but positive, mutation frequencies, even though some studies indicate that the common wisdom favouring an (almost) pure crossover approach might be misleading [254].

6.5 Recombination

Recombination in GP creates offspring by swapping genetic material among the selected parents. In technical terms, it is a binary operator creating two child trees from two parent trees. The most common implementation is **sub-tree crossover**, which works by interchanging the subtrees starting at two randomly selected nodes in the given parents. Note that the size (tree depth) of the children can exceed that of the parent trees. In this, recombination within GP differs from recombination in other EC dialects.

During the development of GP many crossover operators were offered. The most commonly used one, subtree crossover, is illustrated in Fig. 6.6.

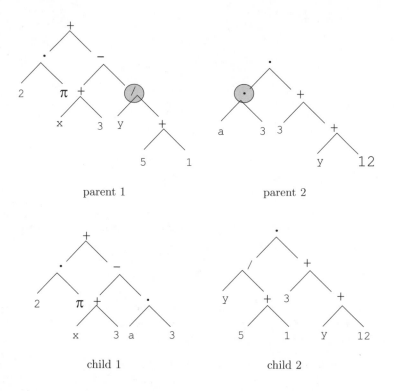

Fig. 6.6. GP crossover illustrated: the nodes designated by a *circle* in the parent trees are selected to serve as crossover points. The subtrees staring at those nodes are swapped, resulting in two new trees, which are the children

Recombination in GP has two parameters:

- The probability of choosing recombination at the junction with mutation
- The probability of choosing an internal point within each parent as crossover point

6.6 Parent Selection

GP typically uses fitness proportionate selection; however, because of the large population sizes frequently used (population sizes of several thousands are not unusual[3]), a method called **over-selection** is often used for population sizes of 1000 and above.

In this method, the population is first ranked by fitness and then divided into two groups, one containing the top $x\%$ and the other containing the other $(100 - x)\%$. When parents are selected, 80% of the selection operations come from the first group, and the other 20% from the second group. The values of x used are found empirically by "rule of thumb" and depend on the population size (Table 6.4).

Population size	Proportion of population in fitter group (x)
1000	32 %
2000	16 %
4000	8 %
8000	4 %

Table 6.4. Proportion of ranked population in "fitter" subpopulation from which majority of parents are selected

As can be seen, the number of individuals from which the majority of parents are chosen stays constant, i.e., the selection pressure increases dramatically for larger populations.

6.7 Survivor Selection

Traditional GP typically uses a generational strategy with no elitism, i.e., the number of offspring created is the same as the population size, and all individuals have a life span of one generation. This is, of course, not a technical necessity; rather it is a convention. In their 1998 book, Banzhaf et al. gave equal treatment to generational and steady-state GP [38], and the latest trend appears to be to use a steady-state scheme. This is mainly motivated by the need for elitism caused by the destructive effects of crossover [10].

6.8 Initialisation

The most common method of initialisation for GP is the so-called **ramped half-and-half** method. In this method a maximum initial depth D_{max} of trees

---

[3] Just as an indication of the population sizes and of how they are growing, in 1994 [231] used 1000; in 1996 [8] used 128,000; and in 1999 [233] used 1,120,000 individuals.

is chosen, and then each member of the initial population is created from the sets of functions F and terminals T using one of the two methods below with equal probability:

- *Full method*: here each branch of the tree has depth D_{max}. The contents of nodes at depth d are chosen from F if $d < D_{max}$ or from T if $d = D_{max}$.
- *Grow method*: here the branches of the tree may have different depths, up to the limit D_{max}. The tree is constructed beginning from the root, with the contents of a node being chosen stochastically from $F \cup T$ if $d < D_{max}$.

6.9 Bloat in Genetic Programming

A special effect of varying chromosome sizes in GP is that these tend to grow during a GP run. That is, without appropriate countermeasures the average tree size is growing during the search process. This phenomenon is known as **bloat** (sometimes called the "survival of the fattest"). There are many studies devoted to understanding why bloat occurs and to proposing counter-measures, see for instance [245, 373]. Although the results and discussions are not conclusive, one primary suspect is the sheer fact that we have chromosomes with variable length, meaning that the *possibility* for chromosome sizes to grow along the evolution already implies that they will *actually* do so.

Appropriate countermeasures to reduce, or even eliminate, tree growth range from elementary to highly sophisticated. Probably the simplest way to prevent bloat is to introduce a maximum tree size and forbid a variation operator if the child(ren) resulting from its application would exceed this maximum size. In this case, this threshold can be seen as an additional parameter of mutation and recombination in GP. Several advanced techniques have also been proposed over the history of GP, but practically the only one that is widely acknowledged is that of **parsimony pressure**. Such a pressure towards parsimony (i.e., being "stingy" or ungenerous) is achieved through introducing a penalty term in the fitness formula that reduces the fitness of large chromosomes [209, 372] or using multiobjective techniques [97].

6.10 Problems Involving "Physical" Environments

An important category of GP applications arises in contexts where executing a given expression *does* something, that is, changes the environment, which in turn affects the execution (and therefore the fitness) of the expression. The arithmetic examples so far and the symbolic regression application in Sect. 6.11 do not fall into this category. They are what can be termed *data fitting* problems, which form the canonical challenge for many machine learning algorithms, GP included. This section illustrates another type of problem that we describe as *problems involving "physical" environments*. The quotes around "physical" indicate that the environment can actually be simulated – which it most often is. Together with data fitting, such problems amount to the great majority of GP applications.

Paraphrasing Teller [394], we can say that these problems do not have solutions that are simple mappings from the inputs to the outputs; some kind of state information or memory is needed to operate well in these domains. As a simple example, consider the problem of evolving a robot controller (which is a computer program) for a robot that must walk down a trajectory and collect objects on its way. A possible syntax is specified by Table 6.5.

Function set	glue, if-object-found
Terminal set	pick, move-on

Table 6.5. Function and terminal set for a simple robot controller

The expressions in the terminal set denote elementary actions that can be performed by the robot. Executing `pick` results in collecting the object (if any) positioned on the present location of the robot, while `move-on` causes the robot to shift one position along the trajectory. The functions in the function set are both binary, and `glue` simply concatenates two arguments. That is, executing `glue(x,y)` will first perform x and then y. The expression `if-object-found(x,y)` represents a conditional action based on the state of the environment: if there is an object on the present location of the robot then x is executed, otherwise y.

This syntax allows `if-object-found(pick,move)` and `if-object-found(move,pick)` both be correct expressions (programs). The semantics (the environmental effects) tells us that the first one would work well in performing the object collection task, and the second one would not be very effective.

What distinguishes this kind of GP application is not the internal EA mechanics. Variation, selection, population update, and the like are done the same way as for all other applications. The difference lies in the fact that a simulator is necessary to calculate fitness by measuring achieved performance in the given environment. In a simple setting, like the above example or the well-known artificial ant problem [229], this can mean one fitness case only: one trajectory the robot has to handle. Evaluating the fitness of a given chromosome (where the program is the robot controller) happens by running a simulator that computes the results of the robot's actions as driven by this controller. Technically speaking, this means a fitness evaluation that is computationally expensive. In a more advanced setting it might even be required that performance be measured within more environments or more initial situations in the same environment. In this case the fitness evaluations become *very* expensive, meaning that one run can take up to months, wall-clock time. This drawback can be compensated by the quality of the evolved results as shown, for instance, by the success of a team of (simulated) robots playing soccer by an evolved controller [253].

6.11 Example Application: Symbolic Regression

One of the standard applications of genetic programming is symbolic regression. In the one-dimensional case the problem instance to be solved is defined by a number of pairs $\langle x_i, y_i \rangle \in \mathbb{R} \times \mathbb{R}$ ($i \in \{1, \ldots, n\}$), and the task is to find a function $f : \mathbb{R} \to \mathbb{R}$ such that $f(x_i) = y_i$ for all $i \in \{1, \ldots, n\}$. It is common to consider the given pairs $\langle x_1, y_i \rangle \in \mathbb{R} \times \mathbb{R}$ as data points and see the whole task as curve fitting. IN other words, we are looking for a function whose plot curve contains each data point.

To define a GP algorithm for this problem we start by defining the representation, that is, the syntax of the s-expressions, or parse trees, used as candidate solutions. Since the problem is arithmetic we can use arithmetic operators as functions, for instance $\{+, -, \cdot, / \}$, but we can also include power, exp, and elementary geometric functions like sin or cos. As for the terminals, we need exactly one variable x and some constants. To keep things simple we allow all elements of $\mathbb{R}$ as constants. Our syntax can now be specified as shown in Table 6.6.

Function set	$\{+, -, \cdot, /, exp, sin, cos\}$
Terminal set	$\mathbb{R} \cup \{x\}$

Table 6.6. Function and terminal set for a symbolic regression problem

Strictly speaking, we also have to specify the arity of the operators, e.g., sin is unary, and + is binary, but using standard operators as we do, this is now self-evident. The closure property is not a problem either since all operators are arithmetical here.

As the following step we define the fitness of an individual f, that is, an expression in the above syntax. The most natural definition is to base the fitness of f on some measure of the fitting error. A suitable error measure is, for instance, the well-known sum of squares

$$err(f) = \sum_{i=1}^{n} (f(x_i) - y_i)^2,$$

which obviously should be minimised.

As for variation operators, we can suffice with using the mutation and recombination operators given in Sects. 6.4 and 6.5, respectively. Also the selection mechanisms can be simply chosen from the list of standard options for

GAs. For parent selection we can use two-tournament, declaring that the winner of the tournament is the individual with the lower err value. Alternatively, we can follow the GP conventions and use fitness proportionate selection applied to the normalised fitness function obtained from err as raw fitness.

Also in line with traditional GP practice, we can choose a generational population update strategy, where no explicit survivor selection takes place. What remains to specify is how to start and how to finish. As for starting, we can use the standard option again, ramped half-and-half initialisation, and generate 1000 random trees. Note that hereby we defined the population size. To define when to finish, first we establish the required precision for hitting y_i by $f(x_i)$, say 0.0001. Then we can set the termination condition as having n hits – that is, having a function f that approximates each y_i with the required precision – or a having reached the maximum number of fitness evaluations, say 50.000. Given that the population size equals 1000, this amounts to a maximum of 50 generations.

6.12 Exercises

1. Rewrite Eq. (6.3) in Polish and LISP notation.
2. Give a suitable function and terminal set that allows the expression in Eq. (6.3) as syntactically correct.
3. The logical operators for negation ($\neg$) and conjunction ($\wedge$) are sufficient to define other operators, e.g., disjunction ($\vee$), implication ($\rightarrow$), and equivalence ($\leftrightarrow$). Is it a good idea to use the minimal set of operators $\{\ \neg,\ \wedge\ \}$ as function set instead of $\{\ \neg,\ \wedge,\ \vee,\ \rightarrow,\ \leftrightarrow\ \}$ for solving a problem whose solution is a logical formula?
4. Design a GA for the credit score problem from Sect. 6.2. Discuss the advantages and disadvantages of this GA versus a GP.
5. Write, or download, a GP implementation and a standard test problem. Design and perform some experiments to measure the amount of "bloat" i.e., the change in solution size as a function of time, and compare this to the change in the performance of the solutions over the same time period.
6. Using your solution to the former exercise, investigate the effects of different mutation rates and population sizes.

6.13 Recommended Reading for this Chapter

1. J.R. Koza. *Genetic Programming*. MIT Press, 1992.

2. J.R. Koza. *Genetic Programming II*. MIT Press, 1994.

3. W. Banzhaf, P. Nordin, R.E. Keller, and F.D. Francone. *Genetic Programming: An Introduction.* Morgan Kaufmann, 1998.

4. W.B. Langdon. *Genetic Programming + Data Structures = Automatic Programming!* Kluwer, 1998.

5. W.B. Langdon and R. Poli. *Foundations of Genetic Programming.* Springer-Verlag, 2001.

7

Learning Classifier Systems

7.1 Aims of this Chapter

This chapter introduces an evolutionary approach to machine learning tasks working with rule sets, rather than parse trees, to represent knowledge. In learning classifier systems (LCS) the evolutionary algorithm acts as a rule discovery component. LCS systems are used primarily in applications where the objective is to evolve a system that will respond to the current state of its environment (i.e., the inputs to the system) by suggesting a response that in some way maximises (future) reward from the environment.[1] Specifically, the idealised result of running an LCS is the evolution of a rule base that covers the space of possible inputs and suggests the most appropriate actions for each. Through LCS algorithms we also demonstrate evolution where *cooperation* between the population members (i.e., rules) is crucial. In this aspect LCS systems differ significantly from the other four members of the evolutionary algorithm family, where individuals strictly compete with each other.

The summary of LCS is given after the introductory example in Table 7.1, while Fig. 7.1 illustrates a generic system.

7.2 Introductory Example

In order to illustrate LCSs, we use as an example a well-known problem: the multiplexer. A k-bit multiplexer concerns bit-strings of length k treated as being in two parts: l address bits followed by 2^l data bits, i.e., $k = l + 2^l$. For $l = 2$ we have $k = 6$, and 101011 is a correct string. In a k-bit multiplexer problem we have to return the value of the data bit specified by the address part of a given string. Given the input string 101011, the address bits 10 decode to the value 2, and the second data bit from 1011 is 0. The correct

---

[1] This class of problems is often known as **reinforcement learning** problems; typical applications range from data-mining to robotics.

output for 101011 is thus 0. A rule capturing this response can be denoted as 101011 : 0. In general, a rule can be specified by a condition part followed by a colon (:) and an action part. In the present example actions are suggested outputs.

There are several possible tasks concerning a k-bit multiplexer. For instance, one could aim at building a system, a rule set in our case, that returns the correct output for each input. Alternatively, one might want to know what response (correct/incorrect) the external system would return in reply to each possible symbol output for any given input.

Clearly, there are 2^k possible input strings, and consequently 2^{k+1} binary rules that would completely describe the environment. However, since this number scales exponentially with the size of the problem, it is easy to see the attractions of a system that is able to generalise. For instance, by the very nature of the multiplexer problem, the values in the $2^l - 1$ data bits not currently addressed are irrelevant, hence for our 6-multiplexer three of the four data bits can be ignored at any one time. Now consider adding a "don't care" symbol # to the set of values that can occur in the condition part of the rules and defining that the condition *bit i = #* always returns the value "TRUE", and can therefore be ignored. For example, the condition 1#0 will read as (*bit 1 = 1*) AND (*bit 3 = 0*). Then for the instance above, we can replace eight different rules in the old syntax (only 0s and 1s) by the generalisation 10#0## : 0.

Now let us assume that our environment gives us a reward of, say, 100 for the correct answer and 0 for an incorrect response. Then the rules 101011 : 0 and 101011 : 1 would get payoffs of 100 and 0, respectively. To evolve a good rule set we extend the representation, i.e., the rule syntax, by reward information separated by an arrow leading from the actual rule. In this notation 101011 : 0 → 100 and 101011 : 1 → 0 are two possible rules. In general, the reward part of a rule stands for a *predicted payoff* of applying that rule.

The working of one possible LCS system (as we show later there are many variants) for this simple multiplexer problem, where we wish to output the value for every input string that maximises the payoff received can be described as follows:

- The environment is interfaced to the system as a string of length k as the input message, where a single binary variable serves as the output, and an integer value from the environment represents the payoff received from the action.
- We have a set of rules forming the population.
- There are two main cycles: a rule evaluation cycle and a rule discovery cycle.
- A rule evaluation cycle works as follows:
  - The condition part of each rule in the rule base is examined to see if it matches the current input string. Those rules that match are tagged

as belonging to the *match set* for this cycle. Note that different rules in the match set may advocate different actions.

- The rules in the match set are grouped according to the action (output) they advocate, and a predicted payoff for each action is calculated from the individual rules' predictions.
- Based on these predictions, an action is chosen. A simple strategy is to go for the action with the highest predicted payoff. All the rules that advocated the chosen action are tagged as belonging to the *action set* for that time step.
- The action is posted to the environment, and a reward signal will be received. A *credit allocation mechanism* is used to distribute that reward amongst the rules in the action set that led to the reward. A natural way to reward individual rules is to raise their predicted payoff, so that they would have more influence on future decisions concerning the action to be chosen.
- In the rule discovery cycle, the GA is run on the population of rules to generate new rules and delete poorly performing ones.
  - Parent selection is performed based on the strength of individual rules measured by their predicted payoff.
  - The `condition:action` parts of the selected rules are recombined and mutated to create offspring.
  - Children are given the average of their parents' strength.
  - Survivor selection is performed based on the strength of individual rules to update the population, that is, to create a new rule set.

Let us note that although the notation $101011 : 0 \rightarrow 100$ might suggest otherwise, technically the predicted payoff is not part of the genotype since it does not undergo mutation and crossover. In addition, note that the multiplexer is a so-called single step problem with immediate reward at each time step. In general, this need not be the case. A whole chain of rule applications, partly reacting to actions of previously fired rules, can be performed before the environmental feedback (and the corresponding reward distribution) takes place. It is in these cases that cooperation among rules (those in the chain resulting in a rewarded action) occurs by distributing the reward over all rules in the chain. Finally, notice that rules with an identical action part matching the same conditions are actually competing. They can be seen as forming an environmental niche in the sense of having to share resources: the rewards earned by the action they all advocate. This forms a natural bias against having too many rules in the same niche, and at the same time favours more general rules since they may fire in more situations, and receive rewards more frequently. The hoped-for outcome is the long-term evolution of sufficiently general rules.

After this introductory example we give the summary of a typical LCS in Table 7.1. As we will see later, although these details are typical, many different versions of LCS have been proposed in which the specifics vary.

Representation	condition:action:prediction-tuples
	conditions use {0,1,#} alphabet
Recombination	One-point crossover on conditions/actions
Mutation	Binary/ternary resetting as appropriate on action/conditions
Parent selection	Fitness proportional
	with sharing within environmental niches
Survivor selection	Stochastic, inversely related to
	number of rules covering same environmental niche

Table 7.1. Sketch of a generic LCS

7.3 General Background

Learning classifier systems were first described by Holland in 1976 [203] as a framework for studying learning in condition:action rule based systems, using genetic algorithms as the principal method for the discovery of new rules and the reinforcement of successful ones. In their broadest form, they can be considered as an iterative procedure governing the interaction of a set of rules with an external environment. The action of a generic LCS can be viewed as follows:

- The state of the environment is transmitted to the system via a set of **detectors** whose output is put on a **message list**.
- This message list may also contain other signals posted there by rules that have fired on previous cycles, or the detector signals from previous cycles. This means it may act as a form of memory.
- The **condition part** of each rule in the rule base is then examined to see if it matches the current message list. Those rules that match are tagged as belonging to the **match set** for this cycle. Note that different rules in the match set may advocate different actions.
- The rules in the match set are grouped according to the action they advocate, and a predicted payoff for each action is calculated from the individual rules' predictions.
- Based on these predictions, an action is chosen, and all of the rules that advocated that action are tagged as belonging to the **action set** for that time step.
- The action is posted to the message list. The action consists of instructions to be read by the effectors (which interact with the environment), and (optionally) signals to the left on the "internal" message list.
- Periodically a reward signal is received from the environment. A **credit allocation mechanism** is used to distribute that reward amongst the rules, usually amongst the chain of action sets that led to the reward.
- Periodically the GA is run on the population of rules to generate new rules and delete poorly performing ones.

The basic elements of this generic LCS are shown in Fig. 7.1.

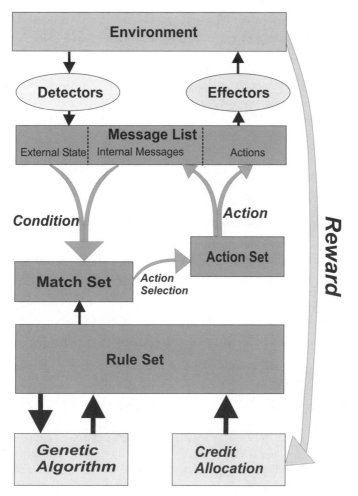

Fig. 7.1. Structure of a learning classifier system

In the form described above, LCS clearly belong to the field of reinforcement learning where they share many features with systems such as Q-learning [413]. However, where they differ, and where they derive their power, is in the use of # (*don't care*) symbols in the condition parts of the rules. This provides an explicit mechanism via which the system can learn generalisations about the environment.

Although the idea of adaptive rule based systems has been around for some decades [329], and Holland's ideas of using GAs as the rule discovery component were well known from 1976 onwards, the systems he described were quite complex, and have tended to be viewed as a manifesto rather than as a complete specification for a working algorithm. The 1980s saw experimentation with a number of variants such as Samuel [183], GOFER-1 [59], and ALECSYS [110], as well as some successful applications in fields such as gas pipeline design [172].

However, most of these systems did not exhibit the hoped-for performance as a result of problems such as the proliferation of overgeneral rules and difficulties in maintaining a complete rule base. The concept of **overgeneralisation** can be understood by considering that we are effectively dividing the input space into a number of discrete subsets and putting different labels on these, representing actions and possibly payoffs. The role of generalisation is to permit us to give a compact description of a subset, rather than listing every separate point. An overgeneral rule is one that matches elements from more than one of these subsets.

The very complexity of the systems also made these shortcomings difficult to analyse, as it is with other highly complex systems to which LCS have been compared, such as artificial neural networks [366]. For these reasons a major step forward was the development of Wilson's ZCS system [426], a minimalist version of the LCS that, as a result of its simplicity, has the potential for careful analysis, whilst exhibiting surprisingly good behaviour.

7.4 ZCS: A "Zeroth-Level" Classifier System

As suggested above, ZCS represents a "stripped down" version of the generic LCS system illustrated in Figure 7.1. The most obvious difference is that it has no internal message list, and therefore no explicit method for transmitting information between cycles. An immediate consequence of this is that the format of the rules is determined entirely by the interface of the system with its environment, i.e., each rule r consists of a real-valued strength s plus one condition bit for each (binary) detector and one action bit for each (binary) effector: $r =< c : a \rightarrow s >$.

In each performance cycle the match set (those members of the rule population whose conditions match the current input from the environment) is found from the population, and this is then logically subdivided according to the actions advocated by the matching rules. Action selection uses a fitness proportionate-like method (Sect. 3.7.1) where the fitness of the actions is given by the the sum of the strengths of those rules advocating that action *in this match set*.

If the case occurs that no rules have conditions matching the current input, i.e., the matchset is empty, ZCS uses a so-called cover operator, which creates a rule with the condition (augmented with #s) and a random valid action.

The credit assignment component of ZCS works as follows:

- All rules not in the match set M^t for this cycle t are initially unchanged:

$$\forall r \notin M^t \quad s'_r = s_r.$$

- All those rules in the match set M^t, but not the action set A (i.e., those advocating weaker actions) have their strengths reduced by multiplication with a factor $\tau \in [0, 1)$:

$$\forall r \in M^t \setminus A^t \quad s'_r = s_r \cdot \tau.$$

- All those rules in the action set have a fraction $\beta \in [0, 1)$ of their strengths removed:

$$\forall r \in A^t \quad s'_r = (1 - \beta) \cdot s_r.$$

- This strength is "pooled" and distributed equally amongst the members of the *previous* action set, after being reduced by a factor $\gamma \in [0, 1)$; i.e., let $x = \sum_{r \in A^t} \beta \cdot s_r$, then:

$$\forall r \in A^{t-1} \quad s''_r = s'_r + \frac{\gamma \cdot x}{\mid A^{t-1} \mid}.$$

- Finally, any feedback P^t from the system is reduced by a factor β and then distributed equally amongst the members of the current action set:

$$\forall r \in M^t \quad s'''_r = s''_r + \beta \cdot P / \mid A^t \mid.$$

This credit assignment method, with strength being moved each action set to its predecessor, has been called an **implicit bucket brigade**. The effect is to reward sequences of actions that lead to reward from the environment, and the use of the discounting term γ leads to a preference for shorter rather than longer chains of actions before rewards.

The rule set is repeatedly modified as the system learns new rules by a genetic algorithm, which is invoked periodically. Two rules are selected from the rule base using fitness proportionate selection based on rule strength. One-point crossover and bitwise mutation (with one of the two/three valid values chosen at random for the action/condition parts of the rules) are then used to create two offspring, each of which receives the mean of its parents' strength as its initial strength. These new rules then replace two of the current rule set, which are chosen stochastically, this time with probabilities inversely proportional to their strength.

The fact that the reward received by each action set is divided equally amongst all of its members, coupled with fitness proportionate selection acting over the whole population of rules in the GA phase, means that a kind of fitness sharing is at work. This tends to preserve a number of rules in each niche (action set) based on the relative frequency of occurrence of the environmental conditions and the payoff received from the action. Although Wilson's original work reported some problems with the persistence of overgeneral classifiers (which match more than one environmental niche as discussed above), Bull and Hurst [68] showed theoretically and empirically that in fact ZCS is capable of evolving optimal behaviour under a variety of conditions.

However, we should note an important feature of ZCS. Since the GA preserves rules according to their strength, or payoff, it only preserves the rules in each niche that lead to maximum reward. Thus, in terms of our multiplexer example above, it would preserve the rule $10\#0\#\# : 0 \rightarrow 100$, but not $10\#0\#\# : 1 \rightarrow 0$. A more formal way of expressing this feature is that ZCS does not evolve a complete mapping from the space of rules to their payoffs. That is, if we denote the set of possible environmental states by S, the set of possible actions that the LCS can perform by $\mathcal{A}$, and the set of possible reward values by P, then ZCS does not preserve the complete mapping $S \times \mathcal{A} \rightarrow \mathcal{P}$.

For many applications this feature is entirely acceptable, and it has the benefit that the evolved rule bases are much smaller and consequently easier to analyse for any given size problem. However, as Wilson noted, the use of fitness proportionate selection, with its well-known problems in the presence of highly fit initial solutions, can lead ZCS to prematurely converge onto suboptimal rules before the space can be properly explored and stable populations formed on each niche. Wilson refers to these as "path habits". Another issue he raises is that, since the GA can create offspring via recombination from rules belonging to entirely different niches, often these may turn out to have no value. These considerations, along with the fact that under some circumstances (e.g., dynamic or noisy environments), and for some applications (e.g., data mining), it might be desirable to obtain a complete mapping led Wilson to consider other ways in which this might be achieved, leading to the design of XCS [427].

7.5 XCS

7.5.1 Motivation

As suggested above, ZCS and other previously proposed LCS algorithms exhibit a number of undesirable features, namely:

- The continued presence of rules depends on their being selected by the GA on the basis of payoff. This biases against:
  - Rules occurring early in a chain of events that lead to a reward, and thus receiving heavily discounted payoff.
  - Rules that lead to relatively low rewards, even if they are the most appropriate action in the circumstances (although note that Bull and Hurst have proved that this effect is heavily dependent on the choice of parameters [68]).
- Running a panmictic GA (i.e., allowing recombination between any rules) can create rules with little meaning, slowing down the learning process.
- The systems do not have explicit pressure towards evolving a complete mapping from inputs and actions to payoff predictions.
- The systems often failed to evolve accurate generalisations.

A number of algorithms had been proposed that address some of these issues, such as running the GA in the match sets rather than in the whole population [58], and using a combination of factors in the calculation of fitness used by the GA [59, 161]. XCS was novel in tackling all of these issues, in particular that of the mapping, via the separation of the factors used in action selection (prediction of payoff for each suggested action) and rule discovery selection (the fitness of the rule used by the GA).

7.5.2 Description

Like its predecessor, XCS is a reduced version of the generic LCS in Figure 7.1. In particular, it does not have any memory, so the internal message list does not exist. However, its prime distinguishing characteristic is that each rule now is a five tuple $\langle c : a : p : \varepsilon : F \rangle$, where c, a, and p are the condition, the action, and the predicted payoff, respectively, as before, plus a measure of prediction error ε, and a separate fitness F, which is used by the GA. It is vital that the fitness is a function of prediction *accuracy* rather than *magnitude*.

For a complete description, the reader is directed to [427, 428]. We will restrict ourselves here to listing its major features.

- The match set M is found as before. Let $\mathcal{A}'$ denote the set of actions present in the rules of M. Then M is logically subdivided according to actions.
- For each action $a \in \mathcal{A}'$, a fitness-weighted average of the rules in that subset R_a is used as the predicted payoff:

$$p_a = \sum_{r \in R_a} w_r \cdot p_r, \quad \text{where } w_r = \frac{F_r}{\sum_{r \in R_a} F_r}.$$

- Action selection can use a number of stochastic schemes (e.g., proportional to payoff), or choose the action with the highest predicted payoff deterministically.
- Once the action is posted to the environment and any reward received, the rules in the *previous* action set are updated. This has three components:
  - First, the fitness values are updated using the current errors ε_r for each rule r. As stated above, the fitness is based on accuracy κ_r, which is defined by the prediction error ε_r as:

$$\kappa_r = e^{ln(\alpha) \frac{\varepsilon_r - \varepsilon_0}{\varepsilon_0}},$$

    where the constants ε_0 and α are parameters of the system. Thus for each rule the accuracy κ_r is calculated, and then the fitness is updated according to:

$$F'_r = F_r + \beta \cdot (\kappa'_r - F_r),$$

where β is called the **learning rate** parameter, and κ'_r is the *relative* accuracy, i.e., normalised with respect to the other rules in the action set

$$\kappa'_r = \frac{\kappa_r}{\sum_{r \in R_a} \kappa_r}.$$

– Second, a payoff value P is calculated using the maximum predicted payoff of all actions in the current match set M (i.e., not necessarily the chosen action), discounted by a factor γ (as per ZCS), plus any reward R received by the system in the previous time step:

$$P = \gamma \cdot max\{ p_a \mid a \in \mathcal{A}'\} + R.$$

– This payoff value P is used to update the prediction errors:

$$\varepsilon'_r = \varepsilon_r + \beta \cdot (\mid P - p_r \mid -\varepsilon_r).$$

– Finally, the payoff P is used to update the actual predictions p_r in the previous action set:

$$p'_r = p_r + \beta \cdot (P - p_r).$$

• The GA is modified to achieve explicit niching by acting on the contents of the action set (match set in early versions). As noted before, the selection operator allocates more reproductive opportunities to accurate rules, and the probability of deletion is set proportional to the size of the action set.
• In addition to the mechanisms above, specialised mechanisms are used for initialising and managing the first few updates of the values of p, ε, F, as well as for deciding when and where the GA should run, according to how recently it has run in each match set, and so on.

It is worth noting that several features of the reinforcement procedure differ from previous systems, in particular the way in which the payoff P is calculated using the *maximum* predicted payoff of all actions in the match set. This stems from extensive comparisons with Q-learning and other reinforcement learning algorithms, for which convergence to optimal solutions can be proved. Similarly, the use of the update rule is informed by research in other areas of machine learning.

Although the full version of XCS contains a number of sophisticated mechanisms and a large number of parameters, it has been shown to exhibit excellent performance in a wide variety of applications and to exhibit a good ability to evolve a rule set that contains accurate generalisations about the search space [428]. A further benefit to the interested reader is the fact that several implementations are freely available on the Internet.

7.6 Extensions

In the previous sections we restricted our attention to binary inputs and outputs in order to simplify the description. However, this restriction is purely arbitrary and is inappropriate in many situations.

Real-Valued Inputs/Outputs

In many applications the state of the environment is best described by detectors with real-valued outputs. In this case the usual approach is to use rules in which each part of the conditions consists of a range of values that the variable can take in order to match. The binary output variables in the actions may also be replaced by real values, and the GA's variation operators are chosen appropriately.

Wilson [429] recommends that each variable in the condition be represented by a tuple $\langle centre, spread \rangle$ representing a range of values $centre \pm spread$. It was recently shown [386] that if the variables are bounded, then this representation introduces a bias that worsens performance, and that better results can be obtained by using a tuple that explicitly contains the endpoints of the range.

Fuzzy Classifiers

A natural extension in the presence of real-valued or integer-coded variables is to represent rules using fuzzy rather than crisp matching. Thus, rather than stating

IF ($light\_intensity > 8.3$) AND ($light\_source\_angle$ *between* -15 *and* $+15$) THEN
$turn\_angle= 47$,

one might have a rule

IF ($light\_intensity = quite\ bright$) AND ($light\_source\_angle = nearly\ forward$)
THEN *turn left.*

Effectively these conditions work by defining a number of fuzzy classes for each variable, and then defining a set of overlapping membership functions (one for each class) over the range of the variable as illustrated for three concepts "close", "near", and "far" concerning a variable "distance" in the Fig. 7.2.

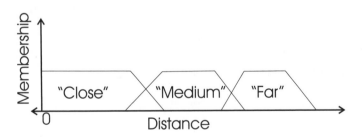

Fig. 7.2. Membership of three fuzzy classes as a function of distance

The action of the fuzzy LCS then starts by the "fuzzification" process whereby the real-valued inputs are compared to the membership functions to find the degree of membership of each class. The condition parts of the rules work on the classes, i.e., they take values of the form {*close, medium, far, don't_care*} in the example above. Thus all rules now match to some degree rather than completely or not at all, although typically a threshold is used to cut off poorly matched rules.

This means that a number of rules are active in the match set, and the final output is decided by a "defuzzification" process, whereby the rules are weighted according to the degree of their match. Similarly, the reinforcement process usually distributes rewards to rules according to their degree of match to the environment.

A primary advantage of using fuzzy sets is that they can exhibit extremely graceful behaviour in the presence of noise compared to "crisp" sets with exact cut-offs for the membership functions. This is very useful when the system's perception of the current environment state may be inaccurate, as typified by robotics applications where sensor values are notoriously unreliable [57].

S-Classifiers

In our discussion of binary and real-coded inputs to the LCS systems, we have considered whether the individual inputs match the relevant parts of the condition of a rule, but we have only considered a rule to match the entire input if all of its parts match. That is, we effectively compute a truth value for each separate bit/real of the input string and then perform a logical AND of these truth values. As an example, recall from Sect. 7.2 that the condition 1#0 is equivalent to saying (*bit 1 = 1*) AND (*bit 3 = 0*), as # always returns the value "TRUE" and can be ignored.

A number of authors have proposed and experimented with alternative representations that would allow different sorts of logical relationships to be expressed such as (*bit 1 = 1*) OR (*bit 3 = 0*), using what Wilson termed s-classifiers [426]. Typically this is done by using LISP s-expressions and evolving them via GP, rather than using binary strings and evolving them with GAs. For example, in [5] s-expression-based ZCS systems are used for a number of classification problems.

7.7 Example Applications

7.7.1 Modelling Financial Market Traders

An example of the use of LCS for data mining and modelling problems can be seen in [339], where Schulenberg and Ross used XCS to evolve sets of rules modelling the behaviour of stock market traders. For inputs they used ten years of trading history, in the form of daily statistics such as volume of trade, current price, change in price over last few days, and whether this price is a new high (or low), and so on. for a given company's stock. The evolved traders consisted of sets of rules, and each day the current stock market conditions were presented to the trader, triggering a rule that decided whether stock was bought or sold. Periodically a GA is run on the set of initial random rules so that well-performing ones are rewarded and poorly performing ones discarded. It was demonstrated that the system evolved trading agents that outperformed many well-known strategies and varied according to the nature of the particular stock they were trading. Of particular interest and benefit, compared to methods such as neural networks, which are also used for this kind of modelling problem in time-series forecasting, is the fact that the rule base of the evolved traders is easily examinable, that is to say that the models that are evolved are particularly transparent to the user and so have explanatory power.

7.7.2 A Multistep Problem

Like the multiplexer and most data mining applications, the example sketched above was a **single-step** problem, i.e., reward is received from the environment after every step. The design of LCS algorithms also usually permits their use in so-called **multistep** problems, where there may be a variable number of steps before any reward is received.

A nice example of a practical application representing a multistep environment can be found in the work of Hurst et al. [215], who evolved the control system for a real robot *on-line* (rather than in simulation). Their robot ran under the on-board control of a temporal classifier system (TCS). This is a modified version of LCS, where rather than going through a fixed cycle of events at each time step, the system inherently learns to generalise over slight changes in the input sensor values, so as to learn when a significant change in environmental state has occurred. Thus if for a given state a, two different actions both lead to to a next state b, but if the time taken for this to happen is different, then the action taking the least time is rewarded more. This is achieved by modifying the credit allocation so that the discount factor τ is replaced by a term exponentially decreasing according to the time taken.

The problem set for the robot is to move towards a light from any given starting position. While this may seem a simple problem, it could of course stand for any number of real-world problems. The robot is equipped with three light sensors whose outputs represent the inputs to TCS, so an interval coding is used for the condition parts of the rules. The actions are one of (0,1,2) representing the actions *move-left-continuously, move-ahead-continuously, move-right-continuously*. The robot only receives a reward when it reaches the light. The system used a maximum of 500 rules, with a crossover probability 0.5, a mutation rate of 0.05, and the GA firing every four cycles probabilistically.

Under the set of experimental conditions, where the size of the arena and the speed of the robot are known, it was calculated that a robot under the control of an optimal system would reach the light in an average of 6.5 seconds. The robot undergoing on-line learning with TCS initially spent a lot of time hitting walls, and so on, as would be expected from a random system, but eventually learned optimal behaviour. Interestingly, it evidenced three distinct stages of learning:

- First, the robot learned to reach the light quickly, once it had reached its neighbourhood by random moves, i.e., it solved the "end-game".
- In the second phase it learned to apply the *move-forward* action once it was facing the light, and did this farther and farther from the source.
- Finally, it learned to efficiently solve the problem of getting the robot facing the light source as quickly as possible from any starting position.

This work uses several interesting features and extensions to ZCS, but it also illustrates some of the ways in which LCS can solve multistep environments. Initially rules proliferate that quickly lead to rewards, since they are discounted less. Then the system learns to generalise, i.e., it discovers that the move-ahead rule is the best thing to do in much of the search space. Finally, it fine-tunes the rules early on in the reward chain.

7.8 Exercises

1. Suggest a suitable representation for using a LCS on the credit assessment example in Chap. 6.
2. Discuss the relative advantages and disadvantages of using ZCS and XCS for this problem.
3. Why do ZCS and XCS use fitness proportionate selection with a roulette wheel implementation rather than tournamenet selection?
4. How big is a typical match set in a fuzzy LCS?

7.9 Recommended Reading for this Chapter

1. P.L. Lanzi, W. Stolzmann, and S.W. Wilson, editors. *Learning Classifier Systems: From Foundations to Applications*, volume 1813 of *LNAI*. Springer-Verlag, Berlin, 2000.

2. J.H. Holland, L.B. Booker, M. Colombetti, M. Dorigo, D.E. Goldberg, S. Forrest, R.L. Riolo, R.E. Smith, P.L. Lanzi, W. Stolzmann, and S.W. Wilson. What is a learning classifier system? In Lanzi et al. [247], pages 3–32.

3. J.H. Holmes, P.L. Lanzi, W. Stolzmann, and S.W. Wilson. Learning classifier systems: new models, successful applications. *Information Processing Letters*, 82(1):23–30, 2002.

8

Parameter Control in Evolutionary Algorithms

8.1 Aims of this Chapter

The issue of setting the values of various parameters of an evolutionary algorithm is crucial for good performance. In this chapter we discuss how to do this, beginning with the issue of whether these values are best set in advance or are best changed during evolution. We provide a classification of different approaches based on a number of complementary features, and pay special attention to setting parameters on-the-fly. This has the potential of adjusting the algorithm to the problem while solving the problem.

This chapter differs from most in this book in that it presents rather more of a survey than a set of prescriptive details concerning how to implement an EA for a particular type of problem. For this reason, rather than end with one or two example applications, we have chosen to interleave a number of examples throughout the text. Thus we hope to both clarify the points we wish to raise as we present them, and also to give the reader a feel for some of the many possibilities available for controlling different parameters.

8.2 Introduction

The previous chapters presented a number of evolutionary algorithms. The description of a specific EA contains its components, thereby setting a framework while still leaving quite a few items undefined. For instance, a simple GA might be given by stating it will use binary representation, uniform crossover, bit-flip mutation, tournament selection, and generational replacement. For a full specification, however, further details have to be given, for instance, the population size, the probability of mutation p_m and crossover p_c, and the tournament size. These data – called the **algorithm parameters** or **strategy parameters** – complete the definition of the EA and are necessary to produce an executable version. The values of these parameters greatly determine whether the algorithm will find an optimal or near-optimal solution, and whether it will find such a solution efficiently. Choosing the right parameter values is, however, a hard task.

Globally, we distinguish two major forms of setting parameter values: **parameter tuning** and **parameter control**. By parameter tuning we mean the commonly practised approach that amounts to finding good values for the parameters *before* the run of the algorithm and then running the algorithm using these values, which remain fixed during the run. Later on in this section we give arguments that any static set of parameters having the values fixed during an EA run seems to be inappropriate. Parameter control forms an alternative, as it amounts to starting a run with initial parameter values that are changed *during* the run.

Parameter tuning is a typical approach to algorithm design. Such tuning is done by experimenting with different values and selecting the ones that give the best results on the test problems at hand. However, the number of possible parameters and their different values means that this is a very time-consuming activity. Considering four parameters and five values for each of them, one has to test $5^4 = 625$ different setups. Performing 100 independent runs with each setup, this implies 62,500 runs just to establish a good algorithm design.

The technical drawbacks to parameter tuning based on experimentation can be summarised as follows:

- Parameters are not independent, but trying all different combinations systematically is practically impossible.
- The process of parameter tuning is time consuming, even if parameters are optimised one by one, regardless of their interactions.
- For a given problem the selected parameter values are not necessarily optimal, even if the effort made for setting them was significant.

This picture becomes even more discouraging if one is after a "generally good" setup that would perform well on a range of problems or problem instances. During the history of EAs considerable effort has been spent on finding parameter values (for a given type of EA, such as GAs), that were good for a number of test problems. A well-known early example is that of [98], determining recommended values for the probabilities of single-point crossover and bit mutation on what is now called the DeJong test suite of five functions. About this and similar attempts [181, 334], it should be noted that genetic algorithms used to be seen as robust problem solvers that exhibit approximately the same performance over a wide range of problems [172, page 6]. The contemporary view on EAs, however, acknowledges that specific problems (problem types) require specific EA setups for satisfactory performance [26]. Thus, the scope of "optimal" parameter settings is necessarily narrow. There are also theoretical arguments that any quest for generally good EA, thus generally good parameter settings, is lost a priori, cf. the discussion of the No Free Lunch theorem [430] in Chap. 11.

To elucidate another drawback of the parameter tuning approach recall how we defined it: finding good values for the parameters before the run of the algorithm and then running the algorithm using these values, *which remain fixed during the run*. However, a run of an EA is an intrinsically dynamic, adaptive process. The use of rigid parameters that do not change their values is thus in contrast to this spirit. Additionally, it is intuitively obvious, and has been empirically and theoretically demonstrated, that different values of parameters might be optimal at different stages of the evolutionary process [16, 17, 18, 91, 194, 216, 335, 341, 349, 359, 360, 384, 391].

For instance, large mutation steps can be good in the early generations, helping the exploration of the search space, and small mutation steps might be needed in the late generations to help fine-tune the suboptimal chromosomes. This implies that the use of static parameters itself can lead to inferior algorithm performance.

A straightforward way to overcome the limitations of static parameters is by replacing a parameter p by a function $p(t)$, where t is the generation counter (or any other measure of elapsed time). However, as indicated earlier, the problem of finding optimal static parameters for a particular problem is already hard. Designing optimal dynamic parameters (that is, functions for $p(t)$) may be even more difficult. Another possible drawback to this approach is that the parameter value $p(t)$ changes are caused by a "blind" deterministic rule triggered by the progress of time t, without taking any notion of the actual progress in solving the problem, i.e., without taking into account the current state of the search. A well-known instance of this problem occurs in simulated annealing (Sect. 8.5.5) where a so-called cooling schedule has to be set before the execution of the algorithm.

Mechanisms for modifying parameters during a run in an "informed" way were realised quite early in EC history. For instance, evolution strategies changed mutation parameters on-the-fly by Rechenberg's 1/5 success rule (Sect. 4.2) using information on the ratio of successful mutations. Davis experimented within GAs with changing the crossover rate based on the progress realised by particular crossover operators [91]. The common feature of these and similar approaches is the presence of a human-designed feedback mechanism that utilises actual information about the search process for determining new parameter values.

Yet another approach is based on the observation that finding good parameter values for an evolutionary algorithm is a poorly structured, ill-defined, complex problem. This is exactly the kind of problem on which EAs are often considered to perform better than other methods. It is thus a natural idea to use an EA for tuning an EA to a particular problem. This could be done using two EAs: one for problem solving and another one – the so-called meta-EA – to tune the first one [162, 181, 220]. It could also be done by using only one EA that tunes itself to a given problem, while solving that problem. Self-adaptation, as introduced in evolution strategies for varying the mutation parameters, falls within this category. In the next section we discuss various options for changing parameters, illustrated by an example.

8.3 Examples of Changing Parameters

Let us assume we deal with a numerical optimisation problem to minimise

$$f(\overline{x}) = f(x_1, \ldots, x_n),$$

subject to some inequality and equality constraints

$$g_i(\overline{x}) \leq 0, i = 1, \ldots, q,$$

and

$$h_j(\overline{x}) = 0, j = q + 1, \ldots, m,$$

where the domains of the variables are given by lower and upper bounds $l_i \leq x_i \leq u_i$ for $1 \leq i \leq n$.

For such a numerical optimisation problem we may consider an evolutionary algorithm based on a floating-point representation, where each individual $\overline{x}$ in the population is represented as a vector of floating-point numbers $\overline{x} = \langle x_1, \ldots, x_n \rangle$.

8.3.1 Changing the Mutation Step Size

Let us assume that offspring for the next generation is produced by arithmetical crossover and Gaussian mutation, replacing components of the vector $\overline{x}$ by

$$x_i' = x_i + N(0, \sigma),$$

just like in case of evolution strategies (Chap. 4). The simplest method to specify the mutation mechanism is to use the same σ for all vectors in the population, for all variables of each vector, and for the whole evolutionary process, for instance, $x_i' = x_i + N(0, 1)$. As indicated by many studies [152, 317, 341], it might be beneficial to vary the mutation step size. We shall discuss several possibilities in turn.

First, we can replace the static parameter σ by a dynamic parameter, i.e., a function $\sigma(t)$. This function can be defined by some heuristic rule assigning different values depending on the number of generations. For example, the mutation step size may be defined as:

$$\sigma(t) = 1 - 0.9 \cdot \frac{t}{T},$$

where t is the current generation number varying from 0 to T, which is the maximum generation number. Here, the mutation step size $\sigma(t)$, which used for all for vectors in the population and for all variables of each vector, decreases slowly from 1 at the beginning of the run ($t = 0$) to 0.1 as the number of generations t approaches T. Such decreases may assist the fine-tuning capabilities of the algorithm. In this approach, the value of the given parameter changes according to a fully deterministic scheme. The user thus has full control of the parameter, and its value at a given time t is completely determined and predictable.

Second, it is possible to incorporate feedback from the search process, still using the same σ for all vectors in the population and for all variables of each vector. A well-known example of this type of parameter adaptation is Rechenberg's 1/5 success rule (Sect. 4.2), which states that the ratio of successful mutations to all mutations should be 1/5. Hence if the ratio is greater than 1/5 the step size should be increased, and if the ratio is less than 1/5 then it should be decreased. The rule is executed at periodic intervals, for instance, after k iterations each σ is reset by

$$\sigma' = \begin{cases} \sigma/c & \text{if} \quad p_s > 1/5, \\ \sigma \cdot c & \text{if} \quad p_s < 1/5, \\ \sigma & \text{if} \quad p_s = 1/5, \end{cases}$$

where p_s is the relative frequency of successful mutations, measured over a number of trials, and the parameter c should be $0.817 \leq c \leq 1$ [340].

Using this mechanism, changes in the parameter values are now based on feedback from the search. The influence of the user on the parameter values is much less direct here than in the deterministic scheme above. Of course, the mechanism that embodies the link between the search process and parameter values is still a heuristic rule indicating how the changes should be made, but the values of $\sigma(t)$ are not deterministic (although they do come from a fixed set).

Third, it is possible to assign an individual mutation step size to each solution, that is, extend the representation to individuals of length $n + 1$ as

$$\langle x_1, \ldots, x_n, \sigma \rangle,$$

and apply some variation operators (e.g., Gaussian mutation and arithmetical crossover) to the values of x_i as well as to the σ value of an individual. In this way, not only the solution vector values (x_i) but also the mutation step size of an individual undergoes evolution. A possible solution introduced for evolution strategies in Sect. 4.4 in Eq. (4.2) is:

$$\sigma' = \sigma \cdot e^{\tau \cdot N(0,1)}, \tag{8.1}$$

$$x_i' = x_i + \sigma' \cdot N_i(0,1). \tag{8.2}$$

Observe that within this self-adaptive scheme the heuristic character of the mechanism resetting the parameter values is eliminated, and a certain value of σ acts on all values of a single individual.

If we change the granularity of the mutation step-size parameter and use a separate σ_i to each x_i, then we obtain an extended representation as

$$\langle x_1, \ldots, x_n, \sigma_1, \ldots, \sigma_n \rangle.$$

Then mutations can be performed by

$$\sigma_i' = \sigma_i \cdot e^{\tau \cdot N_i(0,1)},$$
$$x_i' = x_i + \sigma_i' \cdot N_i(0,1).$$

This is a straightforward extension of Eqs. (8.1) and (8.2), and indeed, very similar to Eq. (4.4) from Sect. 4.4.

8.3.2 Changing the Penalty Coefficients

In the previous section we described different ways to modify a parameter controlling mutation. Several other components of an EA have natural parameters, and these parameters are traditionally tuned in one or another way. Here we show that other components, such as the evaluation function (and consequently the fitness function) can also be parameterised and thus varied. While this is a less common option than tuning mutation (although it is practised in the evolution of variable-length structures for parsimony pressure [438]), it may provide a useful mechanism for increasing the performance of an evolutionary algorithm.

When dealing with constrained optimisation problems, penalty functions are often used (see Chap. 12 for more details). A common technique is the method of static penalties [277], which requires fixed user-supplied penalty parameters. The main reason for its widespread use is that it is the simplest technique to implement: it requires only the straightforward modification of the evaluation function as follows:

$$eval(\overline{x}) = f(\overline{x}) + W \cdot penalty(\overline{x}),$$

where f is the objective function, and $penalty(\overline{x})$ is zero if no violation occurs, and is positive,[1] otherwise. Usually, the $penalty$ function is based on the distance of a solution from the feasible region, or on the effort to "repair" the solution, i.e., to force it into the feasible region. In many methods a set of functions f_j ($1 \leq j \leq m$) is used to construct the penalty, where the function f_j measures the violation of the jth constraint in the following way:

$$f_j(\overline{x}) = \begin{cases} \max\{0, g_j(\overline{x})\} & \text{if} \quad 1 \leq j \leq q, \\ |h_j(\overline{x})| & \text{if} \quad q+1 \leq j \leq m. \end{cases} \tag{8.3}$$

W is a user-defined weight, prescribing how severely constraint violations are weighted. In the most traditional penalty approach the weight W does not change during the evolution process. We sketch three possible methods of changing the value of W.

First, we can replace the static parameter W by a dynamic parameter, e.g., a function $W(t)$. Just as for the mutation parameter σ, we can develop a

---

[1] For minimisation problems.

heuristic that modifies the weight W over time. For example, in the method proposed by Joines and Houck [217], the individuals are evaluated (at the iteration t) by a formula, where

$$eval(\overline{x}) = f(\overline{x}) + (C \cdot t)^{\alpha} \cdot penalty(\overline{x}),$$

where C and α are constants. Since

$$W(t) = (C \cdot t)^{\alpha},$$

the penalty pressure grows with the evolution time provided $1 \leq C, \alpha$.

Second, let us consider another option, which utilises feedback from the search process. One example of such an approach was developed by Bean and Hadj-Alouane [42], where each individual is evaluated by the same formula as before, but $W(t)$ is updated in every generation t in the following way:

$$W(t+1) = \begin{cases} (1/\beta_1) \cdot W(t) & \text{if } \overline{b}^i \in \mathcal{F} \quad \text{for all } t - k + 1 \leq i \leq t, \\ \beta_2 \cdot W(t) & \text{if } \overline{b}^i \in \mathcal{S} - \mathcal{F} \text{ for all } t - k + 1 \leq i \leq t, \\ W(t) & \text{otherwise.} \end{cases}$$

In this formula, $\mathcal{S}$ is the set of all search points (solutions), $\mathcal{F} \subseteq \mathcal{S}$ is a set of all *feasible* solutions, $\overline{b}^i$ denotes the best individual in terms of the function $eval$ in generation i, $\beta_1, \beta_2 > 1$, and $\beta_1 \neq \beta_2$ (to avoid cycling). In other words, the method decreases the penalty component $W(t+1)$ for the generation $t+1$ if all best individuals in the last k generations were feasible (i.e., in $\mathcal{F}$), and increases penalties if all best individuals in the last k generations were infeasible. If there are some feasible and infeasible individuals as best individuals in the last k generations, $W(t+1)$ remains without change.

Third, we could allow self-adaptation of the weight parameter, similarly to the mutation step sizes in the previous section. For example, it is possible to extend the representation of individuals into

$$\langle x_1, \ldots, x_n, W \rangle,$$

where W is the weight. The weight component W undergoes the same changes as any other variable x_i (e.g., Gaussian mutation and arithmetic recombination).

To illustrate this method, which is analogous to using a separate σ_i for each x_i, we need to redefine the evaluation function. Let us first introduce penalty functions for each constraint as per Eq. (8.3). Clearly, these penalties are all non-negative and are at zero if no constraints are violated. Then consider a vector of weights $\overline{w} = (w_1, \ldots, w_m)$, and define

$$eval(\overline{x}) = f(\overline{x}) + \sum_{j=1}^{m} w_j f_j(\overline{x}),$$

as the function to be minimised and also extend the representation of individuals into

$$\langle x_1, \ldots, x_n, w_1, \ldots, w_m \rangle.$$

Variation operators can then be applied to both the $\overline{x}$ and the $\overline{w}$ part of these chromosomes, realising a self-adaptation of the constraint weights, and thereby the fitness function.

It is important to note the crucial difference between self-adapting mutation step sizes and constraint weights. Even if the mutation step sizes are encoded in the chromosomes, the evaluation of a chromosome is *independent* from the actual σ values. That is,

$$eval(\langle \overline{x}, \overline{\sigma} \rangle) = f(\overline{x}),$$

for any chromosome $\langle \overline{x}, \overline{\sigma} \rangle$. In contrast, if constraint weights are encoded in the chromosomes, then we have

$$eval(\langle \overline{x}, \overline{w} \rangle) = f_{\overline{w}}(\overline{x}),$$

for any chromosome $\langle \overline{x}, W \rangle$. This could enable the evolution to "cheat" in the sense of making improvements by minimising the weights instead of optimising f and satisfying the constraints. Eiben et al. investigated this issue in [118] and found that using a specific tournament selection mechanism neatly solves this problem and enables the EA to solve constraints.

8.3.3 Summary

In the previous sections we illustrated how the mutation operator and the evaluation function can be controlled (adapted) during the evolutionary process. The latter case demonstrates that not only can the traditionally adjusted components, such as mutation, recombination, selection, etc., be controlled by parameters, but so can other components of an evolutionary algorithm. Obviously, there are many components and parameters that can be changed and tuned for optimal algorithm performance. In general, the three options we sketched for the mutation operator and the evaluation function are valid for any parameter of an evolutionary algorithm, whether it is population size, mutation step, the penalty coefficient, selection pressure, and so forth.

The mutation example of Sect. 8.3.1 also illustrates the phenomenon of the **scope** of a parameter. Namely, the mutation step size parameter can have different domains of influence, which we call scope. Using the $\langle x_1, \ldots, x_n, \sigma_1, \ldots, \sigma_n \rangle$ model, a particular mutation step size applies only to one variable of a single individual. Thus, the parameter σ_i acts on a subindividual, or component, level. In the $\langle x_1, \ldots, x_n, \sigma \rangle$ representation, the scope of σ is one individual, whereas the dynamic parameter $\sigma(t)$ was defined to affect all individuals and thus has the whole population as its scope.

These remarks conclude the introductory examples of this section. We are now ready to attempt a classification of parameter control techniques for parameters of an evolutionary algorithm.

8.4 Classification of Control Techniques

In classifying parameter control techniques of an evolutionary algorithm, many aspects can be taken into account. For example:

1. *What* is changed? (e.g., representation, evaluation function, operators, selection process, mutation rate, population size, and so on)
2. *How* the change is made (i.e., deterministic heuristic, feedback-based heuristic, or self-adaptive)
3. *The evidence* upon which the change is carried out (e.g., monitoring performance of operators, diversity of the population, and so on)
4. *The scope/level* of change (e.g., population-level, individual-level, and so forth).

In the following we discuss these items in more detail.

8.4.1 *What* is Changed?

To classify parameter control techniques from the perspective of what component or parameter is changed, it is necessary to agree on a list of all major components of an evolutionary algorithm, which is a difficult task in itself. For that purpose, let us assume the following components of an EA:

- Representation of individuals
- Evaluation function
- Variation operators and their probabilities
- Selection operator (parent selection or mating selection)
- Replacement operator (survival selection or environmental selection)
- Population (size, topology, etc.)

Note that each component can be parameterised, and that the number of parameters is not clearly defined. For example, an offspring $\overline{v}$ produced by an arithmetical crossover of k parents $\overline{x}_1, \ldots, \overline{x}_k$ can be defined by the following formula:

$$\overline{v} = a_1 \overline{x}_1 + \ldots + a_k \overline{x}_k,$$

where $a_1, \ldots, a_k$, and k can be considered as parameters of this crossover. Parameters for a population can include the number and sizes of subpopulations, migration rates, and so on for a general case, when more then one population is involved. Despite the somewhat arbitrary character of this list of components and of the list of parameters of each component, we will maintain the "what-aspect" as one of the main classification features, since this allows us to locate where a specific mechanism has its effect.

8.4.2 *How* are Changes Made?

As discussed and illustrated in Sect. 8.3, methods for changing the value of a parameter (i.e., the "how-aspect") can be classified into one of three categories.

- **Deterministic parameter control**
  This takes place when the value of a strategy parameter is altered by some deterministic rule. This rule modifies the strategy parameter in a fixed, predetermined (i.e., user-specified) way without using any feedback from the search. Usually, a time-varying schedule is used, i.e., the rule is used when a set number of generations have elapsed since the last time the rule was activated.

- **Adaptive parameter control**
  This takes place when there is some form of feedback from the search that serves as inputs to a mechanism used to determine the direction or magnitude of the change to the strategy parameter. The assignment of the value of the strategy parameter may involve credit assignment, based on the quality of solutions discovered by different operators/parameters, so that the updating mechanism can distinguish between the merits of competing strategies. Although the subsequent action of the EA may determine whether or not the new value persists or propagates throughout the population, the important point to note is that the updating mechanism used to control parameter values is externally supplied, rather than being part of the "standard" evolutionary cycle.

- **Self-adaptive parameter control**
  The idea of the evolution of evolution can be used to implement the self-adaptation of parameters (see [24] for a good review). Here the parameters to be adapted are encoded into the chromosomes and undergo mutation and recombination. The better values of these encoded parameters lead to better individuals, which in turn are more likely to survive and produce offspring and hence propagate these better parameter values. This is an important distinction between adaptive and self-adaptive schemes: in the latter the mechanisms for the credit assignment and updating of different strategy parameters are entirely implicit, i.e., they are the selection and variation operators of the evolutionary cycle itself.

This terminology leads to the taxonomy illustrated in Fig. 8.1.

Some authors have introduced a different terminology. Angeline [9] distinguished "absolute" and "empirical" rules, which correspond to the "uncoupled" and "tightly-coupled" mechanisms of Spears [376]. Let us note that the uncoupled/absolute category encompasses deterministic and adaptive control, whereas the tightly-coupled/empirical category corresponds to self-adaptation. We feel that the distinction between deterministic and adaptive parameter control is essential, as the first one does not use any feedback from the search process. However, we acknowledge that the terminology

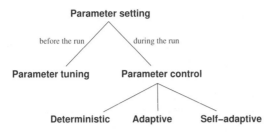

Fig. 8.1. Global taxonomy of parameter setting in EAs

proposed here is not perfect either. The term "deterministic" control might not be the most appropriate, as it is not determinism that matters, but the fact that the parameter-altering transformations take no input variables related to the progress of the search process. For example, one might *randomly* change the mutation probability after every 100 generations, which is not a deterministic process. The name "fixed" parameter control might provide an alternative that also covers this latter example. Also, the terms "adaptive" and "self-adaptive" could be replaced by the equally meaningful "explicitly adaptive" and "implicitly adaptive" controls, respectively. We have chosen to use "adaptive" and "self-adaptive" for the widely accepted usage of the latter term.

8.4.3 What *Evidence* Informs the Change?

The third criterion for classification concerns the evidence used for determining the change of parameter value [348, 361]. Most commonly, the progress of the search is monitored, e.g., by looking at the performance of operators, the diversity of the population, and so on. The information gathered by such a monitoring process is used as feedback for adjusting the parameters. From this perspective, we can make further distinction between the following two cases:

- **Absolute evidence**
  We speak of absolute evidence when the value of a strategy parameter is altered by some rule that is applied when a predefined event occurs. The difference from deterministic parameter control lies in the fact that in deterministic parameter control a rule fires by a deterministic trigger (e.g., time elapsed), whereas here feedback from the search is used. For instance, the rule can be applied when the measure being monitored hits a previously set threshold – this is the event that forms the evidence. Examples of this type of parameter adjustment include increasing the mutation rate when the population diversity drops under a given value [250], changing the probability of applying mutation or crossover according to a fuzzy rule

set using a variety of population statistics [248], and methods for resizing populations based on estimates of schemata fitness and variance [370]. Such mechanisms require that the user has a clear intuition about how to steer the given parameter into a certain direction in cases that can be specified in advance (e.g., they determine the threshold values for triggering rule activation). This intuition may be based on the encapsulation of practical experience, data-mining and empirical analysis of previous runs, or theoretical considerations (in the order of the three examples above), but all rely on the implicit assumption that changes that were appropriate to make on *another* search of *another* problem are applicable to *this* run of the EA on *this* problem.

- **Relative evidence**
  In the case of using relative evidence, parameter values are compared according to the fitness of the offspring that they produce, and the better values get rewarded. The direction and/or magnitude of the change of the strategy parameter is not specified deterministically, but relative to the performance of other values, i.e., it is necessary to have more than one value present at any given time. Here, the assignment of the value of the strategy parameter involves credit assignment, and the action of the EA may determine whether or not the new value persists or propagates throughout the population. As an example, consider an EA using more crossovers with crossover rates adding up to 1.0 and being reset based on the crossovers performance measured by the quality of offspring they create. Such methods may be controlled adaptively, typically using "bookkeeping" to monitor performance and a user-supplied update procedure [91, 219, 336], or self-adaptively [17, 145, 240, 340, 357, 376] with the selection operator acting indirectly on operator or parameter frequencies via their association with "fit" solutions.

8.4.4 What is the *Scope* of the Change?

As discussed earlier, any change within any component of an EA may affect a gene (parameter), whole chromosomes (individuals), the entire population, another component (e.g., selection), or even the evaluation function. This is the aspect of the scope or level of adaptation [9, 197, 361]. Note, however, that the scope or level is not an independent dimension, as it usually depends on the component of the EA where the change takes place. For example, a change of the mutation step size may affect a gene, a chromosome, or the entire population, depending on the particular implementation (i.e., scheme used), but a change in the penalty coefficients typically affects the whole population. In this respect the scope feature is a secondary one, usually depending on the given component and its actual implementation.

It should be noted that the issue of the scope of the parameter might be more complicated than indicated in Sect. 8.3.3. First of all, the scope depends on the interpretation mechanism of the given parameters. For example, an individual might be represented as

$$\langle x_1, \ldots, x_n, \sigma_1, \ldots, \sigma_n, \alpha_1, \ldots, \alpha_{n(n-1)/2} \rangle,$$

where the vector $\overline{\alpha}$ denotes the covariances between the variables $\sigma_1, \ldots, \sigma_n$. In this case the scope of the strategy parameters in $\overline{\alpha}$ is the whole individual, although the notation might suggest that they act on a subindividual level.

The next example illustrates that the same parameter (encoded in the chromosomes) can be interpreted in different ways, leading to different algorithm variants with different scopes of this parameter. Spears [376], following [149], experimented with individuals containing an extra bit to determine whether one-point crossover or uniform crossover is to be used (bit 1/0 standing for one-point/uniform crossover, respectively). Two interpretations were considered. The first interpretation was based on a pairwise operator choice: If both parental bits are the same, the corresponding operator is used; otherwise, a random choice is made. Thus, this parameter in this interpretation acts at an individual level. The second interpretation was based on the bit distribution over the whole population: If, for example, 73% of the population had bit 1, then the probability of one-point crossover was 0.73. Thus this parameter under this interpretation acts on the population level. Spears noted that there was a definite impact on performance, with better results arising from the individual level scheme, and more recently Smith [353] compared three versions of a self-adaptive recombination operator, concluding that the component-level version significantly outperformed the individual or population-level versions.

However, the two interpretations of Spears' scheme can be easily combined. For instance, similar to the first interpretation, if both parental bits are the same, the corresponding operator is used, but if they differ, the operator is selected according to the bit distribution, just as in the second interpretation. The scope/level of this parameter in this interpretation is neither individual nor population, but rather both. This example shows that the notion of scope can be ill-defined and very complex. This, combined with the arguments that the scope or level entity is primarily a feature of the given parameter and only secondarily a feature of adaptation itself, motivates our decision to exclude it as a major classification criterion.

8.4.5 Summary

In conclusion, the main criteria for classifying methods that change the values of the strategy parameters of an algorithm during its execution are:

1. What component/parameter is changed?
2. How is the change made?
3. Which evidence is used to make the change?

Our classification is thus three-dimensional. The *component* dimension consists of six categories: representation, evaluation function, variation operators (mutation and recombination), selection, replacement, and population.

The other dimensions have respectively three (deterministic, adaptive, self-adaptive) and two categories (absolute, relative). Their possible combinations are given in Table 8.1. As the table indicates, deterministic parameter control with relative evidence is impossible by definition, and so is self-adaptive parameter control with absolute evidence. Within the adaptive scheme both options are possible and are indeed used in practice.

	Deterministic	Adaptive	Self-adaptive
Absolute	+	+	–
Relative	–	+	+

Table 8.1. Refined taxonomy of parameter setting in EAs: types of parameter control along the type and evidence dimensions. The – entries represent meaningless (nonexistent) combinations

8.5 Examples of Varying EA Parameters

Here we review some illustrative examples from the literature concerning all major components. For a more comprehensive overview the reader is referred to [117].

8.5.1 Representation

The choice of representation forms an important distinguishing feature between different streams of evolutionary computing. From this perspective GAs and ES can be distinguished from (historical) EP and GP according to the data structure used to represent individuals. In the first group this data structure is linear, and its length is fixed, that is, it does not change during a run of the algorithm. For (historical) EP and GP this does not hold: finite state machines and parse trees are nonlinear structures, and their size (the number of states, respectively nodes) and shape can change during a run. It could be argued that this implies an intrinsically adaptive representation in traditional EP and GP. On the other hand, the main structure of the finite state machines does not change during the search in traditional EP, nor do the function and terminal sets in GP (without automatically defined functions, ADFs). If one identifies "representation" with the basic syntax (plus the encoding mechanism), then the differently sized and shaped finite state machines, respectively trees, are only different expressions in this unchanging syntax. Based on this view we do not consider the representations in traditional EP and GP intrinsically adaptive.

We illustrate variable representations with the delta coding algorithm of Mathias and Whitley [424], which effectively modifies the encoding of the

function parameters. The motivation behind this algorithm is to maintain a
good balance between fast search and sustaining diversity. In our taxonomy
it can be categorised as an adaptive adjustment of the representation based
on absolute evidence.

The GA is used with multiple restarts; the first run is used to find an *interim
solution*, and subsequent runs decode the genes as distances (*delta values*)
from the last interim solution. This way each restart forms a new hypercube
with the interim solution at its origin. The resolution of the delta values can
also be altered at the restarts to expand or contract the search space. The
restarts are triggered when population diversity (measured by the Hamming
distance between the best and worst strings of the current population) is not
greater than one. The sketch of the algorithm showing the main idea is given
in Fig. 8.2.

```
BEGIN
   /* given a starting population and genotype-phenotype encoding */
   WHILE (  HD > 1 ) DO
      RUN_GA with k bits per object variable;
   OD
   REPEAT UNTIL (  global termination is satisfied ) DO
      save best solution as INTERIM;
      reinitialise population with new coding;
      /*  k-1 bits as the distance δ to the object value in  */
      /*  INTERIM and one sign bit */
      WHILE (  HD > 1 ) DO
         RUN_GA with this encoding;
      OD
   OD
END
```

Fig. 8.2. Outline of the delta coding algorithm

Note that the number of bits for δ can be increased if the same solution
INTERIM is found. This technique was further refined in [262, 263] to cope
with deceptive problems.

8.5.2 Evaluation function

Evaluation functions are typically not varied in an EA because they are often considered as part of the problem to be solved and not as part of the
problem-solving algorithm. In fact, an evaluation function forms the bridge
between the two, so both views are at least partially true. In many EAs the
evaluation function is derived from the (optimisation) problem at hand with

a simple transformation of the objective function. In the class of constraint satisfaction problems, however, there is no objective function in the problem definition [112]. Rather, these are normally posed as decision problems with an Boolean outcome ϕ denoting whether a given assignment of variables represents a valid solution (Chap. 12). One possible approach using EAs is to treat these as minimisation problems where the evaluation function is defined as the amount of constraint violation by a given candidate solution. This approach, commonly known as the penalty approach, can be formalised as follows. Let us assume that we have constraints c_i $(i = \{1, \ldots, m\})$ and variables v_j $(j = \{1, \ldots, n\})$ with the same domain S. The task is to find one variable assignment $\bar{s} \in S$ satisfying all constraints. Then the penalties can be defined as follows:

$$f(\bar{s}) = \sum_{i=1}^{m} w_i \times \chi(\bar{s}, c_i),$$

where

$$\chi(\bar{s}, c_i) = \begin{cases} 1 \text{ if } \bar{s} \text{ violates } c_i, \\ 0 \text{ otherwise.} \end{cases}$$

Obviously, for each $\bar{s} \in S$ we have that $\phi(\bar{s}) = true$ if and only if $f(\bar{s}) = 0$, and the weights specify how severely the violation of a certain constraint is penalised. The setting of these weights has a large impact on the EA performance, and ideally w_i should reflect how hard c_i is to satisfy. The problem is that finding the appropriate weights requires much insight into the given problem instance, and therefore it might not be practicable.

The stepwise adaptation of weights (SAW) mechanism, introduced by Eiben and van der Hauw [130] as an improved version of the weight adaptation mechanism of Eiben, Raué, and Ruttkay [123, 125], provides a simple and effective way to set these weights. The basic idea behind the SAW mechanism is that constraints that are not satisfied after a certain number of steps (fitness evaluations) must be difficult, and thus must be given a high weight (penalty). SAW-ing changes the evaluation function adaptively in an EA by periodically checking the best individual in the population and raising the weights of those constraints this individual violates. Then the run continues with the new evaluation function. A nice feature of SAW-ing is that it liberates the user from seeking good weight settings, thereby eliminating a possible source of error. Furthermore, the used weights reflect the difficulty of constraints for *the given algorithm* on the *given problem instance* in *the given stage of the search* [132]. This property is also valuable since, in principle, different weights could be appropriate for different algorithms.

8.5.3 Mutation

A large majority of work on adapting or self-adapting EA parameters concerns variation operators: mutation and recombination (crossover). As we discussed in Chap. 4, the 1/5 rule of Rechenberg constitutes a classical example for adaptive mutation step size control in ES. In the same chapter we also showed that self-adaptive control of mutation step sizes is traditional in ES.

Hesser and Männer [194] derived theoretically optimal schedules within GAs for deterministically changing p_m for the counting-ones function. They suggest:

$$p_m(t) = \sqrt{\frac{\alpha}{\beta}} \times \frac{\exp\left(\frac{-\gamma t}{2}\right)}{\lambda\sqrt{L}},$$

where α, β, γ are constants, L is the chromosome length, λ is the population size, and t is the time (generation counter). This is a purely deterministic parameter control mechanism.

A self-adaptive mechanism for controlling mutation in a bit-string GA is given by Bäck [16]. This technique works by extending the chromosomes by an additional 20 bits that together encode the individuals' own p_m. Mutation then works by:

1. Decoding these bits first to p_m
2. Mutating the bits that encode p_m with mutation probability p_m
3. Decoding these (changed) bits to p'_m
4. Mutating the bits that encode the solution with mutation probability p'_m

This approach is highly self-adaptive since even the rate of variation of the search parameters is given by the encoded value, as opposed to the use of an external parameter like τ in Eqs. (4.2) and (4.4), and α in Eq. (5.1). More recently Smith [354] showed theoretical predictions, verified experimentally, that this scheme gets "stuck" in suboptimal regions of the search space with a low, or zero, mutation rate attached to each member of the population. He showed that a more robust problem-solving mechanism can simply be achieved by ignoring the first step of the algorithm above, and instead using a fixed learning rate as the probability of applying bitwise mutation to the encoding of the strategy parameters in the second step.

8.5.4 Crossover

The classical example for adapting crossover rates in GAs is Davis's adaptive operator fitness. The method adapts the rates of crossover operators by rewarding those that are successful in creating better offspring. This reward is diminishingly propagated back to operators of a few generations back, who helped setting it all up; the reward is a shift up in probability at the cost of other operators [92]. This, actually, is very close in spirit to the "implicit bucket brigade" credit assignment principle used in classifier systems [172].

The GA using this method applies several crossover operators simultaneously within the same generation, each having its own crossover rate $p_c(op_i)$. Additionally, each operator has its "local delta" value d_i that represents the strength of the operator measured by the advantage of a child created by using that operator with respect to the best individual in the population. The local deltas are updated after every use of operator i. The adaptation mechanism recalculates the crossover rates after K generations. The main idea is to redistribute 15% of the probabilities biased by the accumulated operator strengths, that is, the local deltas. To this end, these d_i values are normalised so that their sum equals 15, yielding d_i^{norm} for each i. Then the new value for each $p_c(op_i)$ is 85% of its old value and its normalised strength:

$$p_c(op_i) = 0.85 \cdot p_c(op_i) + d_i^{norm}.$$

Clearly, this method is adaptive based on relative evidence.

8.5.5 Selection

It is interesting to note that neither the parent selection nor the survivor selection (replacement) component of an EA has been commonly used in an adaptive manner, even though there are selection methods whose parameters can be easily adapted. For example, in linear ranking (Sect. 3.7.2) the parameter s represents the expected number of offspring to be allocated to the best individual. By changing this parameter within the range of $[1 \ldots 2]$ the selective pressure of the algorithm can be varied easily. Similar possibilities exist for tournament selection, where the tournament size provides a natural parameter.

Most existing mechanisms for varying the selection pressure are based on the so-called **Boltzmann** selection mechanism, which changes the selection pressure during evolution according to a predefined "cooling schedule" [257]. The name originates from the Boltzmann trial from condensed matter physics, where a minimal energy level is sought by state transitions. Being in a state i the chance of accepting state j is

$$P[\text{accept } j] = \begin{cases} 1 & \text{if } E_i \geq E_j, \\ \exp\left(\frac{E_i - E_j}{K_b \cdot T}\right) & \text{if } E_i < E_j, \end{cases}$$

where E_i, E_j are the energy levels, K_b is a parameter called the Boltzmann constant, and T is the temperature. This acceptance rule is called the Metropolis criterion.

We illustrate variable selection pressure in the survivor selection (replacement) step by **simulated annealing** (SA). SA is a generate-and-test search technique based on a physical, rather than a biological analogy [2]. Formally, however, SA can be envisioned as an evolutionary process with population size of 1, undefined (problem-dependent) representation and mutation, and a specific survivor selection mechanism. The selective pressure changes during the course of the algorithm in the Boltzmann style. The main cycle in SA is given in Fig. 8.3.

In this mechanism the parameter c_k, the temperature, decreases according to a predefined scheme as a function of time, making the probability of

```
BEGIN
   /* given a current solution i ∈ S */
   /* given a function to generate the set of neighbours Nᵢ of i */
   generate j ∈ Nᵢ;
   IF (f(i) < f(j)) THEN
      set i = j;
   ELSE
        IF ( exp ( f(i)-f(j) / cₖ ) > random[0, 1)) THEN
           set i = j;
        FI
   ESLE
   FI
END
```

Fig. 8.3. Outline of the simulated annealing algorithm

accepting inferior solutions smaller and smaller (for minimisation problems). From an evolutionary point of view, we have here a (1+1) EA with increasing selection pressure.

A successful example of applying Boltzmann acceptance is that of Smith and Krasnogor [239], who used it in the local search part of a memetic algorithm (MA) (Chap. 10), with the temperature inversely related to the fitness diversity of the population. If the population contains a wide spread of fitness values, the "temperature" is low, so only fitter solutions found by local search are likely to be accepted, concentrating the search on good solutions. However, when the spread of fitness values is low, indicating a converged population which is a common problem in MAs, the "temperature" is higher, making it more likely that an inferior solution will be accepted, thus reintroducing diversity and offering a potential means of escaping from local optima.

8.5.6 Population

An innovative way to control the population size is offered by Arabas et al. [13, 271] in their GA with variable population size (GAVaPS). In fact, the population size parameter is removed entirely from GAVaPS, rather than adjusted on-the-fly. Certainly, in an evolutionary algorithm the population always has a size, but in GAVaPS this size is a derived measure, not a controllable parameter. The main idea is to assign a lifetime to each individual when it is created, and then to reduce its remaining lifetime by one in each consecutive generation. When the remaining lifetime becomes zero, the individual is removed from the population. Two things must be noted here. First, the lifetime allocated to a newborn individual is biased by its fitness: fitter individuals are allowed to live longer. Second, the expected number of offspring of an individual is proportional to the number of generations it survives. Consequently, the resulting system favours the propagation of good genes.

Fitting this algorithm into our general classification scheme is not straightforward because it has no explicit mechanism that sets the value of the population size parameter. However, the procedure that implicitly determines how many individuals are alive works in an adaptive fashion using information about the status of the search. In particular, the fitness of a newborn individual is related to the fitness of the present generation, and its lifetime is allocated accordingly. This amounts to using relative evidence.

8.5.7 Varying Several Parameters Simultaneously

One of the studies explicitly devoted to adjusting more parameters (and also on more than one level) is that of Hinterding et al. on a "self-adaptive GA" [198]. This GA uses self-adaptation for mutation rate control, plus relative-based adaptive control for the population size.[2] The mechanism for controlling mutation is similar to that from Bäck [16], (Sect. 8.5.3), except that mutating the bits encoding the mutation strength is not based on the bits in question, but is done by a universal mechanism fixed for all individuals and all generations. In other words, the self-adaptive mutation parameter is only used for the genes encoding a solution. As for the population size, the GA works with three subpopulations: a small, a medium, and a large one, P1, P2, and P3, respectively (the initial sizes respectively being 50, 100, and 200). These populations are evolved in parallel for a given number of fitness evaluations (an epoch) independently by the same GA setup. After each epoch, the subpopulations are resized based on some heuristic rules, maintaining a lower and an upper bound (10 and 1000) and keeping P2 always the medium-sized subpopulation. There are two categories of rules. Rules in the first category are activated when the fitnesses in the subpopulations converge and try to move the populations apart. For instance, if P2 and P3 have the same fitness, the size of P3 is doubled. Rules from another set are activated when the fitness values are distinct at the end of an epoch. These rules aim at maximising the performance of P2. An example of one such rule is: if the performance of the subpopulations ranks them as P2 < P3 < P1 then size(P3) = (size(P2) + size(P3))/2. In our taxonomy, this population size control mechanism is adaptive, based on relative evidence.

Lis and Lis [251] also offer a parallel GA setup to control the mutation rate, the crossover rate, and the population size during a run. The idea here is that for each parameter a few possible values are defined in advance, say *lo, med, hi*, and only these values are allowed in any of the GAs, that is, in

---

[2] Strictly speaking, the authors' term "self-adaptive GA" is only partially correct. However, this paper is from 1996, and the contemporary terminology distinguishing dynamic, adaptive, and self-adaptive schemes as we do it here was only published in 1999 [117].

the subpopulations evolved in parallel. After each epoch the performances of the applied parameter values are compared by averaging the fitnesses of the best individuals of those GAs that use a given value. If the winning parameter value is:

1. *hi*, then all GAs shift one level up concerning this parameter in the next epoch;
2. *med*, then all GAs use the same value concerning this parameter in the next epoch;
3. *lo*, then all GAs shift one level down concerning this parameter in the next epoch.

Clearly, the adjustment mechanism for all parameters here is adaptive, based on relative evidence.

Mutation, crossover, and population size are all controlled on-the-fly in the GA "without parameters" of Bäck et al. in [25]. Here, the self-adaptive mutation from [16] (Sect. 8.5.3) is adopted without changes, a new self-adaptive technique is invented for regulating the crossover rates of the individuals, and the GAVaPS lifetime idea (Sect. 8.5.6) is adjusted for a steady-state GA model. The crossover rates are included in the chromosomes, much like the mutation rates. If a pair of individuals is selected for reproduction, then their individual crossover rates are compared with a random number $r \in [0, 1]$ and an individual is seen as ready to mate if its $p_c > r$. Then there are three possibilities:

1. If both individuals are ready to mate then uniform crossover is applied, and the resulting offspring is mutated.
2. If neither is ready to mate then both create a child by mutation only.
3. If exactly one of them is ready to mate, then the one not ready creates a child by mutation only (which is inserted into the population immediately through the steady-state replacement), the other is put on the hold, and the next parent selection round picks only one other parent.

This study differs from those discussed before in that it explicitly compares GA variants using only one of the (self-)adaptive mechanisms and the GA applying them all. The experiments show remarkable outcomes: the completely (self-)adaptive GA wins, closely followed by the one using only the adaptive population size control, and the GAs with self-adaptive mutation and crossover are significantly worse. These results suggest that putting effort into adapting the population size could be more effective than trying to adjust the variation operators. This is truly surprising considering that traditionally the on-line adjustment of the variation operators has been pursued and the adjustment of the population size received relatively little attention. The subject certainly requires more research.

8.6 Discussion

Summarising this chapter a number of things can be noted. First, parameter control in an EA can have two purposes. It can be done to avoid suboptimal algorithm performance resulting from suboptimal parameter values set by the user. The basic assumption here is that the applied control mechanisms are intelligent enough to do this job better than the user could, or that they can do it approximately as good, but they liberate the user from doing it. Either way, they are beneficial. The other motivation for controlling parameters on-the-fly is the assumption that the given parameter can have a different "optimal" value in different phases of the search. If this holds, then there is simply no optimal static parameter value; for good EA performance one must vary this parameter.

The second thing we want to note is that making a parameter (self-)adaptive does not necessarily mean that we have an EA with fewer parameters. For instance, in GAVaPS the population size parameter is eliminated at the cost of introducing two new ones: the minimum and maximum lifetime of newborn individuals. If the EA performance is sensitive to these new parameters then such a parameter replacement can make things worse. This problem also occurs on another level. One could say that the procedure that allocates lifetimes in GAVaPS, the probability redistribution mechanism for adaptive crossover rates (Sect. 8.5.4), or the function specifying how the σ values are mutated in ES (Eq. (8.3)) are also (meta) parameters. It is in fact an assumption that these are intelligently designed and their effect is positive. In many cases there are more possibilities, that is, possibly well-working procedures one can design. Comparing these possibilities implies experimental (or theoretical) studies very much like comparing different parameter values in a classical setting. Here again, it can be the case that algorithm performance is not so sensitive to details of this (meta) parameter, which fully justifies this approach.

Finally, let us place the issue of parameter control in a larger perspective. Over the last 20 years the EC community shifted from believing that EA performance is to a large extent independent from the given problem instance to realising that it is. In other words, it is now acknowledged that EAs need more or less fine-tuning to specific problems and problem instances. Ideally, it should be the algorithm that performs the necessary problem-specific adjustments. Parameter control as discussed here is a step towards this.

8.7 Exercises

1. Give arguments why mutation strength (e.g., p_m or σ) should be increased during a run. Give arguments why it should be decreased.
2. It could be argued that there is no survivor selection (replacement) step in GAVaPS, Sect. 8.5.6. Discuss this issue.

3. Why is it not possible to have self-adaptation operating at the population level?

8.8 Recommended Reading for this Chapter

1. A.E. Eiben, R. Hinterding, and Z. Michalewicz. Parameter control in evolutionary algorithms. *IEEE Transactions on Evolutionary Computation*, 3(2):124–141, 1999.

2. J.E. Smith and T.C. Fogarty. Operator and parameter adaptation in genetic algorithms. *Soft Computing*, 1(2):81–87, 1997.

3. J.E. Smith. On appropriate adaptation levels for the learning of gene linkage. *Journal of Genetic Programming and Evolvable Machines*, 3(2):129–155, 2002.

4. T. Bäck. Self-adaptation. Chapter 21, pages 188–211 in T. Bäck, D.B. Fogel, and Z. Michalewicz, editors. *Evolutionary Computation 2: Advanced Algorithms and Operators*. Institute of Physics Publishing, 2000.

9

Multimodal Problems and Spatial Distribution

9.1 Aims of this Chapter

So far in our discussion of evolutionary algorithms we have considered the entire population to act as a common genepool, with fitness as the primary feature affecting the likelihood of an individual taking part in the creation of new offspring, and surviving to the next generation. However we know that evolution in vivo is also affected by another major parameter, namely that of the physical space within which evolution occurs, which imposes a sense of locality on genetic operators. However beautiful (i.e., highly fit) the flowers in the municipal garden, it is *extremely* unlikely that they will be fertilised with pollen from a garden on the opposite side of the world.

This separation brings with it several benefits, one of which is that it can aid the preservation of diversity within the population. As a result, different subgroups of the same global population may be adapted to their local conditions, as was famously described concerning finches on islands of the Galapagos archipelago by Charles Darwin [86]. One theory holds that the phenomenon of speciation arises as an end result of increasingly specialised adaptation to particular environmental niches, so that eventually distinct subpopulations have evolved so differently that their offspring are no longer viable, even if mating is physically possible at all.

Ideas such as that of a global population being subdivided into smaller, infrequently communicating subpopulations, along with related concepts such as speciation and other mating restrictions, have been widely investigated by EA practitioners as a means of preserving diversity and aiding the search for different high–quality solutions in multimodal problems. In this chapter we provide an overview of these approaches, ending with a description of two areas of optimisation in which EAs are currently showing great promise, namely multiobjective and dynamic problems.

9.2 Introduction: Multimodal Problems and the Need for Diversity

9.2.1 Multimodal Problems

The discussions of adaptive landscapes in Section 1.4.1, (as illustrated by Figure 1.1) and local optima, give raise to the concept of **multimodal problems**, i.e., problems in which there are a number of points that are better than all their neighbouring solutions, but do not have as good a fitness as the globally optimal solution.[1] In physical landscapes, features such as mountain ranges and ridges act as "watersheds" dividing them into a number discrete rainfall catchment areas, which are usually drained to oceans via rivers. In an exactly analogous fashion, we can divide multimodal problems into "basins of attraction" around local optima, defined as the set of points from which a local search algorithm would end up at the given local optima. Just as on physical landscapes, these are usually of different sizes and profiles, and it is not necessarily the case that the global optimum has the largest basin of attraction. Figure 9.1 illustrates this point for a one-dimensional landscape. Commonly the disjoint (i.e., unconnected) regions of high fitness are known as **niches**, a terminology we will adopt since it is more general than the alternatives (peaks and so on).

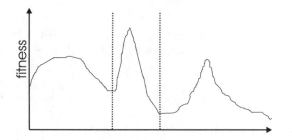

Fig. 9.1. Landscape features: There are three optima with different sizes of basins of attraction, and different "shapes". The global optimum is in the *middle*, and the *leftmost* local optimum has a broader peak than the *rightmost*, despite having a smaller basin of attraction

Multimodality is a typical aspect of the type of problems for which EAs are often employed, either in attempt to locate the global optimum (particularly when a local optimum has the largest basin of attraction), or to identify a *number* of high–fitness solutions corresponding to various local optima. The

---

[1] Note that a landscape definition requires both a set of solution points and a neighbourhood structure. This may be obvious for, say, real-valued problems, but for combinatorial problems the number of local optima depends on the choice of neighbourhood structure, i.e., on the variation operators used.

latter situation can often arise, for example, when the fitness function used by the EA does not completely specify the underlying problem. An example of this might be in the design of a new "widget", where the parameters of the fitness function may change during the design process, as progressively more refined and detailed models are used as decisions such as the choice of materials, etc., are made. In this situation it is valuable to be able to examine a number of possible options, first so as to permit room for human aesthetic judgements, and second because it is probably desirable to use solutions from niches with broader peaks rather than from a sharp peak. This is because the latter may be overfitted (that is overly specialised) to the current fitness function and may not be as good once the fitness function is refined.

9.2.2 Genetic Drift

The population-based nature of EAs holds out much promise for identifying multiple optima, however, in practice the finite population size, when coupled with recombination between *any* parents (known as **panmictic** mixing) leads to the phenomenon known as **genetic drift** and eventual convergence around one optimum. The reasons for this can easily be seen: imagine that we have two equally fit niches, and a population of 100 individuals originally equally divided between them. Eventually, because of the random effects in selection, it is likely that we will obtain a parent population consisting of 49 of one sort and 51 of the other. Ignoring the effects of recombination and mutation, in the next generation the probabilities of selecting individuals from the two niches are now 0.49 and 0.51 respectively, i.e., we are increasingly likely to select individuals from the second niche. This effect increases as the two subpopulations become unbalanced, until eventually we end up with only one niche represented in the population. In terms of the fitness landscape metaphor, the subpopulation in the first niche "melted down" the hill, crossed the valley, and climbed the other hill.

9.2.3 Biological Motivations and Algorithmic Approaches

As described in Sect. 9.1, biological evolution provides us with a number of metaphors to act as inspiration. These include:

- **Speciation**
  This is the process whereby different species adapt to occupy different environmental niches. The important feature here is that species only reproduce with other members of the same species, i.e., there are **mating restrictions**. Since environmental niches necessarily contain finite resources, individuals are in competition with individuals from their own species for survival and resources, and the effect of this combination of competition and restricted mating is to focus the evolutionary exploration on a particular environmental niche, with the outcome that it tends to

yield phenotypic homogeneity within species. It is worth noting that even highly specialised species may also be in competition with other species for resources and survival, for example, plants growing in the same vicinity compete for light and fertile soil.

- **Punctuated Equilibria**
  This is the theory that periods of evolutionary stasis are interrupted by rapid growth when the main population is "invaded" by individuals from previously spatially isolated group of individuals from same species [134]. Clearly this process requires that the main population be spatially separated into a number of isolated subpopulations (or **demes**), with only occasional migrations of individuals between them. It also requires that individuals from separate demes still retain the ability to successfully mate if incoming differences are to be integrated.

- **Local Adaptation**
  This is the effect that occurs within a spatially distributed population when geographically separated sub-populations of the same species show adaptations to their local environments. Examples of this might include birds or animals developing slightly different feeding habits or mouth or bill shapes in response to the presence of different food types in different regions.

Based on these ideas a number of mechanisms have been proposed to aid the use of EAs on multimodal problems. These can be broadly separated into two camps: *explicit* approaches, in which specific changes are made to operators in order to preserve diversity, and *implicit* approaches, in which a framework is used that permits, *but does not guarantee*, the preservation of diverse solutions. However, before describing these we will briefly digress to discuss the issue of what exactly we mean by "space" in greater depth.

9.2.4 Algorithmic Versus Genetic Versus Solution Space

Just as biological evolution takes place on a geographic surface, but can also be considered to occur on an adaptive landscape (Sect. 1.4.1), so we can define and think about a number of spaces within which the evolutionary algorithms operate:

- **Algorithmic Space**
  This is the equivalent of the geographical space on which life on earth has evolved. Effectively we are considering that the working memory of the EA can be structured in some way. A number of different forms of structure and communication have been proposed, and many of these take advantage of the fact that the population might be practically as well as conceptually distributed, for example, over a number of processors in a parallel computing environment.

- **Genotype space**
  Botanists, zoologists, and nowadays geneticists have categorised different

species into a taxonomy based on their evolutionary history and closeness, which effectively defines a neighbourhood structure in the space of DNA sequences via phylogenetic trees. In a similar way we may define a "genotype space", using distance metrics based on some fundamental move operator to define a neighbourhood structure over the set of representable solutions. Typical move operators include a single bit-flip for binary spaces, a single inversion for adjacency-based permutation problems and a single swap for order-based permutations problems.

- **Phenotype space**
  This is the end result: a search space whose structure is based on distance metrics between solutions. The neighbourhood structure in this space may bear little relationship to that in the genotype space according to the complexity of the representation–solution mapping.

9.2.5 Summary

We have identified a number of mechanisms present in biological evolution that permit the simultaneous exploration of a number of different environmental niches. These include explicit measures, such as the formation of species with no interspecies mating. Here the survival chances of an individual depend on the amount of resources available within its particular environmental niche, the extent to which its physical attributes and behaviour are matched to that niche, and on the competition for those resources. They also include implicit measures arising from the fact that "real" individuals exist on a geographical surface with physical distance also imposing implicit restrictions on mating and competition for survival, even within the same species. One effect of this can be that the same phenotypic "solution" can evolve in different places within different species with different genotypes.

Turning our attention to optimisation problems, we have seen that there are a number of reasons why it might be desirable to attempt to explore several different high–fitness regions in a multimodal problem. In the metaphor of Sewal-Wright's adaptive landscapes, these niches represent different environmental niches that species could inhabit, and so we are interested in how the forces that permit simultaneous exploration of different environmental niches in biological evolution can be harnessed with EAs.

Finally, we noted that EAs can be considered to operate within three distinct spaces, namely algorithmic, representation, and solution, which are conceptually equivalent to geographical, genotype, and phenotype spaces in biological evolution. We will now turn our attention to the different ways in which these insights and inspirations have been harnessed with evolutionary search. The reader should note that although we will describe these separately, many of them can of course be used together in tandem, just as they are in nature.

9.3 Implicit Measures

There are a number of possible options for attempting to find a diverse set of good solutions for a multimodal problem, without explicitly enforcing diversity. Some of the most common of these are:

- Run a standard EA many times, and save good solutions. This has the merits of being an extremely simple approach, but can have problems if one optimum has a large basin of attraction, since lots of runs may end up converging to the same solution.
- Run several standard EAs in tandem and let them periodically share information. This model is clearly inspired by the punctuated equilibria theories of evolution and has been widely investigated as is described in Sect. 9.3.1.
- Introduce a sense of spatial distribution into a single population. In this scheme "local" operators are used for parent and survivor selection so as to conceptually divide the population into a number of smaller overlapping subpopulations. As with the previous item, this works by imposing sense of algorithmic space, but here the communication model is different.
- Maintain different "species" within a single population. Here the representation of solutions is extended to include information that is used to identify different "species", and recombination is restricted to happen between members of the same species.

Of these approaches, the first (multiple runs) does not require any modification of the particular form of EA chosen, so we will concentrate on the last three.

9.3.1 Multiple Populations in Tandem: Island Model EAs

The idea of evolving multiple populations in tandem is also known as **island model EAs**, **parallel EAs** and, more precisely **coarse–grain parallel EAs**. These schemes attracted great interest in the 1980s when parallel computing became popular [82, 83, 252, 306, 322, 392] and are still applicable on MIMD systems such as computing clusters. Of course they can equally well be implemented on a single-processor architecture, without the performance speed-up (in terms of time at least).

The essential idea is to run multiple populations in parallel, in some kind of communication structure. The communication structure is usually a ring or a torus, but in principle any form is possible, and sometimes this is determined by the architecture of the parallel system, e.g., a hypercube [392]. After a (usually fixed) number of generations (known as an **epoch**), a number of individuals are selected from each population to be exchanged with others from neighbouring populations – this can be thought of as **migration**.

In [260] this approach is discussed in the context of Eldredge and Gould's theory of punctuated equilibria [134] and Holland's original formulation of the GA as a trade-off between *exploration* of unexplored regions of the search space and *exploitation* of knowledge gained via search in the vicinity of known high–quality solutions. They suggest that during the epochs between communication, when each subpopulation is evolving independently of the others, exploitation occurs, so that the subpopulations each explore the search space around the fitter solutions that they contain. When communication takes place, the injection of individuals of potentially high fitness, and with (possibly) radically different genotypes, facilitates exploration, particularly as recombination happens between the two different solutions.

Whilst extremely attractive in theory, and possessing the highly desirable quality of explicit parallelism, it is obvious that there are no guarantees per se that the different subpopulations are actually exploring different regions of the search space. One possibility is clearly to achieve a start at this through a careful initialisation process, but even if this is used, there are a number of parameters that have been shown to affect the ability of this technique to explore different peaks and obtain good results even when only a single solution is desired as the end result.

A number of detailed studies have been made of the effects of different parameters and implementations of this basic scheme (see, e.g., earlier references in this section), but of course we must bear in mind that the results obtained may be problem dependent, and so we will restrict ourselves to commenting on a few important facets:

- How often to exchange individuals ? The essential problem here is that if the communication occurs too frequently, then all sub-populations will converge to the same solution. Equally if it is done too infrequently, and one or more sub-populations has converged quickly in the vicinity of a peak, then significant amounts of computational effort may be wasted. Most authors have used epoch lengths of the range 25–150 generations. An elegant alternative strategy proposed in [260] is to organise communication adaptively, that is to say to stop the evolution in each sub-population when no improvement has been observed for, say, 25 generations.

- How many, and which individuals to exchange? Many authors have found that in order to prevent too rapid convergence to the same solution, it is better to exchange a small number of solutions between subpopulations – usually 2–5. Once the amount of communication has been decided, it is necessary to specify *which* individuals are selected from each population to be exchanged. Clearly this can be done either by some fitness-based selection mechanism (e.g., "copy-best" [306], "pick-from-fittest-half" [392]) or at random [82]. It must also be decided whether the individuals being exchanged are effectively "moved" from one population to another, thus (assuming a symmetrical communication structure) maintaining subpopulation sizes, or whether they are merely copied, in which case each subpopulation must then undergo some kind of survivor selection mechanism. The choices of how many and which individuals to exchange will evidently affect the tendency of the subpopulations to converge to the same solution. Random, rather than fitness based, selection strategy is less likely to lead to takeover of one population by a new high-fitness migrant, and exchanging more solutions also leads to faster mixing and possible takeover. However, the extent to which these factors affect the behaviour is clearly tied to the epoch length, since if this is long enough to permit fitness convergence then all of the solutions contained within a given subpopulation are likely to be genotypically very similar, so the selection method used becomes less important.

- How to divide the population into subpopulations? The general rule here appears to be that provided a certain (problem–dependent) minimum subpopulation size is respected, then more subpopulations usually gives better results. This clearly fits in with our understanding, since if each subpopulation is exploring a different peak (the ideal scenario), the more peaks explored, the likely it is that one of them will contain the global optimum.

Finally, it is worth mentioning that it is perfectly possible to use different algorithmic parameters on different "islands". Thus in the **injection island models** the subpopulations are arranged hierarchically with each level operating at a different granularity of representation. Equally, parameters such as the choice of recombination or mutation operator and associated parameters, or even subpopulation sizes, might be different between different subpopulations [129, 336].

9.3.2 Spatial Distribution Within One Population: Diffusion Model EAs

In the previous section we described the implementation of a population structure in the form of a number of subpopulations with occasional communication. In this section we describe an alternative model whereby a single population is considered to be split into a larger number of smaller overlapping subpopulations (demes) by being distributed within algorithmic space. We can consider this to be equivalent to the situation whereby biological individuals are separated, only mating and competing for survival with those within a certain distance to them. To take a simple example from the days of less-rapid transport, a person might only have been able to marry and have children with someone from their own or surrounding villages. Thus should a new gene for say, telekinesis, evolve, even if it offers huge evolutionary advantage, at first it will only spread to surrounding villages. In the next generation it might spread to those surrounding them, and so on, only slowly diffusing or percolating throughout the society.

This effect is implemented by considering each member of the population to exist on a different point on a grid, and only permitting recombination and selection with neighbours, hence the common names of **fine-grain parallel EAs** [258], **diffusion model EAs** [414], **distributed EAs** [208] or **cellular EAs**[419] as well as parallel EAs [178, 288]. We will refer to these algorithms as diffusion model EAs since we feel that this best describes the communication structure, although the term cellular EAs is also particularly apt since Whitley has shown that EAs in this form are equivalent to cellular automata [419]. As suggested by the multiplicity of names, there have been a great many differing implementations of this form of EA, but we can broadly outline the algorithm as follows:

1. The current population is conceptually distributed on a (usually toroidal) grid, with one individual per node.
2. For each node we have defined a deme (neighbourhood). This is usually the same for all nodes, e.g., for a neighbourhood size of nine on a square lattice, we take the node and all of its immediate neighbours.
3. In each generation we consider each deme in turn and perform the following operations within it:
   - Select two solutions from the nodes in the deme that will act as parents.
   - Generate an offspring via recombination.
   - Mutate, then evaluate the offspring.
   - Select one solution residing on a node in the deme and replace it with the new offspring.

Within this general structure there is scope for considerable differences in implementation such as:

- The ASPARAGOS algorithm [178, 288] uses a ladder topology rather than a lattice, and also performs a hill-climbing step after mutation.
- Several algorithms implemented on massively parallel SIMD or SPMD machines use asynchronous updates in step 3 rather than the sequential mode suggested in the third step above (a good discussion of this issue can be found in [305]).
- The selection of parents might be fitness based [89] or random (or one of each [258]), and often one parent is taken to be that residing on the central node of the deme. When fitness-based selection is used it is usually a local implementation of a well-known global scheme such as fitness proportionate or tournament. DeJong and Sarma [102] analysed a number of such schemes and found that local selection techniques generally exhibited less selection pressure than their global versions.
- Whilst it is common to replace the central node of the deme, again fitness-based or random selection have been used to select the individual to be replaced, or a combination such as "replace current solution if better" [178]. White and Pettey reported results suggesting that the use of fitness in the survivor selection is preferred [414].

9.3.3 Automatic Speciation Using Mating Restrictions

The two forms of parallel EAs described above attempt to preserve diversity by imposing a mating (and replacement) restriction based on an analogy of physical distance creating separately evolving subpopulations. In contrast to this, the "automatic speciation" approach imposes mating restrictions based on some aspect of the candidate solutions (or their genotypes) defining them as belonging to different species. The population contains multiple species, and during parent selection for recombination, individuals will only mate with others from the same (or similar) species. The biological analogy becomes particularly clear when we note that some authors refer to the aspect controlling reproductive opportunities as an individual's "plumage" [365].

A number of schemes have been proposed to implement speciation, which can be divided into two main approaches. In the first speciation is based on the solution (or its representation), e.g., Deb's phenotype (genotype)–restricted mating [105, 108, 365]. The alternative approach is to add some elements such "tags" to the genotype that code for the individual's species, rather than representing part of the solution. See [58, 105, 375] for implementations, noting that many of these ideas were previously suggested by other authors. These are usually randomly initialised and subject to recombination and mutation. Common to both approaches is the idea that once an individual has been selected to be a parent, then the choice of mate involves the use of a pairwise distance metric (in phenotype or genotype space as appropriate), with potential mates being rejected beyond a certain distance.

Note that in the "tag" scheme, there is initially no guarantee that individuals with similar tags will represent similar solutions, although after a few generations selection will usually take care of this problem. Neither is there any guarantee that different species will contain different solutions, although Spears goes some way towards rectifying this by also using the tags to perform fitness sharing [375], and even without this Deb reported improved performance compared to a standard GA [105]. Similarly, although the phenotypic-based speciation scheme does not guarantee diversity maintenance, when used in conjunction with fitness sharing, it was reported to give better results than fitness sharing on its own [108].

9.4 Explicit Diversity Maintenance

Explicit schemes are based on the idea of *forcing* the population to maintain different niches when doing either selection or replacement. Two forms are most commonly used, namely **fitness sharing** [176], in which the fitnesses of individuals are adjusted prior to selection in an attempt to allocate individuals to niches *in proportion to the niche fitness*, and **crowding** [98, 256], in which a distance-based survivor selection policy is used in an attempt to distribute individuals *uniformly* amongst niches. It should be noted that in both cases the choice of parents is global, i.e. there is nothing to prevent the recombination of parents from different niches. Although a possible source of good solutions, this is often thought to be more likely to produce low-fitness solutions (so-called "lethals"), hence the frequent use of these schemes with some speciation scheme as noted above.

9.4.1 Fitness Sharing

This scheme is based upon the idea that the number of individuals within a given niche is controlled by "sharing" their fitness immediately prior to selection. In practice the scheme works by considering each possible pairing of individuals i and j within the population (including i with itself) and calculating a distance $d(i, j)$ between them according to some distance metric (phenotypic is preferred if possible, else genotypic, e.g., Hamming distance for binary representations). The fitness F of each individual i is then adjusted according to the number of individuals falling within some prespecified distance σ_{share} using a power-law distribution:

$$F'(i) = \frac{F(i)}{\sum_j sh(d(i, j))},$$

where the sharing function $sh(d)$ is a function of the distance d given by

$$sh(d) = \begin{cases} 1 - (d/\sigma_{share})^\alpha & \text{if } d \leq \sigma_{share}, \\ 0 & \text{otherwise .} \end{cases}$$

As can be seen the constant value α determines the shape of the sharing function: for $\alpha=1$ the function is linear, but for values greater than this the effect of similar individuals in reducing a solution's fitness falls off more rapidly with distance.

The other parameter that needs to be set, and the one that decides both how many niches can be maintained and the granularity with which different niches can be discriminated, is the share radius σ_{share}. Deb [108] gives some suggestions for how this might be set if the number of niches is known *in advance*, but clearly this is not always the case. In [106] he suggests that a default value in the range 5–10 should be used.

Finally, we should point out that the use of fitness proportionate selection is implicit within the fitness-sharing method. Studies have indicated that the use of alternative selection methods does not lead to the formation and preservation of stable subpopulations in niches [294]. However, if fitness proportionate selection is used, then there exists a stable distribution of solutions amongst the niches when solutions from each peak have the same effective fitness F'. This means that in each niche k the number of solutions present n_k is proportional to the niche fitness F_k, so that $F'_k = F_k/n_k$ is constant and equal for all niches[2]. This point is illustrated in Fig. 9.2.

---

[2] This assumes for the sake of ease that all solutions within a given niche lie at its optimal point, at zero distance from each other.

9.4.2 Crowding

The crowding algorithm was first suggested in DeJong's thesis [98] as a way of preserving diversity by ensuring that new individuals replaced *similar* members of the population. The original scheme worked in a steady-state setting (the number of new individuals generated in each step was 20% of the population size). When an new offspring is inserted into the population, CF (DeJong used $CF=2$) members of the parent population are chosen at random, and then the offspring replaces the most similar of those parents. A number of problems were found with this approach, and Mahfoud has suggested an improvement called **deterministic crowding** [256].

This algorithm relies on the fact that offspring are likely to be similar to their parents as follows:

1. The parent population is randomly paired.
2. Each pair produces two offspring via recombination.
3. These offspring are mutated and then evaluated.
4. The four pairwise distances between offspring and parents are calculated.
5. Each offspring then competes for survival in a tournament with one parent, so that the intercompetition distances are minimised. In other words, denoting the parents as p, the offspring as o, and using the subscript to indicate tournament pairing, $d(p_1, o_1) + d(p_2, o_2) < d(p_1, o_2) + d(p_2, o_1)$.

The net result of all this is that offspring tend to compete for survival with the most similar parent, so subpopulations are preserved in niches but their size does not depend on fitness; rather it is equally distributed amongst the peaks available. Figure 9.2 illustrates this point in comparison with the distribution achieved under crowding.

9.5 Multiobjective Evolutionary Algorithms

In this section we describe the application of some of the techniques detailed above to a particular class of problems, namely multiobjective optimisation. We begin by introducing this class of problems and the particularly important notion of Pareto optimality. We then look at some of the current state-of-the-art mMultiobjective EAs (MOEAs) for this class of problems and examine the ways in which they make use of concepts of different evolutionary spaces and techniques for promoting and preserving diversity within the population.

9.5.1 Multiobjective Optimisation Problems

In the majority of our discussions in previous chapters we have made free use of analogies such as adaptive landscapes under the assumption that the goal of the EA in an optimisation problem is to find a single solution that maximises a fitness value that is directly related to a single underlying measure of quality.

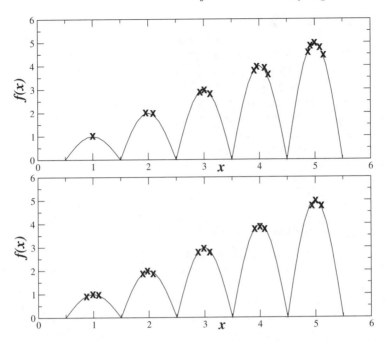

Fig. 9.2. Idealised population distributions under fitness sharing (*upper*) and crowding (*lower*). There are five peaks in the landscape with fitnesses (5,4,3,2,1) and the population size is 15. Fitness sharing allocates individuals to peaks in proportion to their fitness, whereas crowding distributes the population evenly amongst the peaks

In this chapter we introduced a number of modifications to EAs that are aimed at preserving diversity so that a *set* of solutions are maintained, which represent niches of high fitness, but we have still maintained the conceptual link to an adaptive landscape defined via the assignment of a *single* quality metric (objective) to each of the set of possible solutions.

We now turn our attention to a class of problems that are currently receiving a lot of interest within the optimisation community, and in practical applications. These are the so-called **multiobjective problems** (MOPs), where the quality of a solution is defined by its performance in relation to several, possibly conflicting, objectives. In practice it turns out that a great many applications that have traditionally been tackled by defining a single objective function (quality function) have at their heart a multiobjective problem that has been transformed into a single-objective function in order to make optimisation tractable.

To give a simple illustration (inspired by [301]), imagine that we have moved to a new city and are in the process of looking for a house to buy. There are a number of factors that we will probably wish to take into account such as: number of rooms, style of architecture, commuting distance and method to work, provision of local amenities, access to pleasant countryside, and of course price. Many of these factors work against each other (particularly price), and so the final decision will almost inevitably bear a compromise, based on trading-off the house's rating on different factors.

The example we have just presented is a particularly subjective one, with some factors that are hard to quantify numerically. It does exhibit a feature that is common to multiobjective problems, namely that it is desirable to present the user with a diverse set of possible solutions, representing a range of different trade-offs between objectives.

The alternative is to assign a numerical quality function to each objective, and then combine these scores into a single fitness score using some (usually fixed) weighting. This approach, often called **scalarisation** has been used for many years within the operations research and heuristic optimisation communities (see [81, 106] for good reviews), but suffers from a number of drawbacks:

- The use of a weighting function implicitly assumes that we can capture all of the users preferences, even before we know what range of possible solutions exist.
- For applications where we are repeatedly solving different instances of the same problem, the use of a weighting function assumes that the user's preferences remain static, unless we explicitly seek a new weighting every time.

For these reasons optimisation methods that simultaneously find a *diverse* set of high-quality solutions are attracting increasing interest.

9.5.2 Dominance and Pareto Optimality

The concept of **dominance** is a simple one: given two solutions, both of which have scores according to some set of objective values (which without loss of generality we will assume to be maximised), one solution is said to dominate the other if its score is at least as high for all objectives, and is strictly better for at least one. We can represent the scores that a solution A gets for n objectives as a n-dimensional vector $\bar{a}$. Using the $\succeq$ symbol to indicate domination, we can define $A \succeq B$ formally as:

$$A \succeq B \iff \forall i \in \{1, \ldots, n\} \ a_i \geq b_i, \text{ and } \exists i \in \{1, \ldots, n\}, \ a_i > b_i.$$

For conflicting objectives, there exists no single solution that dominates all others, and we will call a solution **nondominated** if it is not dominated by any other. All nondominated solutions possess the attribute that their quality cannot be increased with respect to any of the objective functions without detrimentally affecting one of the others. In the presence of constraints, such solutions usually lie on the edge of the feasible regions of the search space. The set of all nondominated solutions is called the **Pareto set** or the Pareto front.

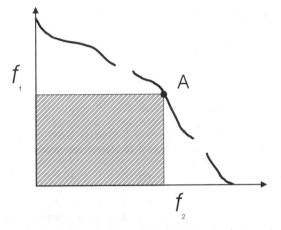

Fig. 9.3. Illustration of the Pareto front. The quality of solutions is represented by their positions relative to the x- and y-axes which represent two conflicting objectives subject to constraints. The *line* represents the Pareto set, of which point A is an example. Solutions above and to the right of the line are infeasible. The *shaded area* represents the set of points dominated by A.

In Figure 9.3 this front is illustrated for two conflicting objectives that are both to be maximised. This figure also illustrates some of the features, such as nonconvexity and discontinuities, frequently observed in real applications that can cause particular problems for traditional optimisation techniques using often sophisticated variants of scalarisation to identify the Pareto set. EAs have a proven ability to identify high-quality solutions in high-dimensional search spaces containing difficult features such as discontinuities and multiple constraints. When coupled with their population-based nature and well-known methods for finding and preserving diverse sets of good solutions (as described in this chapter), it is not surprising that EA-based methods are currently the state of the art in many multiobjective optimisation problems.

9.5.3 EA Approaches to Multiobjective Optimisation

There have been many approaches to multiobjective optimisation using EAs, beginning with Schaffer's vector-evaluated genetic algorithm (VEGA) in 1984 [332]. In this algorithm the population was randomly divided into subpopulations that were then each assigned a fitness (and subject to selection) according to a different objective function, but parent selection and recombination were performed globally. This modification was shown to be enough to preserve an approximation to the Pareto front for a few generations, but not indefinitely.

Subsequent to this, Goldberg suggested the use of fitness based on dominance rather than on absolute objective scores [172], coupled with niching and/or speciation methods to preserve diversity, and this breakthrough triggered a dramatic increase in research activity in this area. We briefly describe some of the best-known algorithms below, noting that the choice of representation, and hence variation operators, are entirely problem dependent, and so we concentrate on the way that fitness assignment and selection are performed.

Nonelitist Approaches

Amongst the first algorithms to explicitly exert selection pressure towards the discovery of nondominated solutions were:

- Fonseca and Fleming's multiobjective genetic algorithm (MOGA) [157]. This assigns a raw fitness to each solution equal to the number of members of the current population that it dominates, plus one. It uses fitness sharing amongst solutions of the same rank, coupled with fitness proportionate selection to help promote diversity.
- Srinivas and Deb's nondominated sorting genetic algorithm (NSGA) [383]. This works in a similar way, but assigns fitness based on dividing the population into a number of "fronts" of equal domination. To achieve this, the algorithm iteratively seeks all the nondominated points in the population that have not been labelled as belonging to a previous front. It then labels the new set as belonging to the current front, and increments the front count, repeating until all solutions have been labelled. Each point in a given front gets as its raw fitness the count of all solutions in inferior fronts. Again fitness sharing is implemented to promote diversity, but this time it is calculated considering only members from that individual's front.
- Horn et al.'s niched Pareto genetic algorithm (NPGA) [206]. This algorithm differs in that it uses a modified version of tournament selection rather than fitness proportionate with sharing. The tournament operator works by comparing two solutions first on the basis of whether they dominate each other, and then second on the number of similar solutions already in the new population.

Although all three of these algorithms show good performance on a number of test problems, they share two common features. The first of these is that the performance they achieve is heavily dependent on a suitable choice of parameters in the sharing/niching procedures. The second is that they can potentially lose good solutions.

Elitist Approaches

During the 1990s much work was done elsewhere in the EA research community, developing methods for reducing dependence on parameter settings (Chap. 8). Theoretical breakthroughs were achieved showing that single-objective EAs converge to the global optimum on some problems, providing that an elitist strategy (Sect. 3.8.2) is used. In the light of this research Deb and coworkers proposed the revised NSGA-II [107], which still uses the idea of non-dominated fronts, but incorporates the following changes:

- A crowding distance metric is defined for each point as the average side length of the cuboid defined by its nearest neighbours in the same front. The larger this value, the fewer solutions reside in the vicinity of the point.
- A $(\mu + \lambda)$ survivor selection strategy is used (with $\mu = \lambda$). The two populations are merged and fronts assigned. The new population is obtained by accepting individuals from progressively inferior fronts until it is full. If not all of the individuals in the last front considered can be accepted, they are chosen on the basis of their crowding distance.
- Parent selection uses a modified tournament operator that considers first dominance rank then crowding distance.

As can be seen this achieves elitism (via the plus strategy) and an explicit diversity maintenance scheme, as well as reduced dependence on parameters.

Two other prominent algorithms, the strength Pareto evolutionary algorithm (SPEA-2) [439] and the Pareto archived evolutionary strategy (PAES) [228], both achieve the elitist effect in a slightly different way by using an archive containing a fixed number of nondominated points discovered during the search process. Both maintain a fixed sized archive, and consider the number of archived points close to a new solution, as well as dominance information, when updating the archive.

Diversity Maintenance in MOEAs

To finish our discussion on MOEAs it is appropriate to return our thoughts to the initial aims of this chapter, namely to considering how sets of diverse solutions can be maintained during evolution. It should be clear from the descriptions of the MOEAs above that all of them use explicit methods to enforce preservation of diversity, rather than relying simply on implicit measures such as parallelism (in one form or another) or artificial speciation.

In single-objective optimisation, explicit diversity maintenance methods are often combined with implicit speciation methods to permit the search for optimal solutions within the preserved niches. The outcome of this is a *few* highly fit diverse solutions, often with multiple copies of each (Fig. 9.2). In contrast to this, the aim of MOEAs is to attempt to distribute the population *evenly* along the current approximation to the Pareto front. This partially explains why speciation techniques have not been used in conjunction with the explicit measures. Finally, it is worth noting that the more modern algorithms discussed have abandoned fitness sharing in favour of direct measures of the distance to the nearest nondominating solution, more akin to crowding.

9.6 Example Application: Distributed Coevolution of Job Shop Schedules

An interesting application, which makes use of many of the ideas in this chapter, (and also some in Section13.2) can be seen in Husbands's distributed coevolutionary approach to multiobjective problems [208]. In this approach he uses a coevolutionary model to tackle a complex multiobjective, multi-constraint problem, namely a generalised version of job shop scheduling. Here a number of items need to be manufactured, each requiring a number of operations on different machines. Each item may need a different number of operations, and in general the order of the operations may be varied, so that the problem of finding an optimal production plan for *one* item is itself NP-hard. The usual approach to the multiple task problem is to optimise each plan individually, and then use a heuristic scheduler to interleave the plans so as to obtain an overall schedule. However, this approach is inherently flawed because it optimises the plans in isolation rather than taking into consideration the availability of machines, etc.

Husbands approach is different: he uses a separate population to evolve plans for each item and optimises these concurrently. In this sense we have a MOP, although the desired final output is a single set of plans (one for each item) rather than a set of diverse schedules. A candidate plan for one item gets evaluated in the context of a member from each other population, i.e., the fitness value (related to time and machining costs) is for a complete production schedule. An additional population is used to evolve "arbitrators", which resolve conflicts during the production of the complete schedule.

Early experiments experienced problems with premature loss of diversity, and this is clearly a highly multimodal problem space. These problems are treated by the use of an implicit approach to diversity preservation, namely the use of a diffusion model EA. Furthermore, by colocating one individual from each population in each grid location, the problem of partner (Sect. 13.2) is neatly solved: a complete solution for evaluation corresponds to a grid cell.

We will not give details of his representation and variation operators here, as these are highly problem specific. Rather we will focus on the details of his algorithm that were aimed at aiding the search for high-class solutions. The first of these is, of course, the use of a coevolutionary approach. If a single population were used, with a solution representing the plans for all items, there would be a greater likelihood of genetic hitchhiking (see Sect. 11.2 for a description), whereby a good plan for one item in the initial population would take over, even if the plans for the other items were poor. By contrast, the decomposition into different subpopulations means that the good plan can at worst take over one population.

The second feature that aids the search over diverse local optima is the use of a diffusion model approach. The implementation uses a 15-by-15 square toroidal grid, thus a population size of 225. Plans for 5 items, each needing between 20 and 60 operations were evolved, so in total there were 6 populations, and each cell contained a plan for each of the 5 items plus an arbitrator. A generational approach is used: within each generation each cell's populations are "bred", with a random permutation to decide the order in which cells are considered.

The breeding process within each cell is iterated for each population and consists of the following steps:

1. Generate a set of points to act as neighbours by iteratively generating random lateral and vertical offsets from the current position. A binomial approximation to a Gaussian distribution is used, which falls off sharply for distances more than 2 and is truncated to distance 4.
2. Rank the cells in this neighbourhood according to cost, and select one using linear ranking with $s = 2$.
3. Take the member of the current population from the selected cell and the member in the current cell, and generate an offspring via recombination and mutation.
4. Choose a cell from the neighbourhood using inverse linear ranking.
5. Replace the member of the current population in that cell with the newly created offspring.
6. Re-evaluate all the individuals in that cell using the newly created offspring.

The results presented from this technique showed that the system managed to evolve low-cost plans for each item, together with a low total schedule time. Notably, even after several thousand iterations, the system had still preserved a number of diverse solutions.

9.7 Exercises

1. Given a function with 5 optima with fitness 8,12,16,20,24 and a population of size 200, what would be the hoped-for distributions of individuals to peaks under fitness sharing and deterministic crowding?
2. In a tag-mediated speciation scheme, how does the length of the speciation tag affect the number of different niches in which we can hope to maintain solutions?
3. Discuss the factors that affect the rate of convergence of an island model EA to a single solution.
4. Describe the main components necessary to add to a "standard" EA in order to tackle a multiobjective problem.
5. What is a nondominated point?
6. A simple multiobjective problem has two objective functions $f_1(\bar{x}) = x_1$ and $f_2(\bar{x}) = x_2^3$, and is subject to the constraints $x_1^2 + x_2^2 \leq 10$. What will the Pareto front for this problem look like?

9.8 Recommended Reading for this Chapter

1. K. Deb. *Multiobjective Optimization using Evolutionary Algorithms.* John Wiley, Chichester, UK, 2001

2. C.A. Coello Coello, D.A. Van Veldhuizen, and G.B. Lamont. *Evolutionary Algorithms for Solving Multi-Objective Problems.* Kluwer Academic Publishers, New York, May 2002

3. I. Parmee. *Evolutionary and Adaptive Computing in Engineering Design: The Integration of Adaptive Search Exploration and Optimization with Engineering Design Processes.* Springer, Berlin, Heidelberg, New York, 2000
   Presents several applications of EAs to multimodal and multiobjective applications within an overall practice-orientated philosophy

Hybridisation with Other Techniques: Memetic Algorithms

10.1 Aims of this Chapter

In the preceding chapters we described the main varieties of evolutionary algorithms and described various examples of how they might be suitably implemented for different applications. In this chapter we turn our attention to systems in which, rather than existing as "stand-alone" algorithms, EA-based approaches are either incorporated within larger systems, or alternatively have other methods or data structures incorporated within them. This category of algorithms is very successful in practice and forms a rapidly growing research area with great potential. This area and the algorithms that form its subject of study are named memetic algorithms (MA). In this chapter we explain the rationale behind MAs, outline a number of possibilities for combining EAs with other techniques, and give some guidelines for designing successful hybrid algorithms.

10.2 Motivation for Hybridising EAs

There are a number of factors that motivate the hybridization of evolutionary algorithms with other techniques. In the following we discuss some of the most salient of these. Many complex problems can be decomposed into a number of parts, for some of which exact methods, or very good heuristics, may already be available. In these cases it makes sense to use a combination of the most appropriate methods for different subproblems.

Overall successful and efficient general problem solvers do not exist. The rapidly growing body of empirical evidence and some theoretical results, like the No Free Lunch theorem (NFL),[1] strongly support this view. From an

---

[1] The NFL is treated in detail in Chap. 11, including a discussion about what it really says. For the present we interpret it as stating that all stochastic algorithms have the same performance when averaged over all discrete problems.

EC perspective this fact implies that EAs do not exhibit the performance as suggested in the 1980's, cf. Fig. 2.8 in Sect. 2.5. An alternative view on this issue is given Fig. 10.1. The figure considers the possibility to combine problem-specific heuristics and an EA into a hybrid algorithm. Furthermore, it is assumed that the amount of problem-specific knowledge is variable and can be adjusted. Depending on the amount of problem-specific knowledge in the hybrid algorithm, the global performance curve will gradually change from roughly flat (pure EA) to a narrow peak (problem-specific method).

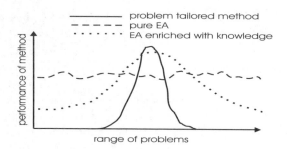

Fig. 10.1. 1990s view of EA performance after Michalewicz [271]

In practice we frequently apply an evolutionary algorithm to a problem where there is a considerable amount of hard-won user experience and knowledge available. In such cases performance benefits can often arise from utilising this information in the form of specialist operators and/or good solutions, provided that care is taken not to bias the search too much away from the generation of novel solutions. In these cases it is commonly experienced that the combination of an evolutionary and a heuristic method – a **hybdrid EA** – performs better than either of its "parent" algorithms alone. Note, that in this sense Figure 10.1 is misleading as it does not indicate this effect.

There is a body of opinion that whilst EAs are very good at rapidly identifying good areas of the search space (exploration), they are less good at the "endgame" of fine-tuning solutions (exploitation), partly as a result of the stochastic nature of the variation operators. To illustrate this point, as anyone who has implemented a GA to solve the "One-Max" problem[2] knows, the algorithm is quick to reach near-optimal solutions, but the process of mutation finding the last few bits to change can be slow, since the choice of which genes are mutated is random. A more efficient method might be to incorporate a more systematic search of the vicinity of "good" solutions by adding a local search improvement step to the evolutionary cycle (in this case, a bit-flipping hill-climber).

---

[2] A binary coded maximisation problem, where the fitness is simply the count of the number of genes set to "1" (Appendix B).

A final concept, which is often used as a motivation by researchers in this field, is Dawkin's idea of "memes" [94] . These can be viewed as units of "cultural transmission", in the same way that genes are the units of biological transmission. They are selected for replication according to their perceived utility or popularity, and then copied and transmitted via interperson communication.

> Examples of memes are tunes, ideas, catch-phrases, clothes fashions, ways of making pots or of building arches. Just as genes propagate themselves in the gene pool by leaping from body to body via sperm or eggs, so memes propagate themselves in the meme pool by leaping from brain to brain via a process which, in the broad sense, can be called imitation [94, p. 192].

Since the idea of memes was first proposed by Dawkins, it has been extended by other authors (e.g., [53, 67]). From the point of view of the study of adaptive systems and optimisation techniques, it is the idea of memes as agents that can transform a candidate solution that is of direct interest. We can consider the addition of a "learning" phase to the evolutionary cycle as a form of meme–gene interaction, whereby the problem representation (genotype) is now considered to be "plastic", and the influence of the learning mechanism (meme) can be thought of as a developmental process.

As this short selection of motivating considerations suggests, there are a number of diverse reasons why the hybridization of evolutionary algorithms with other techniques is of interest to both the researcher and the practitioner. Concerning the use of other techniques and knowledge to augment the EA (as opposed to the use of EAs within large systems), these have been given various names in research papers such as: *hybrid GAs, Baldwinian EAs, Lamarckian EAs, genetic local search algorithms*, and others. Moscato [286] coined the name *memetic algorithm* to cover a wide range of techniques where evolutionary-based search is augmented by the addition of one or more phases of local search, or by the use of problem-specific information. The field is now sufficiently mature and distinct to have its own annual workshop and special issues of major journals dedicated to it, and a comprehensive on-line bibliography is maintained at [285].

10.3 A Brief Introduction to Local Search

In Section 2.6 we briefly described **local search** as an iterative process of examining the set of points in the neighbourhood of the current solution, and replacing it with a better neighbour if one exists. In this section we give a brief introduction to local search in the context of memetic algorithms. For more information there are a number of books on optimisation that cover local search in more detail, such as [3]. A local search algorithm can be illustrated by the pseudocode given in Fig. 10.2.

```
BEGIN
  /* given a starting solution i and a neighbourhood function n */
  set best = i;
  set iterations = 0;
  REPEAT UNTIL ( depth condition is satisfied ) DO
    set count = 0;
    REPEAT UNTIL ( pivot rule is satisfied ) DO
      generate the next neighbour j ∈ n(i);
      set count = count + 1;
      IF (f(j) is better than f(best)) THEN
        set best = j;
      FI
    OD
    set i = best;
    set iterations = iterations + 1;
  OD
END
```

Fig. 10.2. Pseudocode of a local search algorithm

There are three principal components that affect the workings of this local search algorithm.

- The first is the choice of **pivot rule**, which can be **steepest ascent** or **greedy ascent** (also known as *first ascent*). In the former the condition for terminating the inner loop is that the entire neighbourhood $n(i)$ has been searched, i.e., $count = | n(i) |$, whereas in the latter the termination condition is $((count = | n(i) |)$ or $(best \neq i))$, i.e., it stops as soon as an improvement is found. In practice it is sometimes necessary to only consider a randomly drawn sample of size $N <<| n(i) |$ if the neighbourhood is too large to search.
- The second component is the **depth** of the local search, i.e., the termination condition for the outer loop. This lies in the continuum between only one improving step being applied ($iterations = 1$) to the search continuing to local optimality: $((count = | n(i) |)$ and $(best = i))$. Considerable attention has been paid to studying the effect of changing this parameter within MAs [192], and it can be shown to have an effect on the performance of the local search algorithm, both in terms of time taken, and in the quality of solution found.
- The third, and primary, factor that affects the behaviour of the local search is the choice of neighbourhood generating function. In practice $n(i)$ is often defined in a operational way, that is, as a set of points that can be reached by the application of some move operator to the point i. An equivalent representation is as a graph $G = (v, e)$, where the set of vertices v are the

points in the search space, and the edges relate to applications of the move operator i.e., $e_{ij} \in G \iff j \in n(i)$. The provision of a scalar fitness value f defined over the search space means that we can consider the graphs defined by different move operators as fitness landscapes [218]. Merz and Freisleben [270] present a number of statistical measures that can be used to characterise fitness landscapes, and that have been proposed by various authors as potential measures of problem difficulty. They show that the choice of move operator can have a dramatic effect on the efficiency and effectiveness of the local search, and hence of the resultant MA.

In some cases, domain-specific information may be used to guide the choice of neighbourhood structure within the local search algorithms. However, it has recently been shown that the optimal choice of operators can be not only instance specific within a class of problems [270, pp. 254–258], but also dependent on the state of the evolutionary search [240]. This result is not surprising when we consider that points that are locally optimal with respect to one neighbourhood structure may not be with respect to another, unless of course they are globally optimal. Thus if a set of points has converged to the state where all are locally optimal with respect to the current neighbourhood operator, then changing the neighbourhood operator may provide a means of progression, in addition to recombination and mutation. This observation has also been applied in other fields of optimisation and forms the heart of methods such as the *variable neighbourhood search* algorithm [189].

10.3.1 Lamarckianism and the Baldwin Effect

The framework of the local search algorithm outlined above works on the assumption that the current incumbent solution is always replaced by the fitter neighbour when found. Within a memetic algorithm, we can consider the local search stage to occur as an improvement, or developmental learning phase within the evolutionary cycle, and (taking our cue from biology) we should consider whether the changes made to the individual (*acquired traits*) should be kept, or whether the resulting improved fitness should be awarded to the original (pre-local search) member of the population.

The issue of whether acquired traits could be inherited by an individual's offspring was a major issue in nineteenth century, with Lamarck arguing in favour, whereas the **Baldwin effect** [34] suggests a mechanism whereby evolutionary progress can be guided towards favourable adaptation without the changes in individuals' fitness arising from learning or development being reflected in changed genetic characteristics. Modern theories of genetics strongly favour the latter viewpoint. Pragmatically, we saw in Sect. 1.4.2 that the mapping from DNA to protein is highly complex and non-linear, let alone the complexity of the developmental process by which the mature phenotype is created. In the light of this, it is hardly credible to believe that a process of reverse engineering could go on, coding the effects of phenotypically acquired traits back into the genotype.

Luckily, working within the medium of computer algorithms we are not restricted by these biological constraints, and so in practice both schemes are usually possible to implement within a memetic algorithm. In general MAs are referred to as Lamarckian if the result of the local search stage replaces the individual in the population, and Baldwinian if the original member is kept, but has as its fitness the value belonging to the outcome of the local search process. In a classic early study, Hinton and Nowlan [199] showed that the Baldwin effect could be used to improve the evolution of artificial neural networks, and a number of researchers have studied the relative benefits of Baldwinian versus Lamarckian algorithms [207, 264, 400, 421, 422]. In practice most recent work has tended to use either a pure Lamarckian approach, or a probabilistic combination of the two approaches, such that the improved fitness is always used, and the improved individual replaces the original with a given probability.

10.4 Structure of a Memetic Algorithm

There are a number of ways in which an EA can be used in conjunction with other operators and/or domain-specific knowledge as illustrated by Fig 10.3.

10.4.1 Heuristic or Intelligent Initialisation

The most obvious way in which existing knowledge about the structure of a problem or potential solutions can be incorporated into an EA is in the initialisation phase. In our discussion of this issue in Sect. 2.5 we gave reasons why this might not be worth the efforts in general, cf. Fig. 2.6. However, starting the EA by using existing solutions can offer interesting benefits:

1. It is possible to avoid "reinventing the wheel" by using existing solutions. Preventing waste of computational efforts can yield increased efficiency (speed).
2. A nonrandom initial population can direct the search into particular regions of the search space that contain good solutions. Biasing the search can result in increased effectivity (quality of end solution).
3. All in all, a given total amount of computational effort divided over heuristic initialisation and evolutionary search might deliver better results than spending it all on "pure" evolutionary search, or an equivalent multistart heuristic.

There are a number of possible ways in which the initialisation function can be changed from simple random creation, such as:

- **Seeding** the population with one or more previously known good solutions arising from other techniques. These techniques span the range from

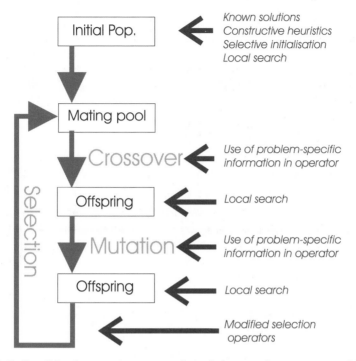

Fig. 10.3. Possible places to incorporate knowledge or other operators within the evolutionary cycle

human trial and error to the use of highly specialised greedy constructive heuristics using instance-specific information. Examples of the latter
include "nearest-neighbour" heuristics for TSP-like problems, "schedule
hardest first" for scheduling and planning problems, and a wealth of other
techniques for different problems, which can be found in the operations
research literature.

- In **selective initialisation** a large number of random solutions are created and then the initial population is selected from these. Bramlette [61]
  suggests that this should be done as a series of N k-way tournaments rather
  than by selecting the best N from $k \cdot N$ solutions. Other alternatives include selecting a set based not only on fitness but also on diversity so as
  to maximise the coverage of the search space.
- Performing a local search starting from each member of initial population,
  so that the initial population consists of a set of points that are locally
  optimal with respect to some move operator.
- Using one or more of the above methods to identify one (or possibly more)
  good solutions, and then cloning them and applying mutation at a high
  rate (**mass mutation**) to produce a number of individuals in the vicinity
  of the start point.

All of these methods have been tried and have exhibited performance gains for certain problems. However, the important issue of providing the EA with sufficient diversity for evolution to occur must also be considered. In [388] Surry and Radcliffe examined the effect of varying the proportion of the initial population of a GA that was derived from known good solutions. Their conclusions were:

- The use of a small proportion of derived solutions in the initial population aided genetic search.
- As the proportion was increased, the *average* performance improved.
- The *best* performance came about from a more random initial population.

In other words, as the proportion of solutions derived from heuristics used increased, so did the mean performance, but the variance in performance decreased. This meant that there were not the occasional really good runs resulting from the EA searching completely new regions of space and coming up with novel solutions. For a certain type of problems (in particular, design problems as discussed in Chap. 14) this is an undesirable property.

10.4.2 Hybridisation Within Variation Operators: Intelligent Crossover and Mutation

A number of authors have proposed so-called "intelligent" variation operators, which incorporate problem- or instance-specific knowledge. At their most simple, these might take the form of introducing bias into the operators. To give a simple example, if a binary-coded GA is used to select features for use in another classification algorithm, one might attempt to bias the search towards more compact features sets via the use of a greater probability for mutating from the allele value "use" to "don't use" rather than vice versa. A related approach can be seen in [355], where genes encode for microprocessor instructions, which group naturally into sets with similar effects. The mutation operator was then biased to incorporate this expert knowledge, so that mutations were more likely to occur between instructions in the same set than between sets.

A slightly different example of the use of problem-specific (rather than instance-specific) knowledge can be seen in the modified one-point crossover operator used for protein structure prediction in [401]. Here the authors realised that the heritable features being combined by recombination were folds, or fragments of three-dimensional structure. A property of the problem is that during folding protein structures can be free to rotate about peptide bonds. The modified operator made good use of this knowledge by explicitly testing all the possible different orientations of the two fragments, (accomplished by trying all the possible allele values in the gene at the crossover point) in order to find the most energetically favourable. If no feasible conformation was found, then a different crossover point was selected and the process repeated. This can be seen as a simple example of the incorporation of a local search phase into the recombination operator. Note that this should be distinguished from the simpler "crossover hill-climber" proposed in [218], in which all of the l-1 possible offspring arising from one-point crossover are constructed and the best chosen.

At the other end of the scale, at their most complex, the operators can be modified to incorporate highly specific heuristics, which make use of instance-specific knowledge. A good example of this is Merz and Friesleben's distance-preserving crossover (DPX) operator for the TSP [163]. This operator has two motivating principles: making use of instance specific knowledge, whilst at the same time preserving diversity within the population to prevent premature convergence. Diversity is maintained by ensuring that the offspring inherits all of the edges common to both parents, but none of the edges that are present in only one parent, and is thus at the same distance to each parent as they are to each other. The "intelligent" part of the operator comes from the use of a nearest-neighbour heuristic to join together the subtours inherited from the parents, thus explicitly exploiting instance-specific edge length information. It is easy to see how this type of scheme could be adapted to other problems, via the use of suitable heuristics for completing the partial solutions after inheritance of the common factors from both parents.

10.4.3 Local Search Acting on the Output from Variation Operators

The most common use of hybridisation within EAs, and that which fits best with Dawkin's concept of the meme, is via the application of one or more phases of improvement to individual members of the population during the EA cycle, i.e., local search acting on whole solutions created by mutation or recombination. As is suggested from Fig. 10.3 this can occur in different places in cycle i.e., before or after selection or after crossover and/or mutation, but a typical implementation might take the form given in Fig. 10.4

The natural analogies between human evolution and learning, and EAs and artificial neural networks (ANNs) prompted a great deal of research into the use of EAs to evolve the structure of ANNs, which were then trained using back-propagation or similar means during the 1980s and early 1990s. This research gave a great deal of insight into the role of learning, Lamarckianism, and the Baldwin effect to guide evolution (e.g. [199, 207, 264, 400, 421, 422] amongst many others), and served to reinforce messages that were proposed by "real-world" practitioners for several years as to the usefulness of incorporating local search and domain-based heuristics. Since then a number of PhD theses [192, 236, 241, 269, 287] have provided the beginnings of a theoretical analysis, and both theoretical and empirical results to justify an increased interest in these algorithms.

One recent result of particular interest to the practitioner is Krasnogor's formal proof that, in order to reduce the worst-case run times, it is necessary to choose a local search method whose move operator is not the same as

```
BEGIN
  INITIALISE population;
  EVALUATE each candidate;
  REPEAT UNTIL ( TERMINATION CONDITION is satisfied ) DO
    SELECT parents;
    RECOMBINE to produce offspring;
    MUTATE offspring;
    EVALUATE offspring;
    IMPROVE offspring via Local Search;
    SELECT individuals for next generation;
  OD
END
```

Fig. 10.4. Pseudocode for a simple memetic algorithm

those of the recombination and mutation operators [236]. This formalises the intuitive point that within a MA recombination, and particularly mutation, have valuable roles in generating points that lie in different basins of attraction with respect to the local search operator. This diversification is best done either by an aggressive mutation rate, or preferably by the use of a variation operators that have different neighbourhood structures.

10.4.4 Hybridisation During Genotype to Phenotype Mapping

A widely used hybridisation of memetic algorithms with other heuristics is during the genotype–phenotype mapping prior to evaluation. A good example of this is the use of instance-specific knowledge within decoder or repair function, as seen in Sect. 2.4.2 where we can consider the decoder function for the knapsack problem as being a packing algorithm that takes its inputs in the order suggested by the EA.

This approach, where the EA is used to provide the inputs controlling the application of another heuristic, is frequently used; another typical example of this was seen in Sect. 3.9, where a GA was used to suggest the order in which tasks were scheduled using a problem-specific heuristic in a job shop scheduling problem. Similar approaches have been used to great effect for timetabling and scheduling problems [191], and in the "sector first–order second" approach to the vehicle routing problem [397].

As can be seen, there is a common thread to all of these approaches, which is to make use of existing heuristics and domain information wherever possible. The role of the EA is often that of enabling a less biased application of the heuristics, or of problem decomposition, so as to permit the use of sophisticated, but badly scaling heuristics when the overall problem size would preclude their use.

10.5 Design Issues for Memetic Algorithms

So far we have discussed the rationale for the use of problem-specific knowlege or heuristics within EAs, and some possible ways in which this can be done. However, as ever we must accept the caveat that like any other technique, MAs are not some "magic solution" to optimisation problems, and care must be taken in their implementation. In the sections below we briefly discuss some of the issues that have arisen from experience and theoretical reasoning.

10.5.1 Preservation of Diversity

The problem of premature convergence, whereby the population converges around some suboptimal point, is recognised within EAs but is exacerbated in MAs by the effect of local search. If the local search phase continues until each point has been moved to a local optimum, then this leads to an inevitable loss of diversity within the population.[3] A number of approaches have been developed to combat this problem such as:

- When initialising the population with known good individuals, only using a relatively small proportion of them
- Using recombination operators such as Merz's DPX, which are designed to preserve diversity
- Modifying the selection operator to prevent duplicates as in CHC [136]
- Modifying the selection operator or local search acceptance criteria to use a Boltzmann method so as to preserve diversity

This last method bears natural analogies to simulated annealing [2, 227], where worsening moves can be accepted with nonzero probability, to aid escape from local optima, and naturally so, since a number of hybrids of simulated annealing with EAs have been proposed. A promising method that tackles the diversity issue explicitly is proposed in [239], where during the local search phase a less-fit neighbour may be accepted with a probability that increases exponentially as the range of fitness values in the population decreases:

$$P(accept) = \begin{cases} 1 & \text{if } \Delta E > 0, \\ e^{\frac{k\Delta E}{F_{max} - F_{avg}}}, & \text{otherwise,} \end{cases}$$

where k is a normalisation constant and we assume a maximisation problem, $\Delta E = F_{\text{neighbour}} - F_{\text{original}}.$

---

[3] Apart from the exceptional case where each member of the population lies within the basin of attraction of a different local optimum.

10.5.2 Choice of Operators

Probably the most important factor in the design of a memetic agorithm incorporating local search or heuristic improvement is the choice of improving heuristic or local search move operator, that is to say, the way that the set of neighbouring points to be examined when looking for an improved solution is generated.

There has been a large body of theoretical and empirical analysis of the utility of various statistical measures of landscapes for predicting problem difficulty. The interested reader can find a good summary in [221]. Merz and Freisleben [270] consider a number of these measures in the context of memetic algorithms, and show that the choice of move operator can have a dramatic effect on the efficiency and effectiveness of the local search, and hence of the resultant MA. We have already mentioned Krasnogor's PLS complexity analysis result, which suggests that to reduce the worst-case time complexity of the algorithm it is desirable for the move operator of the LS to define a different landscape to the mutation and crossover operators.

In general then, it is worth giving careful consideration to the choice of move operators used when designing a MA: for example, using 2-opt for a TSP problem might yield better improvement if not used in conjunction with the inversion mutation operator described in Sect. 3.4.4. In some cases, domain-specific information may be used to guide the choice of neighbourhood structure within the local search algorithms. However, it was recently shown that the optimal choice of operators can be not only instance specific within a class of problems [270, pp. 254–258], but also dependant on the state of the evolutionary search [240]. This result is not surprising when we consider that points that are locally optimal with respect to one neighbourhood structure may not be with respect to another (unless, of course, they are globally optimal). Thus if a set of points has converged to the state where all are locally optimal with respect to their current neighbourhoods, then changing the move operator may provide a means of progression in addition to recombination and mutation.

One simple way to surmount these problems, is the use of *multiple* local search operators in tandem, in a similar fashion to the use of multiple variation operators seen in Sect. 3.4 and Chapter 8. An example of this can be seen in [237],where a range of problem specific move operators, such as local stretches, rotations and reflections, each tailored to different stages of the folding process, are used for a protein structure prediction problem within the context of what is called a *multimemetic algorithm* [240].

The use of a set of possible local search strategies has the pleasing advantage that they are easily seen to be analagous to Dawkin's memes. The extension of this approach to allow the adaptation of the local search "memes" in the form of a coevolving population, amd the implications for search is currently under way in different research groups [67, 238, 351, 350].

10.5.3 Use of Knowledge

A final point that might be taken into consideration when designing a new memetic algorithm concerns the use and reuse of knowledge gained during the optimisation process. To a certain extent this is done automatically by recombination, but generally speaking explicit mechanisms are not used.

One possible hybridisation that explicitly uses knowledge about points already searched to guide optimisation is with **tabu search** [168]. In this algorithm a "tabu" list of visited points is maintained, which the algorithm is forbidden to return to. Such methods appear to offer promise for maintaining diversity. Similarly, it is easy to imagine extensions to the Boltzmann acceptance/selection schemes that utilise information about the spread of genotypes in the current population, or even past populations, when deciding whether to accept new solutions.

10.6 Example Application: Multistage Memetic Timetabling

In order to illustrate some of the ways that EAs can be combined with other techniques, we take as our example an application to examination timetabling described in [69]. Timetabling is in general an NP-complete problem, and the examination timetabling application is particularly beloved of academic researchers, not least because they are regularly made aware of its importance and difficulty. The general form that the problem takes is of a set of examinations E, each of which has a number of seats required s_i, to schedule over a set of time periods P. Usually a co-occurrence matrix C is provided, where c_{ij} gives the number of students sitting both exams i and j. If feasible solutions exist, then this is a constraint satisfaction problem, but in general this might not be the case, so it is more common to take an indirect approach and treat it as a constrained optimisation problem via the use of a penalty function.[4] This function considers a number of terms

- Exams cannot be scheduled in a room that does not have adequate capacity.
- It is highly undesirable to timetable two exams i and j at the same time if $c_{ij} > 0$ since this requires quaranteening those students until they can sit the second paper.
- It is desirable not to have students sitting two exams on the same day.
- It is preferable not to have students sitting exams in consecutive periods, even if there is a night between them.

This timetabling problem has been well studied, and many heuristic approaches have been proposed, but a common problem has been that they do

---

[4] See Chap. 12.

not always scale well. The approach documented by Burke and Newell is particularly interesting and is relevant to this chapter because it has the following features:

- A decomposition approach is taken, whereby a heuristic scheduler breaks down the problem into smaller parts that can be more easily solved by an optimisation technique.
- The optimisation heuristic used is an EA.
- The EA itself incorporates other heuristics, i.e., it is an MA in its own right.

The heuristic scheduler divides the set E into a number of equal-sized smaller sub-groups, which are scheduled in turn. Thus when scheduling the elements of the nth subgroup, the elements of the previous n-1 subgroups are already in place and cannot be altered. The set E is partitioned by using a metric to estimate the difficulty of scheduling each exam, and then ranking the exams so that the most difficult ones are scheduled first. Three different metrics are considered, based on the number of conflicts with other events, the number of conflicts with *previously scheduled* events, and the number of valid periods for an event left in the timetable. The authors also consider the use of "look-ahead" techniques in which two subsets are considered, but only one timetabled.

This strategy could of course be used with any one of a number of techniques embedded within it to handle the timetabling of each subset in turn. The heuristic chosen is itself a memetic algorithm with the parameters listed in Table 10.1.

Representation	Set of linked lists of exams, each encoding for one period
Recombination	None
Mutation	Random choice of "light" or "heavy" mutation
Mutation probability	100%
Parent selection	Exponential ranking
Survival selection	Best 50 of 100 offspring
Population size	50
Initialisation	Randomly generated then local search applied to each
Termination condition	Five generations with no improvement in best fitness
Special Features	Local search (to local optimum) applied after mutation

Table 10.1. Table describing MA embedded with multistage timetabling algorithm

As can be seen, there are several points worth commenting on. Each member of the initial population is created by generating a random permutation of the exams, and then (in that order) assigning each one to the first valid period. The local search algorithm is always applied until a locally optimal solution is reached, but it uses a greedy ascent mechanism so there is some variability in the output. It is applied to each initial solution, and to each offspring, thus the EA is always working with solutions that are locally optimal, at least with respect to this operator.

The authors reported that previous experiments motivated them against the use of recombination for this problem, but instead each offspring is created via the use of one of two problem-specific mutation operators. The "light" operator is a version of scramble mutation that checks for the feasibility of the solutions it produces. The "heavy" mutation operator is highly instance specific. It looks at the parent and calculates a probability of "disrupting" the events in each period based on the amount of penalty it seems to be causing. However, this operator also makes use of knowledge from other solutions, since these probabilities of disruption are modified by reference to the best-performing solution in the current population.

The results obtained by this algorithm are impressive, both in terms of speed and quality of solutions. It is worth emphasising the following points that have led to this success:

- The combination of heuristic sequencing with an EA-based approach finds better results faster than either approach does on its own.
- The algorithm uses local search so that its initial population is already considerably better than random.
- Strong selection pressure is applied: both exponential ranking for parent selection plus (50,100) survivor selection.
- Intelligent mutation operators are used. One uses instance-specific information to prevent it from producing solutions that violate the most important constraints. The second is highly problem specific, aimed at disrupting "poor" periods.
- The "heavy" mutation operator makes use of information from the rest of the population to decide how likely it is to disrupt a period.
- The depth of local search is always maximal, i.e., the parent population will only come from the set of local optima of the local search landscape.
- Despite the strong selection pressure, and the point above, the fact that mutation is always applied, and that all the search operators have different underlying move mechanisms, means that a premature loss of diversity is avoided.
- As detailed in the paper, there is major use of a variety of coding and algorithmic strategies to avoid full evaluation of solutions and to speed up the manipulation of partial solutions.

10.7 Exercises

1. Describe how the use of Lamarkian and Baldwinian versions of local search methods in memetic algorithms change the size of the search space explored by the underlying EA.

2. Implement a simple memetic algorithm using a single iteration of a bit-flipping local search within the code for the SGA you developed for One-Max in Chapter 3. *Before* you run the experiment, justify whether you think steepest or greedy ascent will be most efficient on this problem.

10.8 Recommended Reading for this Chapter

1. P. Moscato. Memetic algorithms' home page.
   http://www.densis.fee.unicamp.br/~moscato/memetic_home.html
   A Web site containing a huge bibliography and lsts of memetic algorithms and related works, plus links to the home pages of researchers in this area.

2. S. Blackmore. *The Meme Machine*. Oxford University Press, Oxford UK, 1999.

3. Corne, Dorigo and Glover (editors). *New Ideas in Optimization*, Chapters 14–18, pages 217–294 McGraw Hill, London 1999

11

Theory

11.1 Aims of this Chapter

In this chapter we present a brief overview of some of the approaches taken to analysing and modelling the behaviour of Evolutionary Algorithms. The "Holy Grail" of these efforts is the formulation of predictive models describing the behaviour of an EA on arbitrary problems, and permitting the specification of the most efficient form of optimiser for any given problem. However, (at least in the authors' opinions) this is unlikely ever to be realised, and most researchers will currently happily settle for techniques that provide *any* verifiable insights into EA behaviour, even on simple test problems. The reason for what might seem like limited ambition lies in one simple fact: evolutionary algorithms are hugely complex systems, involving many random factors. Moreover, while the field of EAs is fairly young, it is worth noting that the field of population genetics and evolutionary theory has a head start of more than a hundred years, and is still battling against the barrier of complexity.

Full descriptions and analysis of the various techniques currently used to develop EA theory would require both an amount of space and an assumption of prior knowledge of mathematics and statistics that are unsuitable here. We therefore restrict ourselves to a fairly brief description of the principal methods and results. For further details, we point the interested reader to the suggested texts at the end of this chapter, ranging from "bird's eye overviews" [124] to extensive monographs [50, 411]. We begin by describing some of the approaches taken to modelling EAs using a discrete representation (i.e., for combinatorial optimisation problems), before moving on to describe the techniques used for continuous representations. This chapter finishes with a description of an important theoretical result concerning all optimisation algorithms, the No Free Lunch (NFL) theorem.

11.2 Competing Hyperplanes in Binary Spaces: the Schema Theorem

11.2.1 What is a Schema?

Since Holland's initial analysis, two related concepts have dominated much of the theoretical analysis and thinking about GAs. These are the concepts of **schema** (plural schemata) and **building blocks**. A schema is simply a hyperplane in the search space, and the common representation of these for binary alphabets uses a third symbol — # the "don't care" symbol. Thus for a five-bit problem, the schema 11### is the hyperplane defined by having ones in its first two positions. All strings meeting this criterion are **instances**, or examples, of this schema (in this case there are $2^3 = 8$ of them). The fitness of a schema is the mean fitness of all strings that are examples of it; in practice this is often estimated from samples when there are a lot of such strings. Global optimisation can be seen as the search for the schema with zero "don't care" symbols, which has the highest fitness.

Holland's initial work showed that the analysis of GA behaviour was far simpler if carried out in terms of schemata. This is an example of **aggregation** in which rather than model the evolution of all possible strings, they are grouped together in some way and the evolution of the aggregated variables is modelled. He showed that a string of length l is an example of 2^l schemata. Although in general there will not be as many as $\mu \cdot 2^l$ distinct schemata in a population of size μ, he derived an estimate that a population will usefully process $O(\mu^3)$ schemata. This result, known as **implicit parallelism** is widely quoted as being one of the main factors in the success of GAs.

Two features are used to describe schemata: the **order**, that is, the number of positions in the schema that do not have the # sign, and the **defining length**, that is, the distance between the outermost defined positions (which equals the number of possible crossover points between these positions). Thus the schema H=1##0#1#0 has order $o(H) = 4$ and defining length $d(H) = 8 - 1 = 7$.

The number of examples of a schema in an evolving population depends on the effects of variation operators. While selection operators can only change the relative frequency of pre-existing examples, variation operators such as recombination and mutation can both create new examples and disrupt current examples. In what follows we will use the notation $Pd(H, x)$ to denote that probability that the action of an operator x on an instance of a schema H is to destroy it, and $Ps(H)$ to denote the probability that a string containing an instance of schema H is selected.

11.2.2 Holland's Formulation for the SGA

Holland's analysis applied to the standard genetic algorithm (SGA) using fitness proportionate parent selection, one-point crossover (1X), and bitwise mutation, with a generational scheme for survivor selection. Considering a genotype of length l that contains an example of a schema H, the schema may be disrupted if the crossover point falls between the ends, which happens with probability

$$Pd(H, 1X) = \frac{d(H)}{(l-1)}.$$

The probability that bitwise mutation with probability P_m will disrupt the schema H is proportional to the order of the schema: $Pd(H, mutation) = 1 - (1 - P_m)^{o(H)}$, which after expansion, and ignoring high-order terms in P_m, approximates to

$$Pd(H, mutation) = o(H) \cdot P_m.$$

The probability of a schema being selected depends on the fitness of the individuals in which it appears relative to the total population fitness, and the number of examples present $n(H, t)$. Using $f(H)$ to represent the **fitness of the schema** H, defined as the mean fitness of individuals that are examples of schema H, and $<f>$ to denote the mean population fitness, we obtain:

$$Ps(H, t) = \frac{n(H, t) \cdot f(H)}{\mu \cdot <f>}.$$

Noting that μ independent samples are taken to create the next set of parents, the expected number of instances of H in the population after selection is then

$$n'(H, t) = \mu \cdot Ps(H, t) = \frac{n(H, t) \cdot f(H)}{<f>}.$$

After normalising by μ (to make the result population-size independent), allowing for the disruptive effects of recombination and mutation derived above, and using an inequality to allow for the creation of new instances of H by the variation operators, the proportion $m(H)$ of individuals representing schema H at subsequent time-steps is given by:

$$m(H, t+1) \geq m(H, t) \cdot \frac{f(H)}{<f>} \cdot \left[1 - \left(p_c \cdot \frac{d(H)}{l-1} \right) \right] \cdot [1 - p_m \cdot o(H)], \quad (11.1)$$

where p_c and p_m are the probabilities of applying crossover, and the bitwise mutation probability, respectively.

This is the **schema theorem**, and the original understanding of this result was that schemata of above-average fitness would increase their number of instances within the population from generation to generation. We can quantify this by noting that the condition for a schema to increase its representation is $m(H, t+1) > m(H, t)$ which is equivalent to:

$$\frac{f(H)}{<f>} > \left[1 - \left(p_c \cdot \frac{d(H)}{l-1} \right) \right] \cdot [1 - p_m \cdot o(H)].$$

11.2.3 Schema-Based Analysis of Variation Operators

Holland's original formulation of the schema theorem was for one-point crossover and bitwise mutation as we have seen above. Following the rapid proliferation of alternative variation (particularly recombination) operators as the field of genetic algorithms expanded and diversified, a considerable body of results was developed in order to try and understand why some operators gave improved performance on certain problems. Particularly worthy of mention within this were two long-term research programs. Over a number of years, Spears and De Jong developed analytical results for $Pd(H, x)$ as function of defining length $d(H)$ and order $o(H)$ for a number of different recombination and mutation operators [103, 104, 374, 378, 379, 380], which are brought together in [377].

Meanwhile, Eshelman and Schaffer conducted a series of empirical studies [138, 140, 141, 335] in which they compared the effects of mutation with various crossover operators on the performance of a GA. They introduced the notion of **operator bias** to describe the interdependence of $Pd(H, x)$ on $d(H), o(H)$ and x, which takes two forms:

- If an operator x displays **positional bias** it is more likely to keep together bits that are close together in the representation. This has the effect that given two schemata H_1, H_2 with $f(H_1) = f(H_2)$ and $d(H_1) < d(H_2)$, then $Pd(H_1, x) < Pd(H_2, x)$.
- By contrast, if an operator displays **distributional bias** then the probability that it will transmit a schema is a function of $o(H)$. One example of this is bitwise mutation, where as we have seen the probability of disruption increases with the order: $Pd(H, mutation) \approx Pm \cdot o(H)$. Another example is Uniform Crossover which will on average select half of the genes from one parent, and so is increasingly likely to disrupt a schema as the ratio $o(H)/l$ increases beyond 0.5.

Although these results provided valuable insight and have informed many practical implementations, it is worth bearing in mind that they are only considering the disruptive effects of operators. Analysis of the constructive effects of operators in creating new instances of a schema H are harder, since these effects depend heavily on the constitution of the current population. However, under some simplifying assumptions, Spears and DeJong [380] developed the surprising result that the expected number of instances of a schema destroyed by a recombination operator is equal to the expected number of instances created, for all recombination operators!

11.2.4 Walsh Analysis and Deception

If we return our attention to the derivation of the schema theorem, we can immediately see from an examination of the disruption probabilities given above that *all other things being equal*, short low-order schema have a greater chance of being transmitted to the next generation than longer or higher order schema of the same mean fitness. This analysis has led to what has become known as the **building block hypothesis** [172, pp. 41–45], which is that GAs begin by selecting amongst competing short low-order schemata, and then progressively combine them to create higher order schemata, repeating this process until (hopefully) a schema of length l-1 and order l, i.e., the globally optimal string, is created and selected for. Note that for two schemata to compete they must have fixed bits (1 or 0) in the same positions. Thinking along these lines raised the obvious question: "What happens if the global optimum is *not* an example of the low-order schemata that have the highest mean fitness?".

To give an immediate example, let us consider a four-bit problem that has 0000 as its global optimum. It turns out that it is relatively simple to create the situation where all of the order-n schemata containing a 0's in their defining positions are less fit than the corresponding schemata with 1's in those position, i.e., $f(0\#\#\#) < f(1\#\#\#)$, $f(\#0\#\#) < f(\#1\#\#)$, etc., right up to $f(\#000) < f(\#111)$, $f(0\#00) < f(1\#11)$, etc. All that is required to achieve this is that the fitness of globally optimal string is sufficiently greater than all the other strings in every schema of which it is a member. In this case we might expect that every time the GA makes a decision between two order-n schemata, it is likely make the "wrong" decision unless $n=4$.

This type of problem is known as **deceptive** and has been of great interest since it would appear to make life hard for a GA, in that the necessary building blocks for successful optimisation are not present. However, it has been postulated that if a fitness function is composed of a number of deceptive problems, then at least a GA using recombination offers the possibility that these can be solved independently and "mixed" via crossover. By comparison, an optimisation technique relying on local search continuously makes decisions on the basis of low order-schema, and so is far more likely to be "fooled". Note that we have not provided a formal definition of the conditions necessary for a function to be deceptive; much work has been done on this subject and slightly differing definitions exist [185, 368, 418].

The importance of deceptive problems to GA theory and analysis is debatable. At various stages some eminent practitioners have made claims that "the only challenging problems are deceptive"[87], (although this view may have been modified with hindsight), but others have argued forcibly against the relevance of deception. Grefenstette showed that it is simple to circumnavigate the problem of deception in GAs by looking for the best solution in each new generation and then creating its inverse [185]. Moreover, Smith and Smith created an abstract randomised test problem generator (NKPRS) in which the probability of that a landscape was deceptive could be directly manipulated [369]. Their findings did not demonstrate that there was a correlation between the likelihood of deception and the ability of a standard GA to discover the global optimum.

Much of the work in this area makes use of **Walsh functions** to analyse fitnesses. This technique was first used for GA analysis in [49], but became more widely known after a series of important papers by Goldberg [170, 171]. Essentially these are a set of functions that provide a natural basis for the decomposition of a binary search landscape. This can be thought of as equivalent to the way that Fourier transforms provide a natural way of decomposing a complex signal in the time domain into a weighted sum of sinusoidal waves, which can be represented and manipulated in the frequency domain. Just as Fourier transforms form a vital part in a huge range of signal processing and other engineering applications, because sine functions are so easily manipulable, so Walsh transforms form an easily manipulable way of analysing binary search landscapes, with the added bonus that there is a natural correspondence between Walsh partitions (the equivalent of harmonic frequencies) and schemata. For more details on Walsh analysis the reader is directed to [170] or [318].

11.2.5 Criticisms and Recent Extensions of the Schema Theorem

Despite the attractiveness of the schema theorem as a description for how GAs work, it is important to note that it has come in for a good amount of criticism, and quantities of experimental evidence and theoretical arguments have been produced to dispute its importance. This is perhaps inevitable given that early on some rather extravagant claims were made by its adherents, and given the perhaps natural tendency of humans to take pot-shots at "sacred cows".

Ironically, empirical counterevidence was provided by Holland himself, in conjunction with Mitchell and Forrest, who created the **Royal Road functions** based on schema ideas (see Appendix B for a description) in order to demonstrate the superiority of GAs over local search methods. Unfortunately, their results demonstrated that the opposite was in fact true [159], although they did lead to the understanding of the phenomenon of **hitchhiking** whereby an unfavourable allele becomes established in the population because of an early association with an instance of a high-fitness schema.

Theoretical arguments against the value of the schema theorem and associated analysis have included:

- Findings that Holland's idea that fitness proportionate selection allocated optimal amounts of trials to competing schemata is incorrect [255, 325].
- Observations that the rate of increase in representation of any given schema is not exponential, since its selective advantage $f(H)/<f>$ decreases as its share of the population increases and the mean fitness rises accordingly.
- The observation that Eq. (11.1) applies to the *estimated* fitness of a given schema as averaged over all the instances in the current population, which might not be representative of the schema as a whole. Thus although

the schema theorem is correct in predicting the frequency of a schema in the next generation, it can tell us almost *nothing* about the frequency in future generations, since as the proportions of other schema change, so will the composition of the set of strings which represent H, and hence the estimates of $f(H)$.

- The fact that the schema theorem ignores the constructive effects of operators. Altenberg [6] showed that in fact the schema theorem is a special case of Price's theorem in population genetics. This latter includes both constructive and disruptive terms. Whilst exact versions of the schema theorem have recently been derived [385], these currently remain somewhat intractable even for relatively simple test problems, although their use is starting to offer interesting new perspectives.

These arguments and more are summarised eloquently in [318, pp. 74–90]. We should point out that despite these criticisms, schemata represent a useful tool for understanding *some* of how GAs work, and we would wish to stress the vital role that Holland's insights into the importance of schemata have had in the development of genetic algorithms.

11.2.6 Gene Linkage: Identifying and Recombining Building Blocks

As noted in Sect. 11.2.4, the Building Block Hypothesis offers an explanation of the operation of GAs as a process of discovering and putting together blocks of coadapted genes of increasing higher orders. In order to do this, it is necessary for the GA to discriminate between competing schemata on the basis of their estimated fitness. The Messy GA [174] was an attempt to explicitly construct an algorithm that worked in this fashion. The use of a representation that allowed variable length strings and removed the need to manipulate strings in the order of their expression began a focus on the notion of gene linkage (in this context gene is taken to mean the combination of a particular allele value in a particular locus).

Munetomo and Goldberg [291] identify three approaches to the identification of linkage groups. The first of these they refer to as the "direct detection of bias in probability distributions", and is exemplified by what Bosman and Thierens [60] refer to as **distribution estimation algorithms** (DEAs). Examples of this approach include [35, 109, 142, 289, 290, 302, 304], a good review is given in [303]. Common to all of these approaches is the notion of first identifying a factorisation of the problem into a number of subgroups, such that a given statistical criterion is minimised, based on the current population. This corresponds to learning a linkage model of the problem. Once these models have been derived, conditional probabilities of gene frequencies within the linkage groups are calculated, and a new population is generated based on these, replacing the traditional recombination and mutation steps of an EA. It should be emphasised that these DEA approaches are based on statistical modelling rather than on a schema-based analysis. However, since they implicitly construct a linkage analysis of the problem, it would be inappropriate not to mention them here.

The other two approaches identified by Munetomo and Goldberg use more traditional recombination and mutation stages, but bias the recombination operator to use linkage information.

In [223, 291] first-order statistics based on pairwise perturbation of allele values are used to identify the blocks of linked genes that algorithms manipulate. Similar statistics are used in a number of other schemes such as [403].

The third approach identified does not calculate statistics on the gene interactions based on perturbations, but rather adapts linkage groups explicitly or implicitly via the adaptation of recombination operators. Examples of this approach that explicitly adapt linkage models can be seen in [190, 328, 356, 358, 359]. A mathematical model of the linkage models of different operators, together with an investigation of how the adaptation of linkage must happen at an appropriate level (see Sect. 8.4.4 for a discussion of the issue of the scope of adaptation) can be found in [353].

11.3 Dynamical Systems

The **dynamical systems** approach to modelling EAs in finite search spaces has principally been concerned with genetic algorithms because of their (relative) simplicity. The principal contributor to this branch of analysis has been Michael Vose, who established the basic formalisms and results in a string of papers culminating in the publication of his book [411]. This work has been taken on and extended by a number of authors (see, for example, the proceedings of the Foundations of Genetic Algorithms workshops [39, 261, 308]). The approach can be characterised as follows:

- Start with an n-dimensional vector $\bar{p}$, where n is the size of the search space, and the component p_i^t represents the proportion of the population that is of type i at iteration t.
- Construct a **mixing matrix** M representing the effects of recombination and mutation, and a **selection matrix** F representing the effects of the selection operator on each string for a given fitness function.
- Compose a "genetic operator" $G = F \circ M$ as the matrix product of these two functions.
- The action of the GA to generate the next population can then be characterised as the application of this operator G to the current population: $\bar{p}^{t+1} = G\bar{p}^t$.

Under this scheme the population can be envisaged as a point on what is known as the "simplex": a surface in n-dimensional space made up of all the possible vectors whose components sum to 1.0 and are nonnegative. The form of G governs the way that a population will trace a trajectory on this surface as it evolves. A common way of visualising this approach is to think of G as defining a "force-field" over the simplex describing the direction and intensity of the forces of evolution acting on a population. The form of G alone determines which points on the surface act as **attractors** towards which the population is drawn, and analytical analysis of G, and its constituents F and M, has led to many insights into GA behaviour.

Vose and Liepens [412] presented models for F and M under fitness proportionate selection, one-point crossover and bitwise mutation, and these have been extended to other operators in [411]. One of the insights gained by analysing the form of M is that schemata provided a natural way of aggregating strings into equivalence classes under recombination and mutation, which provides a nice tie-in to Holland's ideas.

Other authors have examined a number of alternative ways of aggregating the elements in the search space into a smaller number of equivalence classes, so as to make the models more amenable to solution. Using this approach, a number of important results have been derived, explaining facets of behaviour such as the punctuated equilibria effect (described qualitatively in [412] but expanded and including for the first time *accurate* predictions of the time spent between the discovery of new fitness levels in [404]). These ideas have also been extended to model extensions to binary coded GAs, for example, different forms of self-adaptive mutation [349, 354].

It is worth pointing out that while this model exactly predicts the *expected* proportions of different individuals present in evolving populations, these values can only be attained if the population size is infinite. For this reason this approach falls into a class known as **infinite population models**. For finite populations, the evolving vectors $\bar{p}$ can be thought of as representing the probability distribution from which μ independent samples are drawn to generate the next population. Because the smallest proportion that can be present in a real population has a size $1/\mu$, this effectively constrains the population to move between a subset of points on the simplex representing a lattice of size $1/\mu$. This means that given an initial population, the trajectory predicted may not actually be attainable, and corrections must be made for finite population effects. This work is still ongoing.

11.4 Markov Chain Analysis

Markov chain analysis is a well-established technique that is used to study the properties and behaviour of stochastic systems. A good description can be found in many textbooks on stochastic processes [200]. For our purposes it is sufficient to note that we can describe a system as a discrete-time **Markov chain** provided that the following conditions are met:

- The system can be characterised at any given time by being in one of a finite number (N) of states.

- The probability that the system will be in any given state X^{t+1} in the next iteration is solely determined by the state that it is in at the current iteration X^t, regardless of the previous sequence of states.

The impact of the second condition is that we can define a **transition matrix** Q where the entry Q_{ij} contains the probability of moving from state i to state j in a single step $(i, j \in \{1, \ldots, N\})$. It is simple to show that the probability that after n steps the system has moved from state i to state j is given by the (i, j)th entry of matrix Q^n. A number of well-known theorems and proofs exist for making predictions of the behaviour of Markov chains, such as the mean time to reach a given set of states, etc.

There are a finite number of ways in which we can select a finite sized population from a finite search space, so we can treat any EA working within a such a representation as a Markov chain whose states represent the different possible populations, and a number of authors have used these techniques to study evolutionary algorithms.

As early as in 1989 Eiben et al. [1, 114] proposed a model for the abstract genetic algorithm built from a choice, a production, and a selection function, and used it to establish convergence properties through Markov chain analysis. In contemporary terminology it is a general framework for EAs based on parent selection, variation, and survivor selection, respectively. It has been proved that an EA optimising a function over an arbitrary finite space converges to an optimum with probability 1 under some rather permissive conditions. Simplifying and reformulating the results, it is shown that if in any given population

- Every individual has a nonzero probability to be selected as a parent, and
- Every individual has a nonzero probability to be selected as a survivor, and
- The survival selection mechanism is elitist, and
- Any solution can be created by the action of variation operators with a nonzero probability

then the nth generation would certainly contain the global optimum for some n.

Rudolph [323] tightened the assumptions and showed that a genetic algorithm with nonzero mutation and elitism will always converge to the globally optimal solution, but that this would not necessarily happen if elitism was not used. In [324] the convergence theorems are extended to EAs working in arbitrary (e.g., continuous) search spaces.

A number of authors have proposed exact formulations for the transition matrices Q of binary coded genetic algorithms with fitness proportionate selection, one-point crossover, and bit-flipping mutation [93, 292]. They essentially work by decomposing the action of a GA into two functions, one of which encompasses recombination and mutation (and is purely a function of the crossover probability and mutation rate), and the other that represents the action of the selection operator (which encompasses information about the fitness function). These represent a significant step towards developing a general theory; however, their usefulness is limited by the fact that the associated transition matrices are enormous: for an l-bit problem there are $\binom{\mu + 2^l - 1}{2^l - 1}$ possible populations of size μ and this many rows and columns in the transition matrix.

It is left as an exercise for the reader to calculate the size of the transition matrix for a ten-bit problem with ten members in the population, in order to give a feel for how likely it is that advances in computing will make it possible to manipulate these matrices.

11.5 Statistical Mechanics Approaches

The **statistical mechanics** approach to modelling EA behaviour was inspired by the way that complex systems consisting of ensembles of many smaller parts have been modelled in physics. Rather than trying to trace the behaviour of all the elements of a system (the **microscopic** approach), this approach focuses on modelling the behaviour of a few variables that characterise the system. This is known as the **macroscopic approach**. There are obvious links to the aggregating versions of the dynamical systems approach described above; however, the quantities modelled are related to the cumulants of the variables of interest [311, 312, 314, 320, 345].

Thus if we are interested in the fitness of an evolving population, equations are derived that yield the progress of the "moments" of fitness $<f>$, $<f^2>$, $<f^3>$, and so on (where the braces $<>$ denote that the mean is taken over the set of possible populations) under the effects of selection and variation. From these properties, cumulants such as the mean ($<f>$ by definition), variance, skewness, etc., of the evolving population can be predicted as a function of time. Note that these predictions are necessarily approximations whose accuracy depends on the number of moments modelled.

The equations derived rely on various "tricks" from the statistical mechanics literature and are predominantly for a particular form of selection (Boltzmann selection). The approach does not pretend to offer predictions other than of the population mean, variance and so on, so it cannot be used for all the aspects of behaviour one might desire to model. This techniques are nevertheless impressively accurate at predicting the behaviour of "real" GAs on a variety of simple test functions. In [313] Prügel-Bennett compares this approach with a dynamical systems approach based on aggregating fitness classes and concludes that the latter approach is less accurate at predicting dynamic behaviour of the population mean fitness (as opposed to the long-term limit) because the variables that it tracks are not representative as a result of the averaging process. Clearly this work deserves further study.

11.6 Reductionist Approaches

So far we have described a number of methods for modelling the behaviour of EAs that attempt to make predictions about the composition of the next population by considering the effect of all the genetic operators on the current population. We could describe these as holistic approaches, since they explicitly recognise that there will be interactions between the effects of different operators on the evolving population. An unfortunate side effect of this holistic approach is that either the resulting systems become very difficult to manipulate, as a result of their sheer size, or necessarily involve approximations and may not model all of the variables that we would like to predict.

An alternative methodology is to take a reductionist approach, in which parts of the system are examined separately. Although ultimately flawed in neglecting interaction effects, this approach is common to many branches of physics and engineering, where it has been used to yield frequently accurate predictions and insights, provided that a suitable decomposition of the system is made.

The advantage of taking a reductionist approach is that frequently it is possible to derive analytical results and insights when only a part of the problem is considered. A typical division is between selection and variation. A great deal of work has been done on characterising the effects of different selection operators, which can be thought of as complementary to the work described in Section 11.2.3.

Goldberg and Deb [173] introduced the concept of **takeover time**, which is the number of generations needed for a single copy of the fittest string to completely take over the population in a "selecto-EA" (i.e., one in which no are variation operators used). This work has been extended to cover a variety of different mechanisms for parental and survivor selection, using a variety of theoretical tools such as difference equations, order statistics, and Markov chains [19, 20, 21, 54, 75, 76, 326, 364].

Parallel to this, Goldberg, Thierens, and others examined what they called the **mixing time**, which characterises the speed at which recombination brings together building blocks initially present in different members of a population [398]. Their essential insight is that in order to build a well-performing EA, in particular a GA, it is necessary for the mixing time to be less than the takeover time, so that all possible combinations of the building blocks present can be tried before one fitter string takes over the population and removes some of them. While the rigour of this approach can be debated, it does have the immense benefit of providing practical guidelines for population sizing, operator probabilities, choice of selection methods and so on, which can be used to help design an effective EA for new applications.

11.7 Analysing EAs in Continuous Search Spaces

In contrast to the situation with discrete search spaces, the state of theory for continuous search spaces, and evolution strategies in particular, is fairly advanced. As noted in Section 11.4, Rudolph has shown the existence of global proofs of convergence also in such spaces [324], since the evolution of the population is itself a Markov process. Unfortunately, it turns out that the Chapman–Kolmogorov equation describing this is intractable, so the population probability distribution as a function of time cannot be determined directly. However, it turns out that much of the dynamics of ESs can be recovered from simpler models concerning the evolution of two macroscopic variables, and many theoretical results have been obtained on this basis.

The first of the variables modelled is the **progress rate**, which measures the distance of the centre of mass of the population from the global optimum (in variable space) as a function of time. The second is the **quality gain**, which measures the expected improvement in fitness between generations.

Most of the modelling approaches have concerned two fitness functions, the **sphere model**,: $f(\overline{x}) = \sum_i x_i^n$ for some power n, and the **corridor model** [342]. The latter takes various forms but essentially contains a single direction in which fitness is improving, hence the name. Variants of these are also used. Since an arbitrary fitness function in a continuous space can be usually be expanded (using a Taylor expansion) to a sum of simpler terms, the vicinity of a local optimum one of these models is often a good approximation to the *local* landscape.

The continuous nature of the search space, coupled with the use of normally distributed mutations and well-known results from order statistics, have permitted a *relatively* straightforward derivation of equations describing the motion of the two macroscopic variables over time as a function of the values of μ, λ, and σ, starting with Rechenberg's analysis of the (1+1) ES on the sphere model, from which he derived the 1/5 success rule [317]. Following from this, the principles of self-adaptation and multimembered strategies have also been analysed. A thorough overview of these results is given by Beyer and Arnold in [51].

11.8 No Free Lunch Theorems

By now we hope the reader will have realised that the search for a mathematical model of EAs, which will permit us to make accurate predictions of a given algorithm on any given problem, is still a daunting distance from its goal. Whilst the tools are now in place to make some accurate predictions of some aspects of behaviour on some problems, these are usually restricted to those such as OneMax (discrete spaces, see Appendix B) or the sphere model (continuous spaces) for which an EA is almost certainly not the most efficient algorithm anyway.

However, a recent line of work has come up with a result that allows us to make some statements about the comparative performance of different algorithms across all problem: they are all the same! This result is known as the **No Free Lunch theorem** (NFL) by Wolpert and Macready [430], and in layperson's terms it says that if we average over the space of all possible problems, then all nonrevisiting **black box algorithms** will exhibit the same performance.

By nonrevisiting we mean that the algorithm does not generate and test the same point in the search space twice. Although not typically a feature of EAs, this can simply be achieved by implementing an archive of all solutions ever seen, and then each time we generate an offspring discarding it and repeating the process if it already exists in the archive. An alternative approach (taken by Wolpert and Macready in their analysis) is to view performance as the number of distinct calls to the evaluation function. In this case we still need an archive, but can allow duplicates in the population. By black box algorithms we mean those that do not incorporate any problem or instance-specific knowledge.

There has been some considerable debate about the utility of the No Free Lunch theorem, often centred around the question of whether the set of problems that we are likely to try to tackle with EAs is representative of all problems, or forms some special subset. However, they have come to be widely accepted, and the following lessons can be drawn:

- If we invent a new algorithm and it appears to be the best ever at solving some particular class of problems, then it will pay for this by performing poorly at some others. This suggests that a careful strategy is required to evaluate new operators and algorithms as discussed in Chap. 14.
- *For a given problem* we can circumvent the NFL theorem by incorporating problem-specific knowledge. This of course leads us towards memetic algorithms (cf. Chap. 10).

11.9 Exercises

1. Let $S_1=$*0**11***0** and $S_2=$*****0*1**** be two schemata.
   a) Give the order and the defining length of S_1 and S_2.
   b) What is the probability for one-point crossover with crossover rate p_c that crossover breaks S_1, respectively S_2? (i.e., the probability that the child created by the operator does not belong to the given schema.)
   c) What is the probability that mutation with mutation rate p_m breaks S_1, respectively S_2?
   d) What is the probability that S_1 respectively S_2 survives the application of both crossover and mutation?
   e) Is it correct to call one of these two schemata a "building block"? Explain why, or why not.

2. Whilst optimising a three-bit problem, you notice that your population, of size 100, consists of 25 copies each of strings 100 (with fitness 10), 111 (with fitness 20), 011 (with fitness 15), and 010 (with fitness 15).
   a) What is the estimated fitness of schema 1## ?
   b) Assuming fitness proportionate selection with no crossover or mutation, show one way by which you could calculate the estimated fitness of that schema in the next generation.
3. In a simple two-dimensional model of protein structure prediction, a solution consists of a sequence of moves (north/east/west/south) on a square grid. The amino acid residues, which compose the protein, are then mapped onto this path, giving the structure of the folded protein. Good solutions typically exhibit a high degree of local structure. That is to say that they can be seen as the concatenation of secondary structure "motifs". Explain how this domain knowledge may be used to guide the choice of recombination operators for this problem.

11.10 Recommended Reading for this Chapter

1. A.E. Eiben and G. Rudolph. Theory of evolutionary algorithms: a bird's eye view. *Theoretical Computer Science*, 229:1–2 pp. 3–9, 1999

2. L. Kallel, B. Naudts, and A. Rogers (editors). *Theoretical Aspects of Evolutionary Computing* Springer, Berlin, Heidelberg, New York, 2001
   A collection of accessible introductory texts by experts in the field

3. C. Reeves and J. Rowe. *Genetic Algorithms: Principles and Perspectives.* Kluwer, Norwell MA, 2002

4. H.-G. Beyer. *The theory of Evolution Strategies.* Springer, Berlin, Heidelberg, New York, 2001

5. W.M. Spears. *Evolutionary Algorithms: the role of mutation and recombination.* Springer, Berlin, Heidelberg, New York, 2000

6. M.D. Vose. *The Simple Genetic Algorithm.* MIT Press, Cambridge MA, 1999

7. D.E. Goldberg *The Design of Innovation: Lessons from and for Competent Genetic Algorithms (Genetic Algorithms and Evolutionary Computation)* Kluwer Academic Press, 2002

Constraint Handling

12.1 Aims of this Chapter

In this chapter we consider the issue of constraint handling by evolutionary algorithms. This issue has great practical relevance because many practical problems are constrained. It is also a theoretically challenging subject since a great deal of intractable problems (NP-hard, NP-complete, etc.) are constrained. The presence of constraints has the effect that not all possible combinations of variable values represent valid solutions to the problem at hand. Unfortunately, constraint handling is not straightforward in an EA, because the variation operators (mutation and recombination) are typically "blind" to constraints. That is, there is no guarantee that even if the parents satisfy some constraints, the offspring will satisfy them as well. In this chapter we elaborate on the notion of constrained problems and distinguish two different types: constrained optimisation problems and constraint satisfaction problems. (This elaboration requires clarifying some basic notions, leading to definitions that implicitly have been used in earlier chapters.) Based on this classification of constrained problems, we discuss what constraint handling means from an EA perspective, and review the most commonly applied EA techniques to treat constraints. Analysing these techniques, we identify a number of common features and arrive at the conclusion that the presence of constraints is not harmful, but rather helpful in that it provides extra information that EAs can utilise.

12.2 Constrained Problems

To facilitate a clear discussion, let us have a look at the very notion of a constrained problem. For instance, consider the travelling salesman problem for n cities $C = \{c_1, \ldots, c_n\}$ and the distance function d. Is this a constrained problem? The answer should be independent from the algorithm we are to apply to solve this problem, but at the first glance this is not the case. To

illustrate this, assume that we chose for an iterative search algorithm that
either:

1. Operates in the search space $S_1 = C^n$ and seeks a solution $s \in S_1$ that
   minimises the tour length $f(\bar{s}) = \sum_{i=1}^{n} d(s_i, s_{i+1})$ with s_{n+1} defined as
   s_1.
2. Operates in the search space $S_2 = \{permutations\ of\ c_1, \ldots, c_n\}$ and seeks
   a solution $s \in S_2$ that minimises the tour length $f(\bar{s})$ defined as above.

Note that in the first case we need a constraint requiring uniqueness of each
city in a solution $\bar{s} \in S_1$, while in the second case we do not as every $\bar{s} \in S_2$
satisfies this condition by the definition of S_2. Thus, the notion of a constrained
problem seems to depend on what we take as search space.

To clarify this matter we introduce some terminology. In the further discussion we assume that a problem is given in terms of its variables $v_i, \ldots, v_n$,
each having its own domain $D_1, \ldots, D_n$, where the domains can be discrete
or continuous.[1] We will call a Cartesian product of sets $S = D_1 \times \ldots \times D_n$ a
free search space. The most important property of free search spaces is that
testing the membership relation of such a space can be done independently
on each coordinate, taking the conjunction of the results. Note that the usual
mutation and recombination operators for bit, integer, and floating-point representation keep the offspring in the search space. In our perception requiring
that a solution be within a free search space has nothing to do with constraints, instead it is merely the specification of the domains of the variables.
In the further discussion we distinguish problems (over a free search space)
by the presence or absence of

1. An objective function
2. Constraints

The resulting four categories are shown in Table 12.1. Next we will discuss
these problem types more precisely.

	Objective function	
Constraints	Yes	No
Yes	Constrained optimisation problem	Constraint satisfaction problem
No	Free optimisation problem	No problem

Table 12.1. Problem types

---

[1] However, we might require that if D_i is continuous, then it is convex.

12.2.1 Free Optimisation Problems

A **free optimisation problem** (FOP) is a pair $\langle S, f \rangle$, where S is a free search space and f is a real-valued objective function on S, which has to be optimised (minimised or maximised). A **solution of a free optimisation problem** is an $\bar{s} \in S$ with an optimal f value.

Examples of FOP's abound in any literature related to optimisation, and some common examples using a variety of domains (binary, discrete, continuous) are given in Appendix B. FOPs do not pose specific challenges to EAs from our present perspective since EAs have a "basic instinct" to optimise. This is, of course, not to say that solving any FOP is easy with an EA, but the absence of constraints implies free search in the sense that the common variation operators do not generate values outside of the domains of the variables.

12.2.2 Constraint Satisfaction Problems

A **constraint satisfaction problem** (CSP) is a pair $\langle S, \phi \rangle$, where S is a free search space and ϕ is a formula (Boolean function on S). A **solution of a constraint satisfaction problem** is an $\bar{s} \in S$ with $\phi(\bar{s}) = true$. The formula ϕ is often called the **feasibility condition**, and it is typically a composed entity, derived from more elementary constraints. A **constraint** is a restriction on the possible value combinations of certain variables.

A well known CSP example is the graph three-colouring problem, where the nodes of a given graph $G = (N, E)$, $E \subseteq N \times N$ have to be coloured by three colours in such a way that no neighbouring nodes, i.e., nodes connected by an edge, have the same colour. This problem can be formalised by means of a CSP $\langle S, \phi \rangle$ as follows:

- $S = D^n$ with $D = \{1, 2, 3\}$ being the same domain for each of the $n = |N|$ variables.
- ϕ is composed of constraints that belong to edges. That is, for each edge $e \in E$, the corresponding constraint c_e is defined by $c_e(\langle s_1, \ldots, s_n \rangle) = true$ if an only if $e = (k, l)$ and $s_k \neq s_l$. Then the feasibility condition is the conjunction of all constraints $\phi(\bar{s}) = \bigwedge_{e \in E} c_e(\bar{s})$.

The main EA challenge in treating CSPs is the absence of an objective function that could be naturally used to define fitness. The feasibility condition imposes only a very simple landscape on candidate solutions having a large flat plateau at zero level (ϕ is false) with some singular peaks (ϕ is true). This is an extreme case of a needle in a haystack problem. The basis of all approaches to design an EA for a CSP is to transform constraints into optimisation objectives and rely on the optimisation power of EAs to achieve these objectives, and thereby to satisfy the constraints. If all constraints of a CSP are handled this way then such a transformation amounts to turning the CSP into an FOP. It should be noted, however, that this is not the only option.

Recall the eight-queens example from Section 2.4.1, which is clearly a CSP (see exercise at the end of this chapter). The evolutionary approach we have outlined uses permutations as chromosomes. These chromosomes represent board configurations where horizontal constraint violations (two queens on the same row) and vertical constraint violations (two queens on the same column) do not occur. Thus, if we can enforce that these constraints are respected at initialisation and remain maintained during the evolutionary search process then the only thing that remains to be achieved is the satisfaction of diagonal constraints. These have been treated by defining the number of such violations as an objective function to be minimised. With our present terminology we can describe this solution as transforming the given CSP into a problem that still has some explicitly present constraints to be satisfied (the horizontal and vertical constraints) together with some objectives to be achieved (number of diagonal constraint violations minimised).

12.2.3 Constrained Optimisation Problems

A **constrained optimisation problem** (COP) is combination of an FOP and a CSP. It is a triple $\langle S, f, \phi \rangle$, where S is a free search space, f is a real-valued objective function on S, and ϕ is a formula (Boolean function on S). A **solution of a constrained optimisation problem** is an $\bar{s} \in S$ with $\phi(\bar{s}) = true$ and an optimal f value.

To illustrate COPs we use the Travelling Salesman Problem for n cities $C = \{c_1, \ldots, c_n\}$ which can be formalised by $\langle S, f, \phi \rangle$.

- The free search space is $S = C^n$.
- The objective function to be minimised is $f(\bar{s}) = \sum_{i=1}^{n} d(s_i, s_{i+1})$, with s_{n+1} defined as s_1.
- The feasibility condition $\phi = \phi_c \wedge \phi_u$ is the conjunction of the following two conditions:
  - $\phi_c(\bar{s}) = true$ if and only if for each $c \in C$ there is an $i \in \{1, \ldots, n\}$ such that $c = s_i$ (completeness condition).
  - $\phi_u(\bar{s}) = true$ if and only if for each $k, l \in \{1, \ldots, n\}$ $s_k \neq s_l$ (unicity condition).

With the aid of this framework we can now unambiguously classify the TSP as a constrained problem, a COP, since its definition involves a feasibility condition restricting the free search space.

Treating COPs by EAs poses very similar questions to those regarding CSPs, namely, the constraints must be handled. Transforming (some of) them into optimisation objectives is again a most straightforward option, although not as essential as for CSP, since a COP does have a natural fitness definition by the given f. If one is to leave constraints as constraints (i.e., not transforming them into optimisation objectives), then these constraints have to be treated explicitly in order to make sure that the candidate solutions satisfy them.

12.3 Two Main Types of Constraint Handling

Various technical options for constraint handling are discussed in Sect. 12.4. Without going into details yet, here we distinguish two conceptually different possibilities. If all constraints in a CSP or COP are replaced by optimisation objectives, then the given problem is transformed into an FOP. Formally we have $\langle S, \bullet, \phi \rangle \rightarrow \langle S, f, \bullet \rangle$, respectively $\langle S, f, \phi \rangle \rightarrow \langle S, g, \bullet \rangle$, where the $\bullet$ is a place-holder for the absent component of the given problem type. In these cases "constraint handling" means "constraint transformation" before running the EA. After the transformation is done, the EA can perform free search without paying any further attention to constraints. It is the algorithm designer's responsibility (and one of the main design guidelines) to ensure that solutions to the transformed FOP represent solutions to the original CSP or COP.

If not all constraints are replaced by optimisation objectives, then the problem that should be solved by the EA still has constraints – it is a COP. This can be the case if:

1. Some constraints of a CSP are not incorporated into the objective function, but left as constraints making up a new, weakened feasibility condition: $\langle S, \bullet, \phi \rangle \rightarrow \langle S, f, \psi \rangle$, which was the case in our eight-queens example.
2. The original COP is not transformed, so we are to design an EA for the given $\langle S, f, \phi \rangle$.
3. Some but not all constraints in a given COP are transformed into optimisation objectives, while the others are left as constraints making up a new, weakened feasibility condition: $\langle S, f, \phi \rangle \rightarrow \langle S, g, \psi \rangle$.

In cases 1 and 3 we have constraint handling in the sense of constraint transformation and in all of these cases we are facing "constraint handling" as "constraint enforcement" during the run of the EA because the (transformed) problem still has a feasibility condition.

Based on these observations we can eliminate an often-occurring ambiguity about constraint handling and identify the following two forms:

- In the case of **indirect constraint handling** constraints are transformed into optimisation objectives. After the transformation, they effectively practically disappear, and all we need to care about is optimising the resulting objective function. This type of constraint handling is done *before* the EA run.

- As an alternative to this option we distinguish **direct constraint handling**, meaning that the problem offered to the EA to solve has constraints (is a COP) that are enforced explicitly *during* the EA run.

It should be clear from the previous discussion that these options are not exclusive: for a given constrained problem (CSP or COP) some constraints might be treated directly and some others indirectly.

It is also important to note that even when all constraints are treated indirectly, so that we apply an EA for an FOP, this does not mean that the EA is necessarily ignoring the constraints. In theory one could fully rely on the general optimisation power of EAs and try to solve the given FOP without taking note of how f is obtained. However, it is also possible that one does take the specific origin of f into account, i.e., the fact that it is constructed from constraints. In this case one can try to make use of specific constraint-based information within the EA by, for instance, special mutation or crossover operators that explicitly aim at satisfying constraints by using some heuristics.

Finally, let us reiterate that indirect constraint handling is always part of the preparation of the problem before offering it to an EA to solve. However, direct constraint handling is an issue within the EA constituting methods that enforce satisfaction of the constraints.

12.4 Ways to Handle Constraints in EAs

In the discussion so far, we have not considered the nature of the domains of the variables. In this respect there are two extremes: they are all discrete or all continuous. Continuous CSPs are almost nonexistent, so by default a CSP is discrete. For COPs this is not the case as we have discrete COPs (**combinatorial optimisation** problems) and continuous COPs as well. Much of the evolutionary literature on constraint handling is restricted to either of these cases, but the ways for handling constraints are practically identical – at least at the conceptual level. In the following treatment of constraint handling methods we will be general, considering discrete and continuous cases together. The commonly shown list of available options is the following:

1. The use of penalty functions that reduce the fitness of infeasible solutions, preferably so that the fitness is reduced in proportion to the number of constraints violated, or to the distance from the feasible region.
2. The use of mechanisms that take infeasible solutions and "repair" them, i.e., return a feasible solution, which one would hope is close to the infeasible one.
3. The use of a specific alphabet for the problem representation, plus suitable initialisation, recombination, and mutation operators such that the feasibility of a solution is always ensured, and there is an unambiguous mapping from genotype to phenotype.

4. The use of "decoder" functions to manage the mapping from genotype to phenotype so that solutions (i.e., phenotypes) are guaranteed to be feasible. This approach differs from the previous one in that typically a number of potentially radically different genotypes may be mapped onto the same phenotype. It has the strong advantage of permitting the use of more standard variation operators.

Notice that the last option amounts to manipulating the search space S. In the discussion so far, within the $\langle S, f, \phi \rangle$ framework, we have only considered problem transformations regarding the f and the ϕ component. Using decoder functions means that a constrained problem (CSP $\langle S, \bullet, \phi \rangle$ or COP $\langle S, f, \phi \rangle$) is transformed into one with a different search space S'. Taking a COP–FOP transformation as an example, this is formally $\langle S, f, \phi \rangle \rightarrow \langle S', g, \bullet \rangle$, where the EA to solve $\langle S, f, \phi \rangle$ actually works on $\langle S', g, \bullet \rangle$. Here, constraint handling is neither transformation nor enforcement, but is carried out through the mapping (decoder) between S and S'. In a way one could say that in this case we do not handle constraints, instead we simply avoid the question by ensuring that a genotype in S' always mapped onto a feasible phenotype in S. For this reason we call this **mapping constraint handling**.

Within our framework we can arrange the above options as follows:

1. Indirect constraint handling (transformation) coincides with **penalising** constraint violations.
2. Direct constraint handling (enforcement) can be carried out in two different ways:
   a) Allowing the generation of candidate solutions that violate constraints: **repairing** infeasible candidates.
   b) Not allowing the generation of candidate solutions that violate constraints: **preserving** feasibility by suitable operators (and initialisation).
3. Mapping constraint handling is the same as **decoding**, i.e., transforming the search space into another one.

In general the presence of constraints will divide the space of potential solutions into two or more disjoint regions, the **feasible region** (or regions) $F \subset S$, containing those candidate solutions that satisfy the given feasibility condition, and the **infeasible region** containing those that do not. In practice, it is common to utilise as much domain-specific knowledge as possible, in order to reduce the amount of time spent generating infeasible solutions. As is pointed out in [277], the global optimum of a COP with continuous variables often lies on, or very near to, the boundary between the feasible and infeasible regions, and promising results are reported using algorithms that specifically search along that boundary. However, we concentrate here on the more general case, since the domain knowledge required to specify such operators may not be present.

In the following sections we briefly describe the above approaches, focusing on the facets that have implications for the applications of EAs in general.

For a fuller review of work in this area, the reader is referred to [112, 126, 275, 277, 352]. Furthermore, [85, 273, 276, 327] are especially recommended because they contain descriptions of problem instance generators for binary CSPs ([85]), continuous COPs ([273, 276]), or a large collection of continuous COP test landscapes [327]), together with detailed experimental results. One general point worth noting is that in [277] it was reported that for problems in the continuous domain, use of a real-valued rather than binary representation consistently gave better results.

12.4.1 Penalty Functions

Assuming a minimisation problem, the use of penalty functions constitutes a mapping from the objective function such that $f'(\bar{x}) = f(\bar{x}) + P(d(\bar{x}, F))$ where F is the feasible region as before, $d(\bar{x}, F))$ is a distance metric of the infeasible point to the feasible region (this might be simply a count of the number of constraints violated) and the penalty function P is monotonically increasing nonnegatively such that $P(0) = 0$.

It should be noted at the outset that this assumes that it is possible to evaluate an infeasible point; although for many problems this may be so (for example, the knapsack problem), for many others this is not the case. This discussion is also confined to *exterior* penalty functions, where the penalty is only applied to infeasible solutions, rather than *interior* penalty functions, where a penalty is applied to feasible solutions in accordance to their distance from the constraint boundary in order to encourage exploration of this region.

The conceptual simplicity of penalty function methods means that they are widely used, and they are especially suited to problems with disjoint feasible regions, or where the global optimum lies on (or near) the constraint boundary. However, their successful use depends on a balance between exploration of the infeasible region and not wasting time, which places a lot of emphasis on the form of the penalty function and the distance metric.

If the penalty function is too severe, then infeasible points near the constraint boundary will be discarded, which may delay, or even prevent, exploration of this region. Equally, if the penalty function is not sufficient in magnitude, then solutions in infeasible regions may dominate those in feasible regions, leading to the algorithm spending too much time in the infeasible regions and possibly stagnating there. In general, for a system with m constraints, the form of the penalty function is a weighted sum

$$P(d(\bar{x}, F)) = \sum_{i=1}^{m} w_i \cdot d_i^{\kappa}(\bar{x})$$

where κ is a user defined constant, often taking the value 1 or 2. The function $d_i(\bar{x})$ is a distance metric from the point $\bar{x}$ to the boundary for that constraint i, whose form depends on the nature of the constraint, but may be a simple binary value according to whether the constraint is satisfied, or a metric based on "cost of repair".

Many different approaches have been proposed, and a good review is given in in [346], where penalty functions are classified as *constant, static, dynamic,* or *adaptive*. This classification closely matches the options discussed in the example given in Sect. 8.3.2.

Static Penalty Functions

Three methods have commonly been used with static penalty functions, namely *extinctive* penalties (where all of the w_i are set so high as to prevent the use of infeasible solutions), binary penalties (where the value d_i is 1 if the constraint is violated, and zero otherwise), and distance-based penalties.

It has been reported that of these three the latter give the best results [172], and the literature contains many examples of this approach. This approach relies on the ability to specify a distance metric that accurately reflects the difficulty of repairing the solution, which is obviously problem dependent, and may also vary from constraint to constraint. The usual approach is to take the square of the Euclidean distance (i.e., set $\kappa = 2$) .

However, the main problem in using static penalty functions remains the setting of the values of w_i. In some situations it may be possible to find these by experimentation, using repeated runs and incorporating domain specific knowledge, but this is a time-consuming process that is not always possible.

Dynamic Penalty Functions

An alternative approach to setting fixed values of w_i by hand is to use dynamic values, which vary as a function of time. A typical approach is that of [217], in which the static values w_i were replaced with a simple function of the form $s_i(t) = (w_i t)^\alpha$, where it was found that for best performance $\alpha \in \{1, 2\}$. Although possibly less brittle as a result of not using fixed (possibly inappropriate) values for the w_i, this approach still requires the user to decide on the initial values.

An alternative approach, which can be seen as the logical extension of this approach, is the behavioural memory algorithm of [338, 387]. In this approach a population is evolved in a number of stages – the same number as there are constraints. In each stage i, the fitness function used to evaluate the population is a combination of the distance function for constraint i with a death penalty for all solutions violating constraints $j < i$. In the final stage all constraints are active, and the objective function is used as the fitness function. It should be noted that different results may be obtained, depending on the order in which the constraints are dealt with.

Adaptive Penalty Functions

Adaptive penalty functions represent an attempt to remove the danger of poor performance resulting from an inappropriate choice of values for the penalty weights w_i. An early approach described in [42, 188] was discussed in Sect. 8.3.2.

A second approach is that of [347, 393], in which adaptive scaling (based on population statistics of the best feasible and infeasible raw fitnesses yet discovered) is coupled with the distance metrics for each constraint based on the notion of "near feasible thresholds". These latter are scaling factors for each distance metric, which can vary with time.

The Stepwise Adaptation of Weights (SAW) algorithm of [130, 131, 132] can be seen as a population-level adaptation of the search space. In this method the weights w_i are adapted according to whether the best individual in the current population violates constraint i. In contrast to the mechanism of Bean and Hadj-Alouane above ([42, 188]), the updating function is much simpler. In this case a fixed penalty increment Δw is added to the penalty values for each of the constraints violated in the best individual of the generation at which the updating takes place. This algorithm was able to adapt weight values that were independent of the GA operators and the initial weight values, suggesting that this is a robust technique.

In the following two sections we discuss direct constraint handling methods. To this end, let us reiterate from Section 12.3 that indirect constraint handling, thus defining penalties, is always part of the preparation of the problem before offering it to an EA to solve. This can be part of solving a CSP or a COP. In contrast to this, direct constraint handling is an issue within the EA, constituting methods that enforce satisfaction of the constraints in the transformed problem. Therefore, the scope of the next two sections is handling COPs with EAs, where the COP might be the result of an earlier problem transformation CSP→COP or COP→COP.

12.4.2 Repair Functions

The use of repair algorithms for solving COPs with GAs can be seen as a special case of adding local search to the GA, where the aim of the local search in this case is to reduce (or remove) the constraint violation, rather than (as is usually the case) to simply improve the value of the fitness function. The use of local search has been intensively researched, with attention focusing on the benefits of so-called Baldwinian versus Lamarkian learning (Sect. 10.3.1). In either case, the repair algorithm works by taking an infeasible point and generating a feasible solution based on it. In the Baldwinian case, the fitness of the repaired solution is allocated to the infeasible point, which is kept, whereas with Lamarkian learning, the infeasible solution is overwritten with the new feasible point.

Although this debate has not been settled within unconstrained learning, many COP algorithms reach a compromise by introducing some stochasticity, for example Michalewicz's GENOCOP algorithm uses the repaired solution around 15% of the time [274].

To illustrate the use of repair functions we will first consider the binary knapsack problem described in Sect. 2.4.2. Although specifying a repair algorithm at first seems simple – simply change gene values from 1 to 0 until the weight constraint is satisfied – it raises some interesting questions. One of these is the replacement question just discussed; the second is whether the genes should be selected for altering in a predetermined order, or at random. In [271] it was reported that using a greedy deterministic repair algorithm gave the best results, and certainly the use of a nondeterministic repair algorithm will add noise to the evaluation of every individual, since the same potential solution may yield different fitnesses on separate evaluations. However, it has been found by some authors [362] that the addition of noise can assist the GA in avoiding premature convergence. In practice it is likely that the best method is not only dependent on the problem instance, but on the size of the population and the selection pressure.

The binary case above is relatively simple, however, in general defining a repair function may be as complex as solving the problem itself. One algorithm that eases this problem (and incidentally uses stochastic repair), is Michalewicz's GENOCOP III algorithm for optimisation in continuous domains [274].

This works by maintaining two populations, one P_s of so-called "search points" and one P_r of "reference points", with all of the latter being feasible. Points in P_r and feasible points from P_s are evaluated directly. When an infeasible point is generated in P_s it is "repaired" by picking a point in P_r and drawing a line segment from it to the infeasible point. This is then sampled until a "repaired" feasible point is found. If the new point is superior to that used from P_r, the new point replaces it. With a small probability (which represents the balance between Lamarkian and Baldwinian search) the new point replaces the infeasible point in P_s. It is worth noting that although two different methods are available for selecting the reference point used in the repair, both are stochastic, so the evaluation is necessarily noisy.

12.4.3 Restricting Search to the Feasible Region

In many COP applications it may be possible to construct a representation and operators so that the search is confined to the feasible region of the search space. In constructing such an algorithm, care must be taken in order to ensure that all of the feasible region is capable of being represented. It is equally desirable that any feasible solution can be reached from any other by (possibly repeated) applications of the mutation operator. The classic example of this is permutation problems. In Sect. 2.4.1 we showed an illustration for the eight-queens Problem and in Sects., 3.4.4 and 3.5.4 we described a number of variation operators that are guaranteed to deliver feasible offspring from feasible parents.

It should be noted that this approach to solving COP, although attractive, is not suitable for all types of constraints. In many cases it is difficult to find an existing or design a new operator that guarantees that the offspring are feasible. Although one possible option is simply to discard any infeasible points and reapply the operator until a feasible solution is generated, the process of checking that a solution is feasible may be so time consuming as to render this approach unsuitable. However, there remains a large class of problems where this approach is valid and with suitable choice of operators can be very successfully applied.

12.4.4 Decoder Functions

Decoder functions are a class of mappings from the genotype space S' to the feasible regions F of the solution space S that have the following properties:

- Every $z \in S'$ must map to a *single* solution $s \in F$.
- Every solution $s \in F$ must have at least one representation $s' \in S'$.
- Every $s \in F$ must have the same number of representations in S' (this need not be 1).

The use of decoder functions can be illustrated on the knapsack problem again. A simple approach here to sort the items by profit/weight ratio, and then represent a potential solution as a binary string of length l where a gene with allele value 1 is included in the subset. It can immediately be seen that this representation permits the creation of infeasible solutions from feasible ones if normal variation operators are used, and that constructing operators that guarantee feasible solutions is decidedly non-trivial. Therefore some form of pruning is needed.

One such decoder approach would start at the left hand end of the string and interpret a 1 as *take this item if possible....* Although a providing relatively simple way of using EAs for this type of problem, such decoder functions are not without their drawbacks. These are centred around the fact that they generally introduce a lot of redundancy into the genotype space. In the first example given, if the weight limit is reached after considering say 5 of 10 genes, then it is irrelevant what values the rest take, and so 2^5 strings all map onto the same solution.

In some cases it may be possible to devise a decoder function that permits the use of relatively standard representation and operators whilst preserving a one-to-one mapping between genotype and phenotype. One such example is the decoder for the TSP problem proposed by Grefenstette, and well described by Michalewicz in [272]. In this case a simple integer representation was used with each gene $a_i \in \{1, \ldots, l + 1 - i\}$. This representation permits the use of "standard" crossover operators and a bitwise mutation operator that randomly resets a gene value to one of its permitted allele values. The outcome of both of these operators is guaranteed to be valid. The decoder function works by considering an ordered list of cities, $\{ABCDE\}$, and using the genotype to index into this.

For example, with a genotype $\{4, 2, 3, 1, 1\}$ the first city in the constructed tour is the fourth item in the list, i.e., D. This city is then removed from the list and the second gene is considered, which in this case points to B. This process is continued until a complete tour is constructed: $\{4, 2, 3, 1, 1\} \rightarrow DBEAC$.

Although the one to one mapping means that there is no redundancy in the genotype space, and permits the use of straightforward crossover and mutation operators, the complexity of the mapping function means that a small mutation can have a large effect, e.g., $\{3, 2, 3, 1, 1\} \rightarrow CBDAE$. Equally, it can be easily shown that recombination operators no longer respect and propagate all features common to both solutions. Thus if the two solutions $\{1, 1, 1, 1, 1\} \rightarrow ABCDE$ and $\{5, 1, 2, 3, 1\} \rightarrow EACDB$, which share the common feature that C occurs in the third position and D in the fourth undergo 1-point crossover between the third and fourth loci, the solution $\{5, 1, 2, 1, 1\} \rightarrow EACBD$ is obtained, which does not possess this feature. If the crossover occurs in other positions, the edge CD may be preserved, but in a different position in the cycle.

In both of the examples given, the complexity of the genotype–phenotype mapping makes it very difficult to ensure locality and makes the fitness landscape associated with the search space highly complex, since the potential effects in fitness of changes at the left-hand end of the string are much bigger than those at the right-hand end [179]. Equally, it can become very difficult to specify exactly the common features the recombination operators are supposed to be preserving.

12.5 Application Example: Graph Three-Colouring

We illustrate the approaches outlined above via the description of two different ways of solving a well-known CSP problem, graph three-colouring as defined in Section 12.2.2.

12.5.1 Indirect Approach

In this section we take an indirect approach, transforming the problem from a CSP to a FOP by means of penalty functions. The most straightforward representation is using ternary strings of length n, where each variable stands for one node, and the integers 1, 2, and 3 denote the three colours. Using this standard GA representation has the advantage that all standard variation operators are immediately applicable. We now define two objective functions (penalty functions) that measure the amount of "incorrectness" of a chromosome. The first function is based on the number of "incorrect edges" that

connect two nodes with the same colour, while the second relies on counting the "incorrect nodes" that have a neighbour with the same colour. For
a formal description let us denote the constraints belonging to the edges as
c_i $(i = \{1, \ldots, m\})$, and let C^i be the set of constraints involving variable v_i
(edges connecting to node i). Then the penalties belonging to the two options
above described can be expressed as follows:

$$f_1(\bar{s}) = \sum_{i=1}^{m} w_i \times \chi(\bar{s}, c_i),$$

where $\chi(\bar{s}, c_i) = \begin{cases} 1 & \text{if } \bar{s} \text{ violates } c_i, \\ 0 & \text{otherwise.} \end{cases}$

respectively,

$$f_2(\bar{s}) = \sum_{i=1}^{n} w_i \times \chi(\bar{s}, C^i),$$

where $\chi(\bar{s}, C^i) = \begin{cases} 1 & \text{if } \bar{s} \text{ violates at least one } c \in C^i, \\ 0 & \text{otherwise.} \end{cases}$

Note that both functions are correct transformations of the constraints in
the sense that for each $\bar{s} \in S$ we have that $\phi(\bar{s}) = \textit{true}$ if and only if $f_i(\bar{s}) = 0$
($i = 1, 2$). The motivation to use weighted sums in this example, and in
general, is that they provide the possibility of emphasising certain constraints
(variables) by giving them a higher weight. This can be beneficial if some
constraints are more important or known to be harder to satisfy. Assigning
them a higher weight gives a higher reward to a chromosome, hence the EA
naturally focuses on these. Setting the weights can be done manually by the
user, but can also be done by the EA itself on-the-fly as in the stepwise
adaptation of weights (SAW) mechanism [132].

Now the EA for the graph three-colouring problem can be composed from
standard components. For instance, we can apply a steady state GA with
population size 100, binary tournament selection and worst fitness deletion,
using random resetting mutation with $p_m = 1/n$ and uniform crossover with
$p_c = 0.8$. Notice that this EA really ignores constraints; it only tries to minimise the given objective function (penalty function).

12.5.2 Mixed Mapping – Direct Approach

We now present another EA for this problem, illustrating how constraints
can be handled by a decoder. The main idea is to use permutations of the
nodes as chromosomes. The phenotype (colouring) belonging to a genotype
(permutation) is determined by a procedure that assigns colours to nodes in
the order they occur in the given permutation, trying the colours in increasing
order (1,2,3), and leaving the node uncoloured if all three colours would lead to
a constraint violation. Formally, we shift from the search space $S = \{1, 2, 3\}^n$

to $S' = \{\bar{s} \in S \mid s_i \neq s_j \ \ i, j = 1, \ldots, n\}$, and the colouring procedure (the decoder) is the mapping from S' to S. At the first glance this might not seem a good idea as we still have constraints in the transformed problem. However, we know from Chapter 3 that working in a permutation space using a direct approach is easy, as there are many suitable variation operators keeping the search in this space. In other words, we have various operators preserving the constraints defining this space.

An appropriate objective function for this representation can simply be defined as the number (weighted sum) of nodes that remain uncoloured after decoding. This function also has the property that an optimal value (0) implies that all constraints are satisfied, i.e., all nodes are coloured correctly. The rest of the EA can again use off-the-shelf components: a steady-state GA with population size 100, binary tournament selection and worst fitness deletion, using swap mutation with $p_m = 1/n$ and order crossover with $p_c = 0.8$.

Looking at this solution at a conceptual level we can note that there are two constraint handling issues. Primary constraint handling concerns handling the constraints of the original problem, the graph three-colouring CSP. This is done by the mapping approach via a decoder. However, the transformed search space S' in which the EA has to work in is not free, rather it is restricted by the constraints defining permutations. This constitutes the secondary constraint handling issue that is solved by a (direct) preserving approach using appropriate variation operators.

12.6 Exercises

1. Specify the eight-queens problem as a CSP $\langle S, \phi \rangle$.
2. Is it true that solving a COP with an EA always implies indirect constraint handling?
3. Is it true that solving a CSP with an EA never involves direct constraint handling?
4. Design an EA for solving a 3-SAT problem. In a propositional satisfiability problem (SAT) a propositional formula is given, and a truth assignment for its variables is sought that makes the formula true. Without loss of generality it can be assumed that the given formula is in *conjunctive normal form* (CNF), i.e., it is a conjunction of clauses where a clause is a disjunction of literals. In the 3-SAT version of this problem it is also assumed that the clauses consist of exactly three literals. In the common notation, a formula has l clauses $(L_1, \ldots, L_l)$ and n variables $(v_1, \ldots, v_n)$.

12.7 Recommended Reading for this Chapter

1. T. Bäck, D.B. Fogel, and Z. Michalewicz, editors. *Evolutionary Computation 2: Advanced Algorithms and Operators* Part II: Chapters 6–12,

220   12 Constraint Handling

pages 38–86. Institute of Physics Publishing, Bristol, 2000
A series of chapters providing comprehensive reviews of different EA
approaches to constraint handling, written by experts in the field

2. B.G.W. Craenen, A.E. Eiben, and J.I. van Hemert. Comparing evolutionary algorithms on binary constraint satisfaction problems. *IEEE
Transactions on Evolutionary Computation*, 2003 (in press)

3. A.E. Eiben. Evolutionary algorithms and constraint satisfaction: Definitions, survey, methodology, and research directions. In Kallel, Naudts,
Rogers, Eds. [222], 2001
Clear definitions and a good overview of evolutionary constraint handling
methods from the CSP point of view

4. J. Smith. *Handbook of Global Optimization Volume 2*, Chap. Genetic
Algorithms, pages 275–362. Kluwer Academic Publishers, Boston, 2002
A good overview of constraint handling methods in GAs from the COP
point of view

5. Z. Michalewicz and M. Schoenauer. Evolutionary algorithms for constrained parameter optimisation problems. *Evolutionary Computation*,
4:1 pp.1–32, 1996.

13

Special Forms of Evolution

13.1 Aims of this Chapter

In this chapter we discuss special forms of evolution that in some sense deviate from the standard evolutionary algorithms. In particular, we present coevolution and interactive evolution that both work under "external influence". In coevolution the influence comes from another population, whose members affect the fitness of the main population. In turn, the main population also influences the fitness of the other one; hence the two populations evolve together. In interactive evolution this influence comes from a user who defines the fitness values by subjective preferences. In both of these cases, the fitness that is awarded to a solution may vary. In the first case because the fitness is dependent on the evolutionary state of the second population, and in the second because users often display inconsistencies. We finish this chapter by describing evolutionary approaches to problems where changing evaluation criteria form the very feature defining them: nonstationary optimisation problems.

13.2 Coevolution

Previously in this book we made extensive use of Sewall-Wright's analogy of the adaptive landscape where an evolving population is conceptualised as moving on a surface whose points represent the set of possible solutions. This metaphor ascribes a vertical dimension to the search space that denotes the fitness of a particular solution, and the combined effects of selection and variation operators move the set of points into high-fitness regions.[1]

Whilst this is an attractive metaphor, it can also be profoundly misleading when we consider the adaptation of a biological species. This is because it tends to lead to the implicit notion that solutions have a fitness value per

---

[1] Although it can be shown that the reverse can sometimes happen [321].

se. Of course, in life the adaptive value (that is, fitness) of an organism is entirely determined by the environmental niche in which it finds itself. The characteristics of this niche are predominantly determined by the presence and character of other organisms from the same and, in particular, different species.[2]

The effect of other species in determining the fitness of an organism can be positive – for example, the pollination of plants by insects feeding on their nectar – or negative – for example, the eating of rabbits by foxes. Biologists tend to use the terms **mutualism** and **symbiosis** to refer to the coadaptation of species in a mutually beneficial way, and the terms **predation** or **parasitism** to refer to relationships in which one species has a negative effect on the survival and reproductive success of the other (antagonism).

If all of the other species in an environmental niche remained the same, and only one species was evolving, then the notion of a fixed adaptive landscape would be valid for that species. However, since evolution affects all species, the net effect is that the landscape "seen" by each species is affected by the configuration of all the other interacting species, i.e., it will move. This process is known as **coevolution**. To give a concrete example, the adaptive value to a rabbit of being able to run at, say 20 kph depends entirely on whether the fox that preys on it has a maximum top speed of 15 kph or 30 kph. The "height" on the landscape of a "20-kph phenotype" is reduced over time from a high value to a low value as the fox evolves the ability to run faster.

Despite the additional complications of coevolutionary models, they hold some significant advantages that have been exploited within EAs to aid the generation of solutions to a range of difficult problems. One of the most obvious of these is the modelling and evolution of gameplaying strategies, such as the overly popular **iterated prisoner's dilemma** [14, 15]. In this case evolving solutions play against each other to get their fitness, i.e., only one species is used and the model is competitive in the sense defined in Section 13.2.2. Since computers provide the freedom to use a number of different models, and biology is serving as an inspiration rather than a strict blueprint, a number of different models have been used successfully. Coevolutionary EAs have been implemented using both cooperation and competition, and both single and multiple species models as we shall now describe.

13.2.1 Cooperative coevolution

Coevolutionary models in which a number of different species, each representing part of a problem, cooperate in order to come with a solution to a larger problem have been proposed by a number of authors. Examples of this include high-dimensional function optimisation [309], job shop scheduling [208], among many others.

---

[2] With the possible exception of some extremely simple organisms.

The advantage of this approach is that it permits effective function decomposition; each subpopulation is effectively solving a much smaller, more tractable problem. The disadvantage, of course, is that it relies on the user to provide a suitable partition of the problem if it is not obvious from the overall specification. In nature, mutually beneficial relationships have as their ultimate expression so-called **endosymbiosis**, where the two species become so interdependent that they end up inextricably physically linked – for example, the various gut bacteria that live entirely within a host's body and are passed from mother to offspring. The equivalent in the artificial world of optimisation is where the different parts of a problem are so interdependent that they are not amenable to division.

Bull [65] conducted a series of more general studies on cooperative coevolution using Kauffmann's static NKC model [224] (see Appendix B) in which the amount of effect that the species have on each other can be varied systematically. In [66] he examined the evolution of coevolving symbiotic systems that had the ability to evolve "linkage flags" denoting that solutions from different populations should stay together. He showed that the strategies that emerge depend heavily on the extent to which the two populations affect each other's fitness landscape, with linkage preferred in highly interdependent situations.

When cooperating populations are used, a major issue is that of deciding how a solution from one population should be paired with the necessary others in order to gain a fitness evaluation.

- Potter and DeJong [309] used a generational GA in each subpopulation, with the different species taking it in turns to undergo a round of selection, recombination, and mutation. Evaluation was performed using the current best from each of the other species.
- Paredis examined the coevolution of solutions and their representations in a steady state generational model using what he terms lifetime fitness evaluation (LTFE) [298]. In the most general form of this algorithm a new individual undergoes 20 "encounters" with solutions selected from the other population. The fitness of the new individual is initially set as the mean fitness from these encounters. The effect of this scheme is that individuals from each population are continuously undergoing new encounters, and the fitness of an individual is given by the running average of its performance in the last 20 encounters. The benefit of this running-average approach is that it effectively slows down the rate at which each fitness landscape changes in response to changes in the composition of the other populations.
- An alternative approach was taken by Husbands [208], who solved the pairing problem and also effectively changed the rate at which the composition of the different populations are *perceived* to change by using a diffusion model EA (Sect. 9.3.2) with one member of each species located on each grid point.

- Bull [66] examined the use of a range of different pairing strategies: best, random, stochastic fitness-based, joined and distributed as per [208]. His results showed that no one strategy performed better across the range of different interaction strengths and generational models, but random was robust in a generational GA, and distributed did best in a steady-state GA. When fitness sharing was added to prevent premature convergence, "best" became the most robust solution.

Finally, within the field of cooperative coevolution it is worth mentioning the use of **automatically defined functions** within GP [230]. In this extension of GP, the function set is extended to include calls to functions that are themselves being evolved in parallel, in separate populations. The great advantage of this is in permitting the evolution of modularity and code reuse.

13.2.2 Competitive coevolution

In the competitive coevolution paradigm individuals compete against each other to gain fitness at each other's expense. These individuals may belong to the same or different species, in which case it is arguably more accurate to say that the different species are competing against each other.

As noted above, the classic example of this that generated much interested in the paradigm was Axelrod's work on the iterated prisoner's dilemma (IPD) [14, 15], aablelthough early work can be traced back as far as 1962 [40]. This is a two-player game, where each participant must decide whether to cooperate or defect in each iteration. The payoff received depends on the actions of the other player as determined by a matrix of which Table 13.1 represents an example.

	Player B	
Player A	Cooperate	Defect
Cooperate	3,3	0,5
Defect	5,0	1,1

Table 13.1. Example payoff matrix for iterated prisoner's dilemma. Payoff to player A is first of pair

Axelrod organised tournaments in which human-designed strategies competed against each other, with strategies only allowed to "see" the last three actions of their opponent. He then set up experiments in which strategies were evolved using as their fitness the mean score attained against a set of eight human strategies. He was able to illustrate that the system evolved the best strategy (tit-for-tat), but there was some brittleness according to the set of human strategies chosen. In a subsequent experiment he demonstrated that a strategy similar to tit-for-tat could also be evolved if a coevolutionary approach was used with each solution playing against every other in its current generation in order to assess its quality.

In another groundbreaking study, Hillis [196] used a two-species model with the pairing strategy determined by colocation on a grid in a diffusion model EA. Note that this parallel model is similar to, and in fact was a precursor of, Husbands's cooperative algorithm described above. Hillis' two populations represented sorting networks, whose task it was to sort a number of inputs numerically, and sets of test cases for those networks. Fitness for the networks is assigned according to how many of the test cases they sort correctly. Using the antagonistic approach, fitness for the individuals representing sets of test cases is assigned according to how many errors they cause in the network's output. His study caused considerable attention as it found correct sorting networks that were smaller than any previously known.

This two-species competitive model has been used by a number of authors to coevolve classification systems [164, 300]. The approach of Paredis is worth noting as it solves the pairing strategy problem by using a variant of the LTFE method sketched above.

As with cooperative coevolution, the fitness landscapes will change as the different populations evolve, and the choice of pairing strategies can have a major effect on the observed behaviour. When the competition arises within a single population, the most common approaches are to either pair each strategy against each other, or just against a randomly chosen fixed-size sample of the others. Once this has been done, the solutions can be ranked according to the number of wins they achieve and any rank-based selection mechanism chosen.

If the competition arises between different populations, then a pairing strategy must be chosen in order to evaluate fitness, as it is for cooperative coevolution. Given that the NKC model essentially assigns random effects to the interactions between species, i.e., it is neither explicitly cooperative nor competitive, it is likely that Bull's results summarised above will also translate to this paradigm.

The main engine behind coevolution is sometimes called "competitive fitness evaluation". As Angeline states in [11], the chief advantage of the method is that it is self-scaling: early in the run relatively poor solutions may survive, for their competitors are not strong either. But as the run proceeds and the average strength of the population increases, the difficulty of the fitness function is continually scaled.

A particular type of problems is formed by "test-solution problems" as termed by Paredis [299]. These are illustrated by constraint satisfaction problems in the following section.

13.2.3 Example Application: Coevolutionary Constraint Satisfaction

A competitive coevolutionary system to solve CSP problems is described by Paredis in [297]. The main idea is to have two populations, one consisting candidate solutions for the given CSP and one containing constraints, and define the fitness of an individual in one population by the extent it can "frustrate"[3] individuals in the other population. Quite naturally, a candidate solution s frustrates a constraint c if s satisfies c, and a constraint c frustrates a candidate solution s if s violates c. This idea is implemented by arranging random "encounters" between constraints and candidate solutions, where each encounter matches the given c and s to determine whether c satisfies s. The fitness of an individual (in any population) is based on 20 encounters, where fitter individuals of the other population have a higher chance to be selected for an encounter. By this mechanism, the randomised champions of the respective populations are fighting each other, giving rise to an arms race. It is expected that this arms race will be won by the solution population yielding an individual that not only frustrates all its opponents in an encounter, but satisfies the other constraints as well.

It is important to understand here that the two populations are inherently different from the perspective of evolution. The population of candidate solutions really evolves, since it undergoes variation and selection resulting in ever-new population members (disregarding accidental creation of clones). However, the constraint population cannot evolve, since its elements must not be varied as the set of constraints is part of the problem specification that does not change. Thus, the dynamics within the constraint population is restricted to reranking the given members after each evaluation without effectively changing the composition.

The other algorithmic components of this application are not essential for the present example, hence the reader is referred to [297] for the details. We want to remark, however, that this coevolutionary approach to solving CSPs proved to be inferior to many others in an extensive experimental comparison on randomly generated binary CSP [85].

13.3 Interactive Evolution

The defining feature of the type of evolutionary systems discussed in this section is that the user effectively becomes part of the system by acting as a guiding oracle to control the evolutionary process. A trivial example of such a system is agricultural breeding, where human interference changes the reproductive process. Based on functional (faster horses) or aesthetic (nicer cats) judgements, the individuals to reproduce are selected by the human

---

[3] Term from the authors of this book.

supervisor. The result is the emergence of new types of individuals that meet the human expectations better than their ancestors.

As mentioned in Section 2.2, variation and selection are the two cornerstones of any evolutionary process. If the latter one is influenced by the user's subjective judgement, then we talk about **interactive evolution** (IE) or **collaborative evolution**. In fact, these terms are broad enough to also encompass influencing the variation step. This is not an impossible option; consider, for instance, a planner making a timetable with a GA and inspecting the best solution from time to time. If planners interchange two events by hand in the inspected timetable and place the resulting solution back to the population, they actually influence variation.[4] However, human–EA interaction in this sense is seldom, and therefore we follow this limited interpretation of the terms interactive evolution and collaborative evolution as offered in [36, 48].

In general, the user can influence selection in various ways. The influence can be very direct, for example, actually choosing the individuals that are allowed to reproduce. Alternatively, it can be indirect by defining the fitness values or perhaps only sorting the population, and have an automated probabilistic selection mechanism to appoint parents for the next generation. In all cases (even in the indirect one) the user's influence is named **subjective selection**, and in an evolutionary art context the term **aesthetic selection** is often used.

Incorporating human guidance into an evolutionary process implies advantages as well as disadvantages. The advantages are summarised by Bentley and Corne in [48] as follows:

- Handling situations with no clear fitness function. If the reasons to prefer certain solutions cannot be formalised, no fitness function can be specified and implemented within the EA code. Subjective user selection circumvents this problem. It is also helpful if the objectives and preferences are variable, since changing preferences will not imply the necessity to rewrite the fitness function.
- Improved search ability. If evolution gets stuck, the user can redirect search by changing his guiding principle.
- Increased exploration and diversity. The longer the user "plays" with the system, the more and more diverse solutions will be encountered.

The disadvantages include:

- Slowness. Compared to the automated execution of an evaluation function, humans are extremely slow in inspecting and judging solutions. This causes long evolutions (measured by wall-clock time).
- Inconsistency. Humans can (and do) change their minds on-the-fly, altering their preferences, and causing inconsistency in their guidance.
- Limited coverage. Time constraints and human cognitive limitations typically only allow small populations and a few generations. Consequently,

---

[4] The real-life example could be, for instance, genetic manipulation of corn.

only a small fraction of the search space is covered by an interactive evolutionary search process.

13.3.1 Optimisation, Design, Exploration

Interactive evolution is often related to evolutionary design and evolutionary art, which can be seen as a specific form of evolutionary design. In particular cases IE is applied to perform optimisation, as the cherry brandy experiment in Sect. 4.9.2 illustrates. From a conceptual perspective it can even be argued that *evolution is design*, rather than optimisation. From this perspective the canonical task of (natural or computer) evolution is to design good solutions for specific challenges. The field of evolutionary design by computers naturally touches upon such conceptual issues and has arrived ta a view that distinguishes parameter optimisation and exploration [46, 47]. The main underlying difference between these two lies in the representation of a problem. Many problems can be solved by defining a parameterised model of possible solutions and seeking the parameter values that encode an optimal solution. This encoding is "knowledge-rich" in the sense that the appropriate parameters must be chosen intelligently – if there is no parameter for a feature that influences solution quality that feature can never be modified, different values cannot be compared, and possibly good solutions will be overlooked. An alternative to such parameterised representations is formed by component-based representations. Here a set of low-level components is defined, and solutions are constructed from these components. This is a "knowledge-lean" representation with possibly no, or only weak, assumptions of relationships between components and the ways they can be assembled.

Optimisation is related to the first type of representations. Propagating improvements along successive generations, an EA behaves much like an optimiser in the parameter space. Component-based representations give rise to exploration, aiming at identifying novel and good solutions, where novelty can be more important than optimality (which might not even be definable). Within this framework, evolution works as a discovery engine and not only for discovering new designs, but even aiding in identifying new design principles by analysing the evolved designs [278].

13.3.2 Interactive Evolutionary Design and Art

As mentioned above IE is typically associated with evolutionary design. The common approach relies on component-based representations and is exploration oriented. The basic template for interactive evolutionary design systems consists of five components [48]:

1. A phenotype representation defining the application-specific kind of objects we are to evolve

2. A genotype representation, where the genes represent (directly or indirectly) a variable number of components that make up a phenotype
3. A decoder, often called growth function of **embriogeny**, defining the mapping process from genotypes to phenotypes
4. A solution evaluation facility allowing the user to perform (art of the selection within the evolutionary cycle in an interactive way
5. An evolutionary algorithm to carry out the search

This scheme can be used to evolve objects with an amazing variety, including Dawkins' pioneering Biomorphs [95], coffee tables [45], images imitating works of the artist M.C. Escher [121], scenes of medieval towns [371], and music [284]. The basics of such evolutionary art systems are the same as those of evolutionary design in general: some evolvable genotype is specified that encodes a visually or auditively interpretable phenotype. Visual phenotypes include two-dimensional images, animations, and three-dimensional objects; and auditive phenotypes amount to pieces of music. The main feature that distinguishes evolutionary art applications from other forms of evolutionary design lies in the intention: the evolved objects are simply to please the user, that is, they need not serve any practical purpose.

13.3.3 Example Application: The Mondriaan Evolver

To give a detailed illustration we use an existing application example: the Mondriaan evolver aimed at the creation of images in the style of the Dutch artist Piet Mondriaan [402]. In this case the phenotype space is rather simple, consisting of "paintings" containing straight lines and (blocks of) primary colours. Figure 13.1 shows a screenshot of the user interface exhibiting nine images/phenotypes, here in black and white.

Such phenotypes must be represented by some corresponding genotypes that allow variation through mutation and recombination. Using one of the common EA representations, that is, a standard ES, EP, GA, or GP genotype form, has the advantage that no application-specific variation operators need to be developed; one can simply choose from the existing options. Figure 13.2 illustrates one possible representation for Mondriaan-like images by showing three example genotypes and their corresponding phenotypes. The exact specification of this representation is left to the reader as an exercise, see Exercises at the end of this chapter. Here we only want to stress the importance of this step in setting up a evolutionary design system: if the representation is too narrow possibly interesting solutions may be out of reach of the system. For instance, even without giving the formal specification of the Mondriaan representation here, it should be clear that in principle the Dutch flag can be evolved by this system. However, to evolve the British flag is impossible, simply because it contains diagonal lines, which cannot be represented by the combination of the present genotypes and the decoding function.

So far we have illustrated the components 1 through 4 of the interactive evolutionary design framework, where the user interface in Figure 13.1 realises

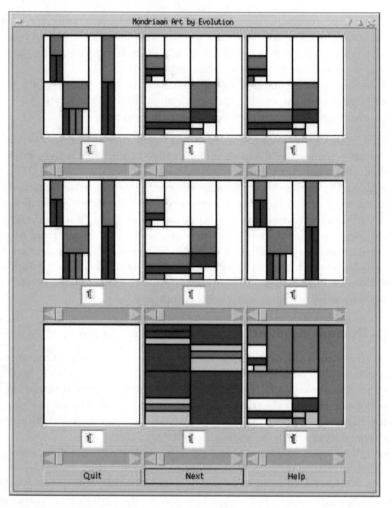

Fig. 13.1. A screenshot of the Mondriaan evolver showing a population of phenotypes, see http://www.cs.vu.nl/ci/Mondriaan/

the solution evaluation facility component. This interface allows users to grade each image according to their likings, and a traditional selection mechanism, for instance, tournament selection, takes these grades into account. It is an interesting empirical fact that a too finely graded system is unsuited for most human users as they find it difficult to express their preferences very accurately. For instance, it can be hard to decide whether a given image should be given a mark of 50 or 51 out of 100. A system with just three grades (low, medium, high) could be sufficient in many cases, and even a simple binary mechanism (like, dislike) is often effective enough. This latter has the practi-

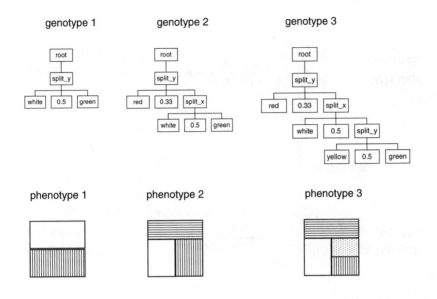

Fig. 13.2. Illustrating a possible representation of Mondriaan-like images by three example genotypes *above*) and their corresponding phenotypes (*below*)

cal advantage that system users are only required to click on the phenotypes they like, grading all others as "disliked" by default. This can speed up the evaluation process considerably and allow more generations within the same time.

The whole system is illustrated by Figure 13.3. In this diagram the genotype and phenotype levels are clearly separated. Parent selection (partly by the user) takes place at phenotype level, delivering a set of images that are used as parents to create the next generation. These parent phenotypes are encoded by their corresponding genotypes. (Let us note that the strings used in the figure are not the actually used genotypes in the running application.) Variation, i.e., mutation and recombination, takes place at the genotype level, creating nine new genotypes that form the new population. These are decoded into the phenotype images they represent and are displayed on the user interface. Hereby they become exposed to selection and a new evolutionary cycle can begin.

Finally, let us remark that the Mondriaan evolver is available on-line as a Java application that can be used though a Web-browser. It is also available as a downloadable package from http://www.cs.vu.nl/ci/Mondriaan/.

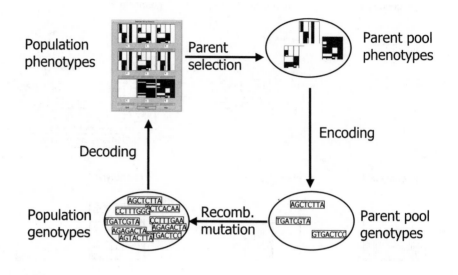

Fig. 13.3. The main cycle of interactive evolution illustrated by the Mondriaan evolver example.

13.4 Nonstationary Function Optimisation

The majority of the EA work to date has been in problem domains in which the fitness landscape is time-invariant. However, it is not unusual for a real-world system to exist in an environment that changes over the course of time. The optimisation algorithm then has to be designed so that it can compensate for the changing environment by monitoring its performance and altering, accordingly, some aspects of the optimisation mechanism to achieve optimal or near-optimal performance. An objective of the resulting adaptation is not to find a single optimum, but rather to select a sequence of values over time that minimise or maximise the time-average of environmental evaluations. In this sense the optimisation algorithm "tracks" the environmental optimum as it changes with time. The general characterisation of this type of problem notes that some (but not necessarily all) members of the search space S have a fitness that varies within the time frame of reference T, i.e.,

$$\exists\, i \in S,\ \exists\, t_1, t_2 \in \{1, \ldots, T\} \mid f^{t_1}(i) \neq f^{t_2}(i).$$

Cobb [79] defines two ways of classifying non-stationary functions:

- Switching versus continuous, which is based on time-scale of change with respect to the rate of evaluation

- Markovian versus state dependant, which is based on whether the fitness function comes from an asymptotic distribution or is strictly a function of time

The distributed nature of the genetic search provides a natural source of power for exploring in changing environments. As long as sufficient diversity remains in the population, the EA can respond to a changing search landscape by reallocating future trials. However, the tendency of EAs, especially of GAs, to converge rapidly results in the population becoming homogeneous, which reduces the ability of the EA to identify regions of the search space that might become more attractive as the environment changes. It such cases it is necessary to complement the standard EA with a mechanism for maintaining a healthy exploration of the search space. (Recall the self-adaptation example from Sect. 4.8.)

A number of researchers have proposed such mechanisms and examined their performance on test cases and "real world" problems. Algorithms are typically compared by running them for a fixed period and calculating two time-averaged metrics, which correspond to different types of real-world applications.

The first of these is the "on-line" measure [98] and is simply the average of all calls to the evaluation function during the run of the algorithm. This measure relates to applications where it is desirable to maintain consistently good solutions, e.g., on-line process control [143, 409].

The second metric considered is the "off-line" performance and is the time-averaged value of the best-performing member of the current population. Unlike the on-line metric, off-line performance is unaffected by the occasional generation of individuals with very low fitness, and so is more suitable for problems where the testing of such individuals is not penalised, e.g., parameter optimisation using a changing design model.

If we use the function b to denote the best individual in a population such that

$$\forall \, i \in P^t \mid f^t(b(P^t)) \geq f^t(i),$$

(maximising the fitness), then we can formalise the two metrics over a period T as

$$online = \sum_{t=1}^{T} \sum_{i \in P^t} f^t(i),$$

$$offline = \sum_{t=1}^{T} f^t(b(P^t)).$$

13.4.1 Algorithmic Approaches

In [79] the behaviour of a standard GA on a parabolic function with the optima moving sinusoidally in space was observed. This was done for a range of bitwise mutation rates. It was found that the off-line performance decreased as the rate of change increased for all mutation probabilities. As the rate of change increased the mutation rate that gave optimal off-line performance increased. Finally, it was noted that as problem difficulty increased, the rate of change that GA could track decreased.

There are two basic modification strategies for the GA that enable it to continually evolve an optimal solution to a problem while the environment changes with time. The first strategy expands the memory of the GA in order to build up a repertoire of ready responses for various environmental conditions. The main examples of this approach are the GA with diploid representation [177] and the structured GA [88]. Goldberg and Smith examined the use of diploid representation and dominance operators to improve performance of the genetic algorithm in an oscillating environment [367], while Dasgupta and McGregor presented a modified ("structured") genetic algorithm with a multilayered structure of the chromosome which constitutes a "long term distributed memory".

The second modification strategy effectively increases diversity in the population directly (i.e., without extending the GA memory) in order to compensate for changes encountered in the environment. Examples of this strategy involve the GA with a hypermutation operator [79, 80], the random immigrants GA [184], the GA with a variable local search (VLS) operator [408, 409], and the thermodynamic GA [283].

The hypermutation operator temporarily increases the mutation rate to a high value, called the hypermutation rate, during periods when the time-averaged best performance of the GA worsens. In his 1992 study, Grefenstette noted that under certain conditions hypermutation might never get triggered. He illustrated this using a function composed of 14 sinusoidal hills with an initial optimum of fitness 5.0, and subsequently appearing optima with height 10.0, which appeared after 20 generations, and moved every 20 generations. He showed that the SGA goes to 5.0, and then rose to 10.0 when the second optimum moved close to the position of the initial one, but could not track subsequent moves. Hypermutation also found the initial optimum with value 5, but the hypermutation was not triggered by the presence of the second peak, as the values of the first remained constant. Once the position of the second optimum moves close to original peak, it was explored, and after this the algorithm was able to track the position of the optimum as triggering works.

The random immigrants mechanism replaces a fraction of a standard GA's population by randomly generated individuals in each generation in order to maintain a continuous level of exploration of the search space. It was reported that 30% replacement gave the best off-line tracking: if the value is too high the algorithm is unable to converge between changes; however, off-line performance decreases with proportion replaced.

In a follow-up study, Cobb and Grefenstette compared hypermutation with random immigrants and simple GA (with high mutation rate) [80]. They noted that there was a qualitative difference in the nature of the mutation operator in the three algorithms:

- SGA – uniform in population and time
- Hypermutation – uniform in population, not in time
- Random immigrants – uniform in time, not in population

They used two landscapes, and three types of change: a linear motion in the first problem, moving 1 step along an axis every 2/5 generations, randomly shifting the optima in A every 20 generations, and swapping between the two problems every 2/20 generations. They ran lots of experiments to find good settings for each algorithm with each problem. Their results can be summarised below:

- SGA: A mutation probability of 0.1 was reasonably good at the translation tasks, but gave very poor online performance. It was unable to track the steadily moving optimum or oscillation. In general the mutation probability needs to be matched to degree of change.
- Hypermutation: High variances in performance were noted and the higher mutation rate needed careful tuning to the problem instance. It was much better at tracking sudden changes than SGA and gave better online performance than SGA or random immigrants when the rate of change was slow enough to allow a lower rate of mutation.
- Random Immigrants: This strategy was not very good at tracking linear movement, but was the best at the oscillating task. They hypothesised (but don't show) that this was because it allowed the preservation of niches. The strategy displayed poor performance on stationary problems and slowly moving problems.

The VLS operator uses a similar triggering mechanism to Hypermutation, and it enables local search around the location of the population members in the search space before the environmental change. The range of the search is variable and can be gradually extended to match degree of the environmental change.

The thermodynamic GA can maintain a given level of diversity in population by evaluating the entropy and free energy of the GA's population. The free energy function is effectively used to control selection pressure during the process of creating a new population.

13.4.2 Selection and Replacement Policies

In [406, 407] the suitability of generational GAs (GGAs) and steady-state GAs (SSGAs) was studied for use in dynamic environments. Results showed that the SSGA with a "delete-oldest" replacement strategy can adapt to environmental changes with reduced degradation of off-line and particularly on-line performance. The improved performance of the SSGA can be explained by the fact that an offspring is immediately used as a part of the mating pool, making a shift towards the optimal solution possible in a relatively early phase of the optimisation process. Selection of the steady-state model for use in nonstationary environments is therefore advantageous, particularly for on-line applications.

Selection is a vital force in any evolutionary algorithm, and an understanding of the nature of its effects is necessary if effective algorithms are to be developed. For GGAs selection has been well studied, and methods have been developed that reduce much of the noise inherent in the stochastic algorithm, e.g., SUS [33]. Unfortunately, the very nature of SSGAs precludes the use of such methods and those available are inherently more noisy.

In [364] several replacement strategies were studied using a Markov chain analysis of the takeover probability versus time, in order to understand the different sources of the noise. For delete-oldest and delete-random strategies, the variations in performance arise in part from losing the only copy of the current best in the population, which happened approximately 50% of the time for delete random, and 10% of the time for delete-oldest. Performance comparisons on static landscapes demonstrated that the extent to which this affects the quality of the solutions obtained depends on the ability of the reproductive operators to rediscover the lost points. In [75] other strategies, e.g., deletion by exponential ranking, were also shown to lose the optimum.

A common way of avoiding this problem is to incorporate elitism, often in the form of a delete-worst strategy. As has been documented by other authors [75, 76], the latter was shown to exhibit increased selection pressure, however, this can lead to premature convergence and poor performance on higher dimensional problems.

In [363] a number of replacement strategies were compared in combination with two different ways of achieving elitism. The first was the common method of explicitly checking whether the member about to be deleted is (one of) the current best in the population, and if so not replacing it. In this case the member can either be preserved with its original fitness value, or be reevaluated and the new fitness value saved. The second, "conservative selection" is an implicit mechanism introduced in [409]. Here each parent was selected by a binary tournament between a randomly selected member of the population, and the member about to be replaced. If the latter is the current best, then it will win both tournaments, so recombination will have no effect, and (apart from the effects of mutation), elitism is attained. In [364] this was shown to guarantee takeover by the optimal class, but at a much slower rate than delete-worst or elitist delete-oldest. In total ten selection strategies were evaluated for their on-line and off-line performance on two different test problems. Deletion of the oldest, worst, and random members was done in conjunction with both standard (both members randomly selected) and conservative (member to be replaced plus one random member) tournaments. Additionally, a delete-oldest policy was tested with four variants of elitism. These were:

1. Oldest is not replaced if it is one of the current best, but is reevaluated.
2. Oldest is not replaced if it is the sole copy of the current best and is reevaluated.
3. As 1., but without reevaluation (original fitness value kept).
4. As 2., but without reevaluation (original fitness value kept).

This was done for algorithms with and without hypermutation on two different classes of problems. The results obtained clearly confirmed that for some algorithms an extra method for creating diversity (in this case hypermutation) can improve tracking performance, although not all of the strategies tested were able to take advantage of this. However, two factors are immediately apparent from these results which hold with or without hypermutation.

Exploitation: Strategies such as delete-oldest or delete-random, which can lose the sole copy of the current population best, performed poorly. This matched results on static landscapes noted above. Analysis of the takeover times for a single newly created best individual showed that these policies will actually lose the individual 50% of the time. Therefore some form of elitism is desirable.

Reevaluation: In potentially dynamic environments it is essential that the fitness of points on the landscape is continuously and systematically reevaluated. Failure to do so leads to the population forever being "dragged back" to the original peak position, as solutions in that region of the search space are selected to be parents on the basis of out-of-date information. Failure to reevaluate solutions can also lead to a failure to trigger the hypermutation mechanism. Although this was obvious for the third and fourth variants of elitism tested, it also applies to the much more common delete-worst policy. In this case if the population had converged close to the optimum prior to the change, the "worst" members that get deleted may be the only ones with a true fitness value attached. The importance of systematic reevaluation was clear from the difference between conservative delete-oldest and conservative delete-random. The former always produced better performance than the latter, and very significantly so when hypermutation was present.

Of all the policies tested, the conservative delete-oldest was the best suited to the points noted above and produced the best performance. The improvement over the elitist policy with reevaluation is believed to result not merely from the reduced selection pressure, but from the fact that the exploitation of good individuals is not limited to preserving the very best, but will also apply (with decreasing probability) to the second-best member, and so on. Since the implicit elitism still allows changes via mutation, there is a higher probability of local search around individuals of high fitness, whilst worse members are less likely to win tournaments, and so they are replaced with offspring created by recombination. The result is that even without hypermutation the algorithm was able to track environmental changes of modest size.

13.4.3 Example Application: Time-Varying Knapsack Problem

This problem is a variant of that described in [283]. As discussed in Sect. 2.4.2, we have a number of items each having a value (v_i^t) and a weight or cost (c_i^t) associated with them, and the problem is to select a subset that maximises the sum of the elements' values while meeting a (time-varying) total capacity constraint $C(t)$. Given a fixed number of elements N, each subset is represented by a binary string of length N, where a 1 in a position i indicates that the corresponding item is included in the subset. For such a string $\bar{x}$, at time t, the fitness is given by:

$$F(x,t)= \begin{cases} \sum_{i=1}^{N} v_i(t)x_i & \text{if } \sum_{i=1}^{N} c_i^t x_i \leq C(t), \\ 0.01 \left[C_{sum} - \left(\sum_{i=1}^{N} c_i^t x_i - C(t) \right) \right] & \text{if } \sum_{i=1}^{N} c_i^t x_i > C(t). \end{cases} \quad (13.1)$$

where the term C_{sum} in the penalty clause for solutions that transgress the constraint is the sum of all the items' cost.

In [363], Smith and Vavak outline a series of experiments on this problem aimed at investigating the effect of different survivor selection policies. In the particular case investigated, a 32-bit problem was considered (N=32), the values v_i and costs c_i attached to the items remained constant, and were generated using a uniform random distribution over the interval [0,100.0]. The capacity constraint $C(t)$ alternated between 50%, 30%, and 80% of C_{sum}, changing once every 20000 evaluations.

The algorithm used was a binary-coded SSGA. Parent selection was by binary tournaments, with the fitter member always declared the winner. Note from the previous section that in some cases the conservative tournament selection operator was used. Because the costs and values of different items were assigned at random, there was no a priori reason to believe that the representation chosen grouped together items that were highly interdependant in their effect on fitness. Therefore uniform crossover was used (with probability 1.0) to generate offspring, as this shows no positional bias (Sect. 11.2.3). The rest of the parameter settings were decided after some initial experimentation to establish robust values and are given in Table 13.2.

The hypermutation operator was implemented as it is currently the most commonly used method for tracking. It is triggered if the running average of the best performing members of the population over an equivalent of three generations of the generational GA (i.e., over a number of evaluations equal to three times the population size) drops by an amount that exceeds a predefined threshold. In this case a value of threshold TH=3 was used. The best performing member of the population is evaluated after an equivalent of one generation of the generational GA. Once it has been triggered, the hypermutation rate (0.2) is switched back to the "baseline" mutation rate (0.001) as soon as the best performing member of the population reaches 80% of its value before the environmental change occurred. The setting of the parameters (80% and hypermutation rate 0.2) was found to provide good results

Representation	32-Bit binary
Recombination	Uniform crossover
Mutation	Bit-flipping
Mutation probability	0.005, 0.001, 0.01, 0.05 per bit
Parent selection	Binary tournament, fittest always chosen
Survival selection	Various methods compared
Population size	100
Initialisation	random
Termination condition	60,000 evaluations
Performance metric	On-line and off-line fitness
Special features	Hypermutation operator to create diversity when needed

Table 13.2. Table describing GA for the time-varying knapsack problem

for the given problem. A prolonged period of high mutation for values higher than 80% has a negative effect on on-line performance because diversity is introduced into the population despite the correct region of the search space having already been identified. Similarly to the choice of the threshold level described previously, the values of both parameters were selected empirically.

As hinted above, the best results came from the use of the conservative selection policy, where a delete-oldest policy is used for survivor selection, but the member about to be replaced is always one of the participants in every tournament. The algorithm using this policy, along with hypermutation, was able to successfully track the global optimum in both a switching environment, as here, and also in a problem with a continuously moving optimum.

13.5 Exercises

1. Implement a two-population cooperative GA where the solutions in each population code for half of a 50-bit OneMax problem, and the populations take it in turns to evolve for a generation. Use the same parameters within each population as for exercise 7 in Chap. 3 Investigate the effect of random versus best pairing strategies.
2. Now repeat this experiment, but this time use a competitive model. Let the fitness that one population gets be the OneMax score and the fitness that the other gets be (50 - OneMax) i.e., ZeroMax. What happens to the two populations?
3. Define a representation for the Mondriaan evolver matching the three examples in Figure 13.2.
4. Define a representation that would allow the evolution of the British flag.
5. Using your code from exercise 7 in Chap. 3, run the GA with the fitness function swapping from Onemax to ZeroMax every 50 generations. Observe what happens to the mean, best and worst fitness.
6. Investigate the effects of changing mutation rates on your results.

13.6 Recommended Reading for this Chapter

1. P.J. Bentley, Ed. *Evolutionary Design by Computers.* Morgan Kaufmann, San Francisco, 1999

2. P.J. Bentley, D.W. Corne, Eds. *Creative Evolutionary Systems.* Academic Press, 2002

3. P.J. Bentley, D.W. Corne. An introduction to creative evolutionary systems. In *Creative Evolutionary Systems* (above), pp. 1–75

4. J. Branke, S. Kirby. *Evolutionary Optimization in Dynamic Environments.* Kluwer Academic Publishers, Boston, 2001

5. J. Branke, H. Schmeck. Designing evolutionary algorithms for dynamic optimization problems. In Ghosh, Tsutsui [167], pp. 239–262

6. W. D. Hillis. coevolving parasites improve simulated evolution as an optimization procedure. In C. G. Langton et. al., Eds. *Proceedings of the Workshop on Artificial Life (ALIFE '90)*, pp. 313–324, Addison-Wesley, Redwood City, CA, USA, 1992

7. J. Paredis. Coevolutionary algorithms. In T. Bäck, D. Fogel, Z. Michalewicz, Eds. [26]

14

Working with Evolutionary Algorithms

14.1 Aims of this Chapter

The main objective of this chapter is to provide practical guidelines for working with EAs. Working with EAs often means comparing different versions experimentally. Guidelines to perform experimental comparisons are therefore given much attention, including the issues of algorithm performance measures, statistics, and benchmark test suites. The example application (Sect. 14.5) is also adjusted to the special topics here; it illustrates the application of different experimental practices, rather than EA design.

14.2 What Do You Want an EA to Do?

Throughout the whole book so far, we have seemingly never considered this issue: "What do you want an EA to do?". The reason is that we tacitly assumed the trivial answer: "I want the EA solve my problem". Many of the subjects treated in this chapter concern specific interpretations and refinements of this answer, and it will become clear that different objectives imply different ways of designing and working with an EA.

The first step one could take to narrow down the objectives concerns the given problem context. We can roughly distinguish three main types of problems:

- Design (one-off) problems
- Repetitive problems, including on-line control problems as special cases

As an example of a design problem, let us consider the optimisation of a road network, assuming that a certain region is to extend its present road network with newly laid connections to meet new demands. This is most certainly a highly complex multiobjective optimisation problem, subject to many constraints. Computer support for this problem requires an algorithm that creates *one* excellent solution at least *once*. In this context the quality of the solution is of utmost importance, and other commonly considered aspects of algorithm performance are secondary. For instance, algorithm speed is not too important in this case. Since the time scale of the whole project spans years, the algorithm does not have to be fast. It can be given months of computing time, perhaps performing several runs and keeping the best result, if this helps in achieving superior solution quality. The algorithm does not need to be generally applicable either. The present problem most probably contains very specific aspects, hindering reapplication of the algorithm to other problems. Furthermore, a similar problem will occur as part of a similar project allowing enough time to develop a good EA for that problem.

Repetitive problems form a counterpoint to design problems. To illustrate such problems, consider a domestic transportation firm, having dozens of trucks and drivers that need to be given a daily schedule every morning. Such a schedule should contain a pick-up and delivery plan, plus the corresponding route description for each truck and driver. For each truck and driver this is "just" a TSP problem (probably with time windows), but the optimisation criteria and the constraints must be taken across the whole firm, together making the actual problem very complex. Depending on the type of business, the data and requirements concerning a day's schedule might become available weeks, days, but maybe only hours before the schedules are to be handed out to the drivers. In any case, the dispatcher must provide a schedule every morning to every available driver. Suitable computer support for this problem, an EA in our case, must be able to find *good* solutions *quickly* and be able to do this *repeatedly* for *different instances* of the problem (i.e., with different data and requirements every day). The implications for the algorithm are radically different from those in the case of a design problem. The preference in the speed versus quality trade-off is clearly given to speed now. Solutions must be good, e.g., better than hand-made ones, but not necessarily optimal. Speed, however, is crucial. For example, it could be required that the time between feeding the data in the system and receiving the schedules does not exceed 30 minutes. Closely related to this issue, it is important that the algorithm performance is stable. Since an EA is a stochastic algorithm, the quality of end solutions over a number of runs shows a certain variance. For a design problem we typically have the time to perform many runs and select the best solution. Therefore it is not a problem if some runs terminate with bad results, as long as others end with good solutions. For repetitive problems, however, we might have time for one single run only. To reduce the probability of really bad runs, we need a consistent EA to keep the variance of end solution quality as low as possible. Finally, for repetitive problems the wide-scale applicability of the algorithm is also important as the system will be used under various circumstances. In other words the algorithm will be run on different problem instances.

On-line control problems can be seen as repetitive problems with extremely tight time constraints. To remain in the transportation context, we can think of traffic light optimisation. In particular, let us consider the task of optimising a controller to set the green times of a single crossing with four crossroads. We assume that each of the crossroads has sensors embedded in the road surface that continuously monitor traffic approaching the crossing.[1] This sensory information is sent to the traffic light controller, a piece of software running on a special device at the crossing. The task of this controller is to calculate the green times for each of the roads in such a way that the throughput of vehicles is maximised. It is important to note that an EA can be used for this problem in two completely different ways. First, we can use an EA *to develop a controller*, based on simulations, and then deploy this controller at the crossing in question. (This type of application was mentioned in the genetic programming chapter (Chap. 6).) The other way is to have an EA that *is the controller*, and this is what we have in mind here. The most important requirement here is, of course, speed. A controller is working in on-line mode, and it has to cope with streaming sensory information and needs to control the traffic lights in real time. The speed requirements are given in wall-clock time: The length of one full cycle[2] is typically a few minutes, and this time must be enough to calculate the green times for the following cycle. This can be very demanding for an evolutionary algorithm that works with a whole population of candidate solutions and needs quite a few generations to evolve a good result. Fortunately, by the nature of traffic flows, the situation does not change very rapidly, which also holds for many other control problems. This means that the consecutive problem instances are rather similar to each other, and therefore it can be expected that the corresponding near-optimal solutions are similar as well. This motivates an EA that keeps the best solutions from its previous run and uses them in the new run. The second requirement, similarly to repetitive problems, is a small variance in end solution quality. The third one is that the controller (the EA) must be very fault-tolerant and robust. This means that noise in the data (measurement errors of the sensors) or missing data (breakdown of a sensor) must not have a critical effect. The system, and the EA within, must keep working and delivering the best possible results under the given circumstances.

Finally, let us mention a different but important type of context for working with EAs: academic research. The considerations in the previous paragraphs apply in an application-oriented situation, and it can be argued that making good applications is one of the major goals of the whole evolutionary computing field. However, an examination of the EC literature soon discloses that a huge majority of what has been published in scientific journals, conference proceedings, or monographs is ignorant concerning such concrete application-related issues. Scientific research apparently has its own "dynamics", goals,

---

[1] In many countries this is rather common, and in the Netherlands it is almost standard.

[2] One cycle is defined as the time between two consecutive turn-to-green moments of traffic light no. 1.

methodologies, and conventions. Some of these arise from the fact that EAs can exhibit complex behaviours and emergent phenomena that are interesting per se, and developing a solid theoretical understanding may yield insight into "real" biological evolution. This chapter would not be complete without paying attention to working with EAs in an academic environment.

The objective in many experimental research papers, implicitly or explicitly, is to show that the EA in question is better than other evolutionary algorithms or their competitors – at least for some "interesting" problems. This objective is typically not placed into an application context. The requirements of the algorithm are therefore not inferred from what we want the algorithm to do, rather, they are based on conventions or ad hoc choices. Frequently occurring goals for experimentation in an academic environment are:

- Get a good solution for a given problem, e.g., challenging combinatorial optimisation.
- Show that EC is applicable in a (possibly new) problem domain.
- Show that an EA with some newly invented feature is better than some benchmark EA.
- Show that EAs outperform traditional algorithms on some relevant problems.
- Find best setup for parameters of a given EA, in particular, get data on the impact of varying some EA component, e.g., the population size.
- Obtain insights into algorithm behaviour, e.g., the interaction between selection and variation.
- See how an EA scales-up with problem size.
- See how the performance is influenced by parameters
  - of the problem,
  - of the algorithm.

While these goals are different among themselves, and academic experimental research is apparently different from application-oriented work, there are general issues for all of these cases. The most prominent issue present in all experimental work is the objective of assessing algorithm performance.

14.3 Performance Measures

Assessing the quality of an evolutionary algorithm commonly implies experimental comparisons between the given EA and other evolutionary or traditional algorithms. Even if showing the superiority of some EA is not the main goal, parameter tuning for good performance remains experimental work, implying comparison of different algorithm variants.

Such comparisons always assume the use of some algorithm performance measures, since claims on ranking algorithms are always meant as claims on ranking their performances (and not on, for instance, code length or readability). Because of the stochastic nature of EAs, these performance measures are statistical in nature, implying that a number of experiments need to be conducted to gain sufficient experimental data. In the following we discuss three basic performance measures:

- Success rate
- Effectiveness (solution quality)
- Efficiency (speed)

Additionally, we discuss the use of progress curves, i.e., plots of algorithm behaviour against time.

14.3.1 Different Performance Measures

In quite a few cases, experimental research concerns problems where the optimal solution can be recognised, which is typical in academia, or a criterion for sufficient solution quality can be given, as in many practical applications. For such problems one can easily define a success criterion: finding a solution of the required quality. For this type of problems the **success rate** (SR) measure can be defined as the percentage of runs terminating with success. For problems where the optimal solutions cannot be recognised, the SR measure cannot be used in theory. This is the case if the optimum of the objective function is unknown, or perhaps not even a lower/upper bound is available. Nevertheless, a success criterion in the *practical* sense can often be given even in these cases. As an example, think of a university timetabling problem. The theoretical optimum of the problem instance at hand is surely unknown here. However, one could use last year's timetable, or the one made by hand as benchmark and declare that a run ending with a timetable beating the benchmark by 10% is a success. Practical success criteria can also be used even in cases when the theoretical optimum is known, but the user does not require this optimum. For instance, it might be sufficient if we have a solution with an error less than a given $\epsilon > 0$.

The **mean best fitness** measure (MBF) can be defined for any problem that is tackled with an EA – at least for any EA using an explicit fitness measure (excluding, for instance, evolutionary art applications, Sect. 13.3.2). For each run of a given EA, the best fitness can be defined as the fitness of the best individual at termination. The MBF is the average of these best fitness values over all runs. Depending on the application at hand, or the specific research objective, the best-ever fitness and the worst-ever fitness, calculated over a number runs, can be also interesting. For design problems, for instance, it is more relevant as it gives an indication of the quality of the end result, that is the best solution found in all runs.

Note that although SR and MBF are related, they are different, and there is no general advice on which one to use for algorithm comparison. The difference between the two measures is rather obvious: SR cannot be defined for some problems, while the MBF is always a valid measure. Furthermore, all possible combinations of low or high SR and MBF values can occur. For example, low SR and high MBF is possible and indicates a good approximiser algorithm: it gets close consistently, but seldom really makes it. Such an outcome could motivate increasing the length of the runs, hoping that this allows the algorithm to finish the search. An opposite combination of a high SR and low MBF is also possible, indicating a "Murphy" algorithm: if it goes wrong, it goes very wrong. That is, those few runs that terminate without an (optimal) solution end in a disaster, with a very bad best fitness value deteriorating MBF. Clearly, whether the first or the second type of algorithm behaviour is preferable depends on the problem. As mentioned above, for a timetabling problem the SR measure might not be meaningful, so one should be interested in a high MBF. To demonstrate the other situation, think of solving the 3-SAT problem with the number of unsatisfied clauses as fitness measure. In this case a high SR is pursued, since the MBF measure – although formally correct – is useless because the number of unsatisfied clauses at termination says, in general, very little about how close the EA got to a solution. Notice, however, that the particular application objectives (coming from the original problem-solving context) might necessitate a refinement of this picture. For instance, if the 3-SAT problem to be solved represents a practical problem, with some tolerance for a solution, then measuring MBF and striving for a good MBF value might be appropriate.

in addition to the mean best fitness calculated over a number of runs, in specific cases one might be interested in the best-ever fitness or the worst-ever fitness. For design problems as discussed in the previous section, the best-ever fitness is more appropriate then MBF, since *one* excellent solution is all that is required. For repetitive problems the worst-ever fitness can be interesting. Such a measure can be used for studying worst-case scenarios and can help to establish statistical guarantees on solution quality.

It is important to note that for both measures, SR and MBF, it is assumed that they are taken under an a priori specified limit of computational efforts. That is, SR and MBF always reflect performance within a fixed maximum amount of computing. If this maximum is changed, the ranking of algorithms might change as well. This is illustrated in Fig. 14.1, which shows a "turtle and hare" situation, where algorithm A (the hare) shows rapid progress, and in the case of limited time it beats algorithm B (the turtle). In turn algorithm B outperforms algorithm A if given more time. Summarising, SR and MBF are performance measures for an algorithm's effectiveness, indicating how far can it get within a given computational limit.

The complementary approach is to specify when a candidate solution is satisfactory and measure the amount of computing needed to achieve this solution quality. Roughly speaking, this is the issue of algorithm efficiency or speed. Speed is often measured in elapsed computer time, CPU time, or user time. However, these measures depend on the specific hardware, operating system, compiler, network load, and so on, and therefore are ill-suited for reproducible research. In other words, repeating the same experiments, possibly elsewhere, may lead to different results. For generate-and-test-style

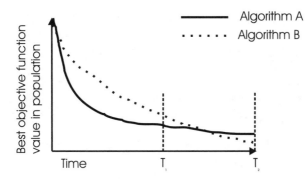

Fig. 14.1. Comparing algorithms A and B by after terminating at time T_1 and T_2 (for a minimisation problem). Algorithm A clearly wins in the first case, while B is better in the second one

algorithms, as EAs are, a common way around this problem is to count the number of points visited in the search space. Since EAs immediately evaluate each newly generated candidate solution, this measure is usually expressed as the number of fitness evaluations. Of necessity, because of the stochastic nature of EAs, this is always measured over a number of independent runs, and the **average number of evaluations to a solution** (AES) is used. It is important to note that the average is only taken over the successful runs (that is, "to a solution"). Sometimes the average number of evaluations to termination measure is used instead of the AES, but this has clear disadvantages. Namely, for runs finding no solutions the specified maximum number of evaluations will be used when calculating this average. This means that the values obtained will depend on how long the unsuccessful runs are allowed to continue. That is, this measure mixes the AES and the SR measures, and the outcome figures are hard to interpret.

Success percentages and run lengths can be meaningfully combined into a measure expressing the amount of processing required to solve a problem with a given probability [229, Chap. 8]. This measure (defined for generational EAs and used frequently in GP) depends on the population size and the number of generations as tunable quantities. The probability $Y(\mu, i)$ that a given run with population size μ hits a solution for the first time in generation i is estimated by observed statistics, which require a substantial number of runs. Cumulating these estimations, the probability $P(\mu, i)$ that a given generation i will contain a solution (found in a generation $j \leq i$) can be calculated. Using the $P(\mu, i)$ values we can then determine the probability that generation i finds a solution at least once in R runs as $1 - (1 - P(\mu, i))^R$. Then the number of independent runs needed to find a solution by generation i with a probability of z is

$$R(\mu, i, z) = \left\lceil \frac{log(1 - z)}{log(1 - P(\mu, i))} \right\rceil, \tag{14.1}$$

where $\lceil \; \rceil$ is the ceiling function. Being a function of the population size, this measure can give information on how to set μ. For instance, after collecting enough data with different settings, the total amount of processing, that is, the number of fitness evaluations, needed to find a solution with a probability of z by generation i using a population size μ is $I(\mu, i, z) = \mu \cdot i \cdot R(\mu, i, z)$. Notice that the dependence on μ is not the crucial issue here; in fact, any algorithm parameter p can be used in an analogous way, leading to estimates for $R(p, i, z)$.

Using the AES measure generally gives a fair comparison of algorithm speed, but its usage can be disputed, or even misleading in some cases.

1. First, it could be misleading if an EA uses "hidden labour", for instance, some local search heuristics incorporated in the mutation operator. The extra computational efforts within the mutation can increase performance, but are invisible to the AES measure.
2. Second, it could be misleading if some evaluations take longer than others. For instance, if a repair mechanism is applied, then evaluations invoking this repair take much longer. One EA with good variation operators might proceed by chromosomes that do not have to be repaired, while another EA may need a lot of repair. The AES values of the two may be close, but the second EA would be much slower, and this is not an artifact of the implementation.
3. Third, it could be misleading when evaluations can be done very quickly compared with executing other steps in the EA cycle.[3] Then the AES does not reflect algorithm speed correctly, for other components of the EA have a relatively large impact.

An additional problem with AES is that it can be difficult to apply for comparison of an EA with search algorithms that do not work in the same search space, in the same fashion. An EA iteratively improves complete candidate solutions, so one elementary search step consists of the creation and testing of one new candidate solution. However, a constructive search algorithm works in the space of partial solutions (including the complete ones that an EA is searching through), so one elementary search step consists of extending the current solution. In general, counting the number of elementary search steps is misleading if the search steps are different. A possible treatment for this, and also for the hidden labour problem, is to compare scale-up behaviour of the algorithms. To this end a problem is needed that is scalable, that is, its size can be changed. The number of variables is a natural scale-up parameter for many problems. Two different types of methods can then be compared by plotting their own speed measure figures against the problem size. Even though the measures used in each curve are different, the steepness information is a fair basis for comparison: the curve that grows at a higher rate indicates an

---

[3] Typically this is not the case, and approximately as much as 70–90% of the time is spent on fitness evaluations.

inferior algorithm (Fig. 14.2). A great advantage of this comparison is that it also can be applied to plain running times (e.g., CPU times), not only to the number of abstract search steps. As discussed above, there are important arguments against using running times themselves for comparisons. However, the scale-up curves of running times do give a fair comparison without those drawbacks.

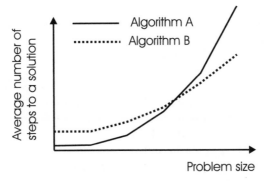

Fig. 14.2. Comparing algorithms A and B by their scale-up behaviour. Algorithm B can be considered preferable because its scale-up curve is less steep

An alternative to AES, especially in cases where one cannot specify satisfactory solution quality in advance, is the pace of progress to indicate algorithm speed. Here the best (or alternatively the worst or average) fitness value of the consecutive populations is plotted against a time axis – typically the number of generations or fitness evaluations (Fig. 14.1). Clearly, such a plot provides much more information than the AES and therefore it can also be used when a clear success criterion is available. In particular, a progress plot can help rank two algorithms that score the same on AES. For example, progress curves might disclose that algorithm A has achieved the desired quality halfway through the run. Then the maximum number of evaluations might be decreased and the competition redone. The chance is high that algorithm A keeps its performance, e.g., its MBF, at lower costs and algorithm B does not, thus a well-motivated preference can be formulated. Another possible difference between progress curves of algorithms can be the steepness towards the end of the run. If, for instance, curve A has already flattened out, but curve B did not, one might extend the runs. The chance is high that B will make further progress in the extra time, but A will not; thus again, the two algorithms can be distinguished.

A particular problem with using such progress plots is that it is hard to use them in a "statistical" way. Averaging the data of, say, 100 such plots and only drawing the average plot can hide interesting effects by smoothening them out. Overlaying all curves forms an alternative, but has obvious disadvantages:

it might result in a chaotic figure with too much black ink and no visible structure. A practical solution is depicting a "typical curve", that is, one single plot that is representative for all others. This option might not have a solid statistical basis, but it can deliver the most information when used with care.

14.3.2 Peak versus Average Performance

For some, but not all, performance measures, there is an additional question of whether one is interested in peak performance, or average performance, considered over all these experiments. In evolutionary computing it is typical to suggest that algorithm A is better than algorithm B if its average performance is better. In many applications, however, one is often interested in the best solution found in X runs or within Y hours/days/weeks (peak performance), and the average performance is not that relevant. This is typical, for instance, in design problems as discussed in Section 14.2. In general, if there is time for more runs on the given problem and the final solution can be selected from the best solutions of these runs, then peak performance is more relevant than average performance.

We have a different situation if a problem-solving session allows only time for one run that must deliver the solution. This might be the case if a computationally expensive simulation is needed to calculate fitness values or a real-time application, like repetitive and on-line control problems. For this kind of problem, an algorithm with high average performance and small standard deviation is the best option, since this carries the lowest risk of missing the only chance we have.

It is interesting to note that academic experimental EC research falls in the first category – there is always time to perform more runs on any given set of test problems. In this light, it is strange that the huge majority of experimental EC research is comparing average performances of algorithms. This might be because researchers do not consider the differences between design and repetitive problems, and do not realise the different implications for the requirements of the problem-solving algorithm. Instead, it seems, they simply assume that the EA will be used in the repetitive mode.

Next we consider an example to show how the interpretation of figures concerning averages and standard deviations can depend on application objectives. In EC it is common to express preferences for algorithms with better averages for a given performance measure, e.g., higher MBF or lower AES, especially if a better average is coupled to a lower standard deviation. This attitude is never discussed, but it is less self-evident than it might seem. Using the timetabling example, let us assume that two algorithms are compared based on 50 independent runs and the resulting MBF values that are given in Fig. 14.3. Given these results, it could be tempting to conclude that algorithm A is better, because of the slightly higher MBF, and the more consistent behaviour (that is, lower variation in best fitness values at termination). This is

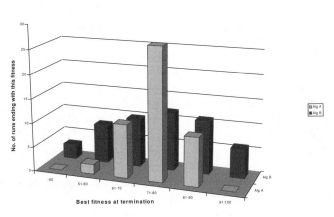

Performance of algorithms

Fig. 14.3. Comparing algorithms by histograms of the best found fitness values

indeed a sound argument in the case of a repetitive application, for instance, if a team of hospital employees must be scheduled every morning, based on fresh data and constraints. Notice, however, that six runs of algorithm B terminated with a solution quality that algorithm A never achieved. Therefore in a design application algorithm B is preferable, because of the higher chance of delivering a better timetable. Making a university timetable would fall into this category, since it has to be made only once a year, and the data is available weeks, perhaps months, before the time table must be effective. This discussion of performance measures is not exhaustive, but it illustrates the point that for a sound comparison it is necessary to specify the objectives of the algorithms in the light of some problem-solving context and to derive the performance measures used for comparison from these objectives.

Finally, let us pay some attention to using statistics. It is clear that by the stochastic nature of EAs only statistical statements about behaviour are possible. Typically, averages and standard deviations supply the necessary basis for claims about (relative) performance of algorithms. In a few cases these can be considered as sufficient, but in principle it is possible that two (or more) series of runs deliver data that are statistically indistinguishable, i.e., may come from the same distribution, and the differences are due to random effects. This means that the two series, and the behaviour of the two EAs behind these series, should be considered as statistically identical, and claims about one being better are ill-founded. It is important to recall that the mean and standard deviation of any given observable are only *two* values that by which we try to describe the whole set of data. Consequently, considering only the standard deviations often cannot eliminate the possibility that any observed difference is only a result of randomness.

Good experimental practice therefore requires the use of specific tests to establish whether observed differences in performance are truly statistically significant. A popular method for this purpose is the two-tailed T-test, which gives an indication about the chance that the values came from the same underlying distribution. The applicability of this test is subject to certain conditions, for instance, that the data are normally distributed, but in practice it proves rather robust and is often used without verifying these conditions. When more than two algorithms are being compared, it is suggested that an analysis of variance (ANOVA) test be performed. This uses all of the data to calculate a probability that any observed differences are due to random effects, and should be performed *before* comparing algorithms pairwise. More sophisticated variants also exist: for instance, if we want to investigate the effects of two parameters (say, population size and mutation rate), then we can perform a two-way ANOVA, which simultaneously analyses the effects of each parameter and their interactions.

If we have limited amounts of data, or our results are not normally distributed, then the use of the t-test and ANOVA are not appropriate. To give an example, if we are comparing MBF values for a number of algorithms, with $SR < 1$ for some (but not all) of them, then our data will almost certainly not be normally distributed, since there is a fixed upper limit to the MBF value defined by the problem's optimum. In this type of cases, it is more appropriate to use the equivalent so-called non-parametric test, noting that it is less likely to show a difference, since it makes fewer assumptions about the nature of the data.

Unfortunately, the present experimental EC practice seems rather unaware of the importance of statistics. This is a great shame, since there are many readily available software packages for performing these tests, so there is no excuse for not performing a proper statistical analysis of results. However this problem is easily remediable. There are any number of excellent books on statistics that deal with these issues, aimed at experimental sciences, or business and management courses, see for instance [267, 437]. The areas of concern are broadly known as hypothesis testing, and experimental design. Additionally, a wealth of information and on-line course material can be found by entering these terms into any Internet search engine.

14.4 Test Problems for Experimental Comparisons

In addition to the issue of performance measures, experimental comparisons between algorithms imply the question of which benchmark problems and problem instances should be used. To this end one could distinguish three different approaches:

1. Using problem instances from an academic benchmark repository.
2. Using problem instances created by a problem instance generator.
3. Using real-life problem instances.

14.4.1 Using Predefined Problem Instances

The first option amounts to obtaining prepared problem instances that are freely available from Web-based repositories, monographs, or other printed literature. In the history of EC some objective functions had a large impact on experimental studies. For instance, the so-called DeJong test suite, consisting of five functions has long been very popular [98]. This test suite was carefully designed in the to span an interesting variety of fitness landscapes. However, both computing power, and our understanding of EAs, has advanced considerably since the 1970s. Consequently, a modern study that only showed results on these functions and then proceeded to make general claims would not be considered to be methodologically sound. Over the last decade other functions have been added to the "obligatory" list and are used frequently, such as the Ackley, Griewank, and Rastrigin functions, just to name the most popular ones. A number of these commonly used functions can be found in Appendix B. Obviously, new functions pose new challenges to evolutionary algorithms, but the improvement is still rather quantative. To put it plainly: How much better is a claim based on ten test landscapes than one only using the five DeJong functions? There is, of course, a straightforward solution to this problem by limiting the scope of statements on EA performance and restricting it to *the functions used* in the comparative experiments. Formally, this is a sound option, but in practice these careful refinements can easily skip the reader's attention. Additionally, the whole EC community using the same test suite can lead to overfitting new algorithms to these test functions. In other words, the community will not develop better and better EAs over the years, but only better and better EAs *for these problems!*

Another problem with the present practice of using particular objective functions or fitness landscapes is that these functions do not form a systematically searchable collection. That is, using 15 such functions will deliver 15 data points without structure. Unfortunately, although we have some ideas about the sorts of features that make problems hard for EAs, we do not currently possess the tools to divide these functions into meaningful categories, so it is not possible to draw conclusions on the relationship between characteristics of the problem (the objective function) and the EA behaviour. A deliberate attempt by Eiben and Bäck [115] in this direction of failed in the sense that the EA behaviour turned to be inconsistent with the borders of the test function categories. In other words, the EAs showed different behaviours within one category and similar behaviours on functions belonging to different categories. This example shows that developing a meaningful classification of objective functions or test landscapes is nontrivial because the present vocabulary to describe and to distinguish test functions seems inappropriate to

254 14 Working with Evolutionary Algorithms

define "good" categories (see [221] for a good survey of these issues). For the time being this remains a research challenge [119].

Building on cumulative experience in the EC community, for instance that of Whitley et al. [417], Bäck and Michalewicz gave some general guidelines for composing test suites for EC research in [29]. Below we reproduce the main points from their recommendations.

1. The test suit should include a few unimodal functions for comparisons of convergence velocity (efficiency), e.g., AES.
2. The test suite should include several multimodal functions with a *large* number of local optima (e.g., a number growing exponentially with n, the search space dimension). These functions are intended to be representatives of the characteristics that are typical for real-world problems, where the best out of a number of local optima is sought.
3. A test function with randomly perturbed objective function values models a typical characteristic of numerous real-world applications and helps to investigate the robustness of the algorithm with respect to noise.
4. Real-world problems are typically constrained such that the incorporation of constraint handling techniques is a topic of active research. Therefore, a test suite should also contain constrained problems.
5. The test suite should contain high-dimensional objective functions, because these are representative of real-world applications. Furthermore, low-dimensional functions (e.g., with $n = 2$) are not suitable representatives of application problems where an evolutionary algorithm would be applied, because they can be solved optimally with traditional methods. Most useful are test functions that are *scalable* with respect to n, i.e., which can be used for arbitrary dimensions.

14.4.2 Using Problem Instance Generators

An alternative to such test landscapes is formed by problem instances of a certain (larger) class, for instance, operations research problems, constrained problems or machine-learning problems. The related research communities have developed their collections, like the OR library http://www.ms.ic.ac.uk/info.html, the constraints archive at http://www.cs.unh.edu/ccc/archive, or the UCI Machine Learning Repository at http://www.ics.uci.edu/~mlearn/MLRepository.html. The advantage of such collections is that the problem instances are "interesting" in the sense that many other researchers have investigated and evaluated them already. Besides, an archive often contains performance reports of other techniques, thereby providing direct feedback on one's own achievements.

Using a problem instance generator, which of course could be coming from an archive, means that problem instances are produced on-the-spot. Such a generator usually has some problem-specific parameters, for example, the number of clauses and the number of variables for 3-SAT, or the number of variables and the extent of their interaction for NK landscapes [224], and can generate random instances for each parameter value. The advantage of this approach is that the characteristics of the problem instances can be tuned by the parameters of the generator. In particular, for many combinatorial problems there is much available information on the location of really hard problem instances, the so-called phase transition, related to the given parameters of the problem [77, 166, 310]. A generator makes it possible to perform a systematic investigation in and around the hardest parameter range. Using a problem instance generator one can expect results relating problem characteristics to algorithm performance. An illustration is given in Fig. 14.4. The question "which of the two algorithms is better" can now be refined to "which algorithm is better on which problem instances". On mid-range parameter values (apparently the hardest instances) algorithm B outperforms algorithm A. On the easier instances belonging to low and high parameter values, this behaviour inverts.

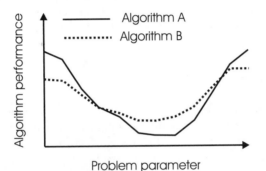

Fig. 14.4. Comparing algorithms on problem instances with a scalable parameter

Over the last few years there has been a growing interest in EC in using problem instance generators for experimental research. The Evolutionary Algorithms Repository of Test Problem Generators at http://www.cs.uwyo.edu/~wspears/generators.html is a collection made by and for EC researchers. As of summer 2003 it offered the following generators:

- Bit-string multimodality generator
- Continuous-valued multi-modality generator
- Random L-SAT epistasis generator
- Matrix epistasis generator
- Graph generators
- Dynamic fitness landscape test function generator – DF1
- NK landscape generator
- Polynomial generator
- Constraint satisfaction problem generator

14.4.3 Using Real-World Problems

Testing on real data has the advantages that results can be considered as very relevant viewed from the application domain (data supplier). However, it also has some disadvantages. Namely, practical problems can be overcomplicated. Furthermore, there can be few available sets of real data, and these data may be commercially sensitive and therefore difficult to publish and to allow others to compare. Last, but not least, there might be so many application-specific aspects involved that the results are hard to generalise. Despite of these drawbacks it remains highly relevant to tackle real-world problems as the proof of the pudding is in the eating!

14.5 Example Applications

As mentioned in the introduction to this chapter, rather than present two case studies, giving implementation details, we are rather more concerned here with describing examples of good and bad practice, in order to illustrate some of our points.

14.5.1 Bad Practice

In this section we show an example of an experimental study following the template that can be found in many EC publications.[4] In this imaginary case the researcher in question invented a new EA feature, e.g., "tricky mutation", and assessed the value of this new feature by running a standard GA and "tricky GA" 20 times independently on each of 10 objective functions chosen from the literature. The outcomes of these experiments proved tricky GA better on seven, equal on one, and worse on two objective functions in terms of SR. Based on these figures it was concluded that the new feature is indeed valuable.

The main question here is what did we, the EC community, learn from this experience? We did learn a new feature (tricky mutation) and obtained some indication that it might be a promising idea to try in a GA. This can of course justify publishing a paper reporting this; however, there are also many things that we did not learn here, including:

- How relevant are these results, e.g., how typical are the test functions of real-world problems, or how important are they from an academic perspective?
- What would have happened if a different performance metric had been used, or if the runs had been ended sooner, or later?
- What is the scope of claims about the superiority of the tricky GA?

---

[4] The authors admit that some of their own papers also follow this template.

- Is there a property distinguishing the seven good and the two bad functions?
- Are these results generalisable? Alternatively, do some features of the tricky GA make it applicable for specific other problems, and if so which?
- How sensitive are these results to changes in the algorithm's parameters?
- Are the performance differences as measured here statistically significant, or can they be just artifacts caused by random effects?

In the next section we present another example that explicitly addresses some of these issues and therefore forms a showcase for a better, albeit still not perfect, practice.

14.5.2 Better Practice

A better example of how to evaluate the behaviour of a new algorithm, takes into account questions such as:

- What type of problem am I trying to solve?
- What would be a desirable property of an algorithm for this type of problem, for example,: speed of finding good solutions, reliably locating good solutions, or occasional brilliance?
- What methods currently exist for this problem, and why am I trying to make a new one, i.e., when do they not perform well?

After considering these issues, a particular problem type can be chosen, a careful set of experiments can be designed, and the necessary data to collect can be identified. A typical process might proceed along the following lines:

- Inventing a new EA (xEA) for solving problem X
- Identifying three other EAs and a traditional benchmark heuristic for problem X in the literature
- Wondering when and why xEA could be better than the other four methods
- Obtaining a problem instance generator for problem X with two parameters: n (problem size) and k (some problem-specific indicator)
- Selecting five values for k and five values for n
- Generating 100 random problem instances for all 25 combinations
- Executing all algorithms on each instance 100 times (benchmark heuristic is also stochastic)
- Recording AES, SR, MBF values with the standard deviations (not for SR)
- Assessing statistical significance of results (after identifying appropriate tests based on the data)
- Putting the program code and the instances on the Web

The advantages of this template with respect to the one in the previous example are numerous:

- The results can be arranged "in 3D": that is, as a performance landscape over the (n, k) plane with special attention to the effect of n, as for scale-up.
- The niche for xEA can be identified, e.g., weak with respect to other algorithms for (n, k) combinations of type 1, strong for (n, k) combinations of type 2, comparable otherwise. Hereby the "when question" can be answered.
- Analysing the specific features and the niches of each algorithm can shed light on the "why question".
- Much knowledge has been collected about problem X and its solvers.
- Generalisable results are achieved, or at least claims with well-identified scope based on solid data.
- Reproduction of results elsewhere, and thereby further research, is facilitated.

14.6 Exercises

1. Consider using the number of generations as a measure to establish the speed of an EA. Compare the use of this measure with using the number of fitness evaluations.
2. Provide the derivation for Eq.(14.1).
3. Design a crossover operator that generalises one point crossover for an arbitrary number of parents. Make an experimental plan to assess the value of this operator within a GA on 3-SAT problems. Do not forget to include tests with respect to the number of parents.
4. Carry out the plan you made above and report on your findings.

14.7 Recommended Reading for this Chapter

1. T. Bäck, Z. Michalewicz. Test landscapes. In: [26]

2. A.E. Eiben, M. Jelasity. A critical note on experimental research methodology in EC. In: [74] pp. 582–587

3. D. Whitley, K. Mathias, S. Rana, J. Dzubera. Building better test functions. In: [137], pp. 239–246

15

Summary

15.1 What Is in This Book?

In this book we have presented evolutionary computing as *one* problem-solving paradigm and positioned four historical types of EAs as "dialects". These dialects have emerged independently to some extent (except GP that grew out of GAs) and developed their own terminology, research focus, and technical solutions to realise particular evolutionary algorithm features. The differences between them, however, are not crisp – there are many examples of EAs that are hard to place into one of the historical categories. Thus after the introductory material in Chaps. 1 and 2, we proceeded to describe these four main dialects of EC in Chaps. 3–6. In Table 15.1 we give a brief summary of these dialects.

It is one of the main messages of this book that such a division is not highly relevant, even though it may be helpful in some cases. It will not have escaped the reader's attention that we have increasingly focused on the idea that the key to a successful EA application lies the choice of a suitable representation of the problem at hand, coupled with a suitable choice of variation operators to act on that solution, and selection operators to manage the population.

Another of the main themes that we have tried to get across in this book is that evolutionary computing forms a problem-solving paradigm, of the "generate-and-test" variety rather than involving any explicit sort of reasoning or calculation of derivatives, and so forth. Populations are multisets of solutions, and the forces of selection act on these populations to increase the proportions of those solutions that are better fitted to the problem at hand, at the expense of those which are less well fitted. This is can be viewed as equivalent to updating the working memory of an algorithm in "conventional" artificial intelligence. Thus the constitution of the population after selection can be said to represent knowledge learned about the problem being solved.

From the solutions in the population, new points in the search space are generated and tested for their suitability via the action of variation operators

Component or feature	EA Dialect			
	GA	ES	EP	GP
Typical problems	Combinatorial optimisation	Continuous optimisation	Optimisation	Modelling
Typical representation	Strings over a finite alphabet	Strings (vectors) of real numbers	Application specific often as in ES	Trees
Role of recombination	Primary variation operator	Important, but secondary	Never applied	Primary/only variation operator
Role of mutation	Secondary variation operator	Important, sometimes the only operator	The only variation operator	Secondary, sometimes not used at all
Parent selection	Random, biased by fitness	Random, uniform	Each individual creates one child	Random, biased by fitness
Survivor selection	Generational: n.a. all individuals replaced Steady-state: deterministic biased by fitness	Deterministic, biased by fitness	Random, biased by fitness	Random, biased by fitness

Table 15.1. Overview of the main EA dialects

on *representations* of those solutions. Again, we can contrast this with traditional AI approaches, and note that instead of performing an inference step we are using a set of stochastic operators to introduce *random* changes in a representation of successful solutions and thereby generate new ones.

Thus in evolutionary algorithms, whatever their dialect, any attempt to mimic the reasoning processes that take place in most human problem-solving activities is absent: we could be said to be trying to "learn without brains". While this may seem like a negative proposition, we could, perhaps rather tritely, counter this argument by pointing to the existence of life on earth as an evidence of the power of evolution as a problem solver. However, this stretches the biological analogy further than we as authors would feel happy with, and the exact processes and importance of evolution are still a matter of some debate. More credibly, we could simply point to the huge number of successful applications of EAs in fields where traditional methods have failed, and claim this as justification for evolutionary computing. Alternatively, we could identify the source of this problem-solving power in the basic underlying principles: selection acting on a population of complete solutions and *random* variations introduced during replication, which permit a search of the space of possible solutions that is not biased by human preconceptions or the dictates of logic.

The emphasis on randomness within almost every operator in an EA does, of course, have some follow-on effects. In particular it informs the choice of theoretical tools that we can use in an attempt to understand, quantify, and predict the behaviour of EAs. Traditionally, the obvious difficulties of describing and theorising about huge, complex, random systems have led to a perception of EAs as being slightly theory-weak. Thankfully, this situation is now being rapidly addressed, and in Chap. 11 we attempted to give an even-handed description of the principal approaches that have been taken to try and come up with descriptive models of evolutionary algorithm behaviour. What is interesting to note is the way that ideas from one approach are beginning to crop up within others, so that, for example, Holland's notion of schemata being processed by binary coded GAs has emerged naturally in Vose's dynamical systems model. It seems likely that as a result of the natural cross-fertilisation with ideas from other disciplines such as statistical physics and theoretical biology, informed by an ever-expanding pool of empirical experience, we will increasingly see a synthesis of approaches, yielding increased understanding.

Whilst the theorists may still be principally concerned with relatively simple test problems, practitioners are applying EAs to an ever-increasing range of "real-world" problems with great success. Successful applications span a range of problem types from optimisation and simulation to modelling and reinforcement-learning problems, and we have tried to give a flavour of some of these in the application examples in each chapter. What is common is that EA-based methods tend to be applied when other methods have failed, either because the sheer size of the problem has made exact methods impractical, or because the search space is characterised by features such as constraints, nonlinearities, discontinuities, multimodality, or uncertainty that render traditional methods ineffective.

In the second half of this book, we have turned our attention to advanced topics for dealing with real-world problems. Having decided on a suitable representation and set of operators for a given problem, it is necessary to specify various parameters (population size, probability of applying variation operators, etc.), and in Chap. 8 we examined the thorny subject of how best to select them. A range of possible options was presented and discussed, and a strong message emerges that it is often preferable to choose a mechanism whereby the parameters can be adapted on-line during evolution to suit the state of the search process. This has the added benefit of removing the need for, or at least reducing the effect of, user decisions about parameter values.

A frequently observed property of search spaces is that they contain multiple local optima. In Chapter 9 we examined a number of mechanisms that have been proposed to encourage the discovery and exploration of a diverse set of high-quality solutions. Biological metaphors have been particularly fruitful here, as most of these approaches take as their inspiration the various processes that have led to the huge variety of successful life-forms on earth, each well adapted to their particular environmental niche. A natural extension led us to considering the application of EAs to multiobjective problems, where the population-based nature of EAs has shown great promise in identifying the efficient trade-off (Pareto) surface.

Another frequently observed property of search spaces is the presence of constraints on the form that solutions can take. Depending on the presence of constraints and a fitness function, we can divide problems into free optimisation problems, constraint satisfaction problems, and constrained optimisation problems. This distinction is formalised in Chap. 12, and a number of methods are outlined and discussed that facilitate the use of EAs on the latter two classes.

Of course, evolutionary algorithms do not exist in isolation: there are a great many search methods available, and frequently EAs are being applied to problems where there is already a body of knowledge about the likely form of good solutions, or where existing methods and heuristics exist. Rather than adopt a purist approach, it is usually more profitable to make use of whatever methods we can to come up with good solutions, and in Chap. 10 we outline a variety of ways in which problem- or instance-specific information or methods can be incorporated within the evolutionary process to create hybrid or memetic algorithms. We then synthesise some of the recent empirical and theoretical work in attempt to draw some guidelines for designing hybrid systems.

If the method or knowledge is used to improve a candidate solution generated by recombination and mutation, then an interesting perspective is to consider that these are behaving as developmental processes acting on a "plastic" phenotype, in a manner akin to learning. A significant body of work has been motivated by this perspective, of which research into evolving artificial neural networks and into evolving learning behaviours as "memes" are particularly important, and we provide pointers to some of this research.

In Chapter 13 we consider three particular situations in which there exists a degree of uncertainty concerning the quality of a solution, and how EAs may be adapted to tackle them. First we consider problems where the fitness of a candidate solution depends entirely on the context in which it is evaluated, in particular when that context is provided by other evolving entities: this is the realm of Coevolution. Second we consider the case where a human acts as a fitness-function, so-called interactive evolution. This is illustrated by perhaps the ultimate subjective problem: the evolution of art. Finally, we consider so-called nonstationary problems, where the fitness function changes over time as a result of external forces. This type of problem is typical of, for example, the on-line control of real machines, where parts wear out and so on.

Finally, having given many practical guidelines and application examples, so having armed our readers to develop new algorithms for their problems, we turn our attention to the issue of how to evaluate the worth of different approaches. Chapter 14 deals with this topic in some depth, focusing on issues such as "what do you want the algorithm to do". Different requirements (speed, ultimate quality of solution, etc.) lead to different types of algorithms, and different measures for comparing the performance of alternative algorithms are relevant. We discuss these in some detail, and provide some guidelines for experimental methodology.

15.2 What Is Not in This Book?

The subjects treated in this book have been selected by their overall relevance to an introductory book *on evolutionary computing*. Quite naturally, our personal interests played a role too, and we are fully aware of the fact that we could not cover everything that is related to Evolutionary Computing.

To begin with, this book does not treat other biologically and socially inspired techniques, such as ant colonies [56], swarm systems [55], cultural evolution [319], artificial immune systems [96], or evolving neural networks [432]. Furthermore, we have not discussed *evolutionary robotics* – a flourishing area of exciting activities [293]. In this field increasingly intelligent robots are created by letting them evolve, self-organise, and adapt to their environment. The physical grounding of the evolved objects – the robots, or at least their controllers – and the "tedious" evaluation of fitness pose special challenges that gave rise to novel views on evolution and many technical innovations. It could be argued that it is evolutionary robotics where human engineers and scientists most closely approach natural evolution. Another related area is that of *evolvable hardware* [330], (that is, evolutionary electronics), where the design of electronic circuits is carried out through evolution. This area is a subfield of EC, where the evolved solution is represented in hardware instead of software. That is, the evolutionary process always takes place in software, and the evaluations of the evolved designs are done either in software (extrinsic, off-line evolution), or in real hardware (intrinsic, or on-line evolution).

Artificial life (ALife) is a field that overlaps with evolutionary computing, rather than being part of it [246]. ALife is a highly diverse area concerned with various subjects, such as autonomous agents, molecular evolutionary biology, formal grammars, or simulated ecology, to name just a few. From a highly conceptual point of view, it is concerned with fundamental issues of life as we know it by creating models and implementations of it in a novel (silicon) medium – that is, through studying life as never existed before.

On the highest level of the "evolutionary ladder" we find societies that developed from living organisms. One approach to study socioeconomic systems is based on the perception that these systems are evolutionary systems and must therefore be analysed using evolutionary tools. This area is extremely rich with a very diverse literature grouped around terms as, for instance, evolutionary economy, social evolution, language evolution, and many more. Any attempt to give a brief sketch is doomed to fail, and our best advice to the interested reader is to visit the Readings section of L. Tesfatsion's Agent-Based Computational Economics site at `http://www.econ.iastate.edu/tesfatsi/sylalife.htm`.

All in all, there are many exiting subjects and research areas related to evolutionary computing and we hope that this book whetted the readers' appetites to learn more about at least some of them.

A

Gray Coding

Gray coding is a variation on the way that integers are mapped on bit strings that ensures that consecutive integers always have Hamming distance one. A three bit Gray coding table is given in Table A.1, and the procedures for converting a binary number $b = \langle b_1, \ldots, b_m \rangle$, where m is the number of bits, into a Gray code number $g = \langle g_1, \ldots, g_m \rangle$ and vice versa in Table A.2.

Integer	0	1	2	3	4	5	6	7
Standard	000	001	010	011	100	101	110	111
Gray	000	001	011	010	110	111	101	100

Table A.1. Three-bit Gray coding

```
int[] binaryToGray (int[] b) {
        g[1] = b[1];
        for (k=2; k<=m; k++) {
                g[k] = xor(b[k-1], b[k]);
        }
        return g;
}

int[] grayToBinary (int[] g) {
        b[1] = value = g[1];
        for (k=2; k<=m; k++) {
                if (g[k] == 1)
                                value = !value;
                b[k] = value;
        }
        return b;
}
```

Table A.2. Gray to Binary coding and vice-versa

B

Test Functions

We cannot hope here to give a comprehensive set of test functions, and by the arguments given in Sect. 14.4.1, it would not be particularly appropriate. Rather we will give a *few* instances of test problems that we have referred to in this book, along with descriptions and pseudocode for two randomised test function generators. For more test functions and generators, including downloadable code, the reader is referred to the supporting a Web sites at

- http://www.cs.vu.nl/~gusz/ecbook/ecbook.html and
- http://www.cems.uwe.ac.uk/~jsmith/ecbook/ecbook.html

and to the repositories listed in Chap. 14.

B.1 Unimodal Functions

B.1.1 OneMax

The OneMax function is a binary function for a string $\bar{x}$ of length L. It is usually maximised with global optimum $= \bar{1}$ and fitness L.

$$f(\bar{x}) = \sum_{i=1}^{L} x_i \quad .$$

B.1.2 The Sphere Model

The sphere model is an n-dimensional function in the continuous domain. The minimum has value 0.0 at $\bar{0}.0$.

$$f(\bar{x}) = \sum_{i=1}^{n} x_i^2 \quad .$$

B.1.3 Royal Road Function

The Royal Road function is a binary problem with one optimum but many large plateaus. Technically, this is a type-R1 Royal Road function. This version assumes there are a blocks, each of b bits, so that $L = a \cdot b$.

$$f(\bar{x}) = \sum_{i=1}^{a} \Pi_{j=i\cdot b+1}^{i\cdot(b+1)} x_j \quad .$$

B.2 Multimodal Functions

B.2.1 Ackley Function

This n-dimensional function is highly multimodal, with a large number of local minima fairly evenly spread over the search space, but with one global minimum at the origin $\bar{x} = \bar{0}$ with value 0.0.

$$f(\bar{x}) = -20 \cdot \exp\left(-0.2\sqrt{\frac{1}{n}\sum_{i=1}^{n} x_i^2}\right)$$
$$-\exp\left(\frac{1}{n}\sum_{i=1}^{n}\cos(2\pi x_i)\right) + 20 + e \quad .$$

B.2.2 Schwefel's function

Schwefel's function is another widely used n-dimensional function, usually constrained so that each variable lies in the range $-65.536 \le x_i \le 65.536$. Its minimum is at 0.0 with value 0.0.

$$f(\bar{x}) = \sum_{i=1}^{n}\left(\sum_{j=1}^{i} x_j\right)^2 = x^{\mathrm{T}}\mathbf{A}x + b^{\mathrm{T}}x \quad .$$

B.2.3 Generalized Rastrigin's function

The generalised Ratrigen's function is another widely used n-dimensional function, usually constrained so that each variable lies in the range $-5.12 \le x_i \le 5.12$. The minimum is at 0.0 with value 0.0.

$$f(\bar{x}) = nA + \sum_{i=1}^{n} x_i^2 - A\cos(\omega x_i) \quad .$$

where $A = 10, \quad ; \quad \omega = 2\pi, \quad -5.12 \le x_i \le 5.12$.

B.2.4 Deb's Deceptive 4-Bit Function

This is a binary problem, usually used in multiples, i.e., a 40-bit version might consist of 10 of the these subproblems, either concatenated or interleaved. The problem can be made harder by using different weightings for different subproblems. The equation below gives the fitness of a single block of length 4, as a function of the number of 1's it contains. The maximum value is 1.0 for $\bar{1}$.

$$f(\bar{x}) = \begin{cases} 0.6 - 0.2u(\bar{x}), & u(\bar{x}) < 4, \\ 1, & u(\bar{x}) = 4, \end{cases}$$

where

$$U(\bar{x}) = \sum_{i=1}^{4} x_i \quad .$$

B.3 Randomised Test Function Generators

B.3.1 Kauffman's NK Landscapes

This generator can be used to produce test landscapes that are tunable in two respects: the length of the problem (N) and the amount of epistatic interactions between genes (K). Kauffman's model makes two principal assumptions: first, that the fitness of a genotype is the additive sum of the contributions from each gene, and second, that the effects of polygeny and pleiotropy make these interactions effectively random. The model consists of a binary vector $\bar{x}$ of length N. The fitness contribution from each bit depends on its value and on the values of K others. A simpler model assumes that these are the K bits next to the one in question, but we outline the more general (and harder) case here. In both cases the landscape is effectively "held" in a fitness matrix F and an epistasis matrix E. These landscapes have been extensively studied, and their properties are fairly well understood. For a good description and further reading see [7, 368].

A test landscape is instantiated as by generating a fitness matrix (Fig. B.1) and epistasis matrix (Fig. B.2) as shown (note that for ease we index elements from 0).

Having generated a test landscape, the fitness of a solution $\bar{x}$ is calculated as the sum of the gene contributions. These are calculated by taking the binary value of the gene and the K others on which it depends and interpreting this as a binary-coded integer. This is decoded to give the index into the fitness table as shown in Fig. B.3.

```
BEGIN
  /* Generation of the Fitness Matrix */
  set numcols = 2^(K+1);
  Allocate a matrix F with N rows and numcols columns ;
  set row = 0;
  REPEAT UNTIL ( row = N - 1 ) DO
    set column = 0;
    REPEAT UNTIL ( column = numcols - 1 ) DO
      generate a random number r, uniformly in the range [0,1);
      set F(row, column) = r;
      set column = column + 1;
    OD
    set row = row + 1;
  OD
END
```

Fig. B.1. NK landscapes 1: generation of fitness matrix

```
BEGIN
  /* Generation of the Epistasis Matrix */
  Allocate a matrix E with N rows and K columns ;
  set row = 0;
  REPEAT UNTIL ( row = N - 1 ) DO
    set column = 0;
    generate a random permutation perm of the integers (0, ..., N - 1);
    REPEAT UNTIL ( column = K - 1 ) DO
      IF (perm[column] = row) THEN
        set E(row, column) = perm[N - 2];
        ELSE
          set E(row, column) = perm[column];
        ESLE
      FI
      set column = column + 1;
    OD
    set row = row + 1;
  OD
END
```

Fig. B.2. NK landscapes 2: generation of the epistasis matrix

```
BEGIN
  /* Fitness Evaluation */
  set gene = 0;
  set fitness = 0.0;
  REPEAT UNTIL ( gene = N − 1 ) DO
    set gene_index = x[gene];
    set i = 0;
    REPEAT UNTIL ( i = K − 1 ) DO
      set multiplier = 2^{i+1};
      set epistatic_gene = E[gene][i];
      set gene_index = gene_index + multiplier · x[epistatic_gene];
      set i = i + 1;
    OD
    set fitness = fitness + F[gene][gene_index];
    set gene = gene + 1;
  OD
END
```

Fig. B.3. NK landscapes 3: fitness evaluation

B.3.2 NKC Landscapes

The NKC landscapes are an extension of the NK landscapes for a coevolutionary system. The principal difference is that the coevolutionary pressures are modelled by having the fitness contribution of each gene depend not only on K other genes within its own genotype, but also on the value of C other genes in the genotype of the individual with which it is paired to be evaluated. Thus the matrix F is of size N by 2^{K+C+1} and E is of size N by $K + C$. This model can be used for single or multiple population systems; in the latter case there are seperate matrices for each population. The implementation details are a simple extension of those in the previous section.

B.3.3 Random L-SAT

This code (Table B.1) and the corresponding explanation are taken from Spears's site http://www.cs.uwyo.edu/~wspears/epist.html. The code implements the random L-SAT problem generator of Mitchell et al. [279]. It creates Boolean expressions in CNF, with L literals per clause. A clause is filled by choosing L variables (with replacement) uniformly from the set of all variables, and negating those variables with 50% probability. It is well known that the toughest problem instances are created when the ratio between the number of clauses and the number of variables is around 4.3. This program can be used as a generator of epistatic problems; the greater the number of clauses, the greater the epistasis. For more details see [100].

```
#define MAX_CLAUSE_LENGTH 10
#define MAX_CLAUSES 50000

int nclauses; /* The number of clauses in the expression */
int nvars;         /* The number of Boolean variables */
int clause_length; /* The number of literals per clause */

/* c_list[i][] will have a list of variables for clause i.
   A negative entry means the variable is negated. */

int c_list[MAX_CLAUSES][MAX_CLAUSE_LENGTH];

/* Create the CNF Boolean expression.
   You will need to call srandom()
   with some seed value, before calling this function. */

void initialization()
{
      int j, k;

      for (j = 1; j <= nclauses; j++) {
 for (k = 1; k <= clause_length; k++) {
   if (random()&01 == 1) {
     c_list[j][k] = random() % nvars + 1;
   }
   else {
       c_list[j][k] = -(random() % nvars + 1);
   }
 }
      }

}
```

Table B.1. L-SAT problem generator

References

1. E.H.L. Aarts, A.E. Eiben, K.M. van Hee. A general theory of genetic agorithms. Tech. Rep. 89/08, Eindhoven University of Technology, 1989
2. E.H.L. Aarts, J. Korst. *Simulated Annealing and Boltzmann Machines*. Wiley, Chichester, UK, 1989
3. E.H.L. Aarts, J.K. Lenstra, Eds. *Local Search in Combinatorial Optimization*. Discrete Mathematics and Optimization. Wiley, Chichester, UK, June 1997
4. D. Adams. *The Hitch Hiker's Guide to the Galaxy*. Guild Publishing, London, 1986
5. M. Ahluwalia, L. Bull. A genetic programming-based classifier system. In: Banzhaf et al. [37], pp. 11–18
6. L. Altenberg. The schema theorem and Price's theorem. In: Whitley, Vose [425], pp. 23–50
7. L. Altenberg. NK landscapes. In: Bäck et al. [26], Chap. B 2.7.2
8. D. Andre, J.R. Koza. Parallel genetic programming: A scalable implementation using the transputer network architecture. In: P.J. Angeline, K.E. Kinnear, Eds., *Advances in Genetic Programming 2*. MIT Press, Cambridge, MA, 1996, pp. 317–338
9. P.J. Angeline. Adaptive and self-adaptive evolutionary computations. In: *Computational Intelligence*. IEEE Press, 1995, pp. 152–161
10. P.J. Angeline. Subtree crossover: Building block engine or macromutation? In: Koza et al. [234], pp. 9–17
11. P.J. Angeline. Competitive fitness evaluation. In: Bäck et al. [28], Chap. 3, pp. 12–14
12. P.J. Angeline, R.G. Reynolds, J.R. McDonnel, R. Eberhart, Eds. *Proceedings of the 6th Annual Conference on Evolutionary Programming*, No. 1213 in Lecture Notes in Computer Science. Springer, Berlin, Heidelberg, New York, 1997
13. J. Arabas, Z. Michalewicz, J. Mulawka. GAVaPS – a genetic algorithm with varying population size. In ICEC-94 [210], pp. 73–78
14. R. Axelrod. *The Evolution of Cooperation*. Basic Books, New York, 1984
15. R. Axelrod. The evolution of strategies in the iterated prisoner's dilemma. In: L. Davis, Ed., *Genetic Algorithms and Simulated Annealing*. Pitman, London, 1987
16. T. Bäck. The interaction of mutation rate, selection and self-adaptation within a genetic algorithm. In: Männer, Manderick [259], pp. 85–94

17. T. Bäck. Self adaptation in genetic algorithms. In: Varela, Bourgine [405], pp. 263–271
18. T. Bäck. Optimal mutation rates in genetic search. In: Forrest [158], pp. 2–8
19. T. Bäck. Selective pressure in evolutionary algorithms: A characterization of selection mechanisms. In ICEC-94 [210], pp. 57–62
20. T. Bäck. Generalised convergence models for tournament and (μ, λ) selection. In: Eshelman [137], pp. 2–8
21. T. Bäck. Order statistics for convergence velocity analysis of simplified evolutionary algorithms. In: Whitley, Vose [425], pp. 91–102
22. T. Bäck. *Evolutionary Algorithms in Theory and Practice*. Oxford University Press, Oxford, UK, 1996
23. T. Bäck, Ed. *Proceedings of the 7th International Conference on Genetic Algorithms*. Morgan Kaufmann, San Francisco, 1997
24. T. Bäck. Self-adaptation. In: Bäck et al. [28], Chap. 21, pp. 188–211
25. T. Bäck, A.E. Eiben, N.A.L. van der Vaart. An empirical study on GAs "without parameters". In: Schoenauer et al. [337], pp. 315–324
26. T. Bäck, D.B. Fogel, Z. Michalewicz, Eds. *Handbook of Evolutionary Computation*. Institute of Physics Publishing, Bristol, and Oxford University Press, New York, 1997
27. T. Bäck, D.B. Fogel, Z. Michalewicz, Eds. *Evolutionary Computation 1: Basic Algorithms and Operators*. Institute of Physics Publishing, Bristol, 2000
28. T. Bäck, D.B. Fogel, Z. Michalewicz, Eds. *Evolutionary Computation 2: Advanced Algorithms and Operators*. Institute of Physics Publishing, Bristol, 2000
29. T. Bäck, Z. Michalewicz. Test landscapes. In: Bäck et al. [26], Chap. B2.7, pp. 14–20
30. T. Bäck, G. Rudolph, H.P. Schwefel. Evolutionary programming and evolution strategies: Similarities and differences. In: Fogel, Atmar [151], pp. 11–22
31. T. Bäck, H.-P. Schwefel. An overview of evolutionary algorithms for parameter optimization. *Evolutionary Computation*, 1:1 pp.1–23, 1993
32. T. Bäck, D. Vermeulen, A.E. Eiben. Tax and evolution in sugarscape. In: S.-H. Cheng, P. Wang, Eds., *Proceedings of the The Second International Workshop on Computational Intelligence in Economics and Finance*. JCIS Press, 2002, pp. 1151–1156
33. J.E. Baker. Reducing bias and inefficiency in the selection algorithm. In: Grefenstette [182], pp. 14–21
34. J.M. Baldwin. A new factor in evolution. *American Naturalist*, 30, 1896
35. S. Baluja, S. Davies. Using optimal dependency-trees for combinatorial optimisation: Learning the structure of the search space. In: Fisher, Ed., *Proceedings of the 1997 International Conference on Machine Learning*. Morgan Kaufmann, San Francisco, 1997
36. W. Banzhaf. Interactive evolution. In: Bäck et al. [27], Chap. 30, pp. 228–234
37. W. Banzhaf, J. Daida, A.E. Eiben, M.H. Garzon, V. Honavar, M. Jakiela, R.E. Smith, Eds. *Proceedings of the Genetic and Evolutionary Computation Conference (GECCO-1999)*. Morgan Kaufmann, San Francisco, 1999
38. W. Banzhaf, P. Nordin, R.E. Keller, F.D. Francone. *Genetic Programming: An Introduction*. Morgan Kaufmann, San Francisco, 1998
39. W. Banzhaf, C. Reeves, Eds. *Foundations of Genetic Algorithms 5*. Morgan Kaufmann, San Francisco, 1999
40. N.A. Baricelli. Numerical testing of evolution theories, part1. *Acta Biotheor.*, 16 pp.69–98, 1962

41. J.C. Bean. Genetic algorithms and random keys for sequencing and optimisation. *ORSA Journal of Computing*, 1994
42. J.C. Bean, A.B. Hadj-Alouane. A dual genetic algorithm for bounded integer problems. Tech. Rep. 92-53, University of Michigan, 1992
43. R.K. Belew, L.B. Booker, Eds. *Proceedings of the 4th International Conference on Genetic Algorithms*. Morgan Kaufmann, San Francisco, 1991
44. R.K. Belew, M.D. Vose, Eds. *Foundations of Genetic Algorithms 4*. Morgan Kaufmann, San Francisco, 1997
45. P. Bentley. From coffee tables to hospitals: Generic evolutionary design. In: Bentley [46], pp. 405–423
46. P.J. Bentley, Ed. *Evolutionary Design by Computers*. Morgan Kaufmann, San Francisco, 1999
47. P.J. Bentley, D.W. Corne, Eds. *Creative Evolutionary Systems*. Morgan Kaufmann, San Francisco, 2002
48. P.J. Bentley, D.W. Corne. An introduction to creative evolutionary systems. In Bentley,Corne [47], pp. 1–75
49. A.D. Bethke. *Genetic Algorithms as Function Optimizers*. PhD thesis, The University of Michigan, 1981
50. H.-G. Beyer. *The Theory of Evolution Strategies*. Springer, Berlin, Heidelberg, New York, 2001
51. H.-G. Beyer, D.V. Arnold. Theory of evolution strategies: A tutorial. In: Kallel et al. [222], pp. 109–134
52. H.-G. Beyer, H.-P. Schwefel. Evolution strategies: A comprehensive introduction. *Natural Computing*, 1:1 pp.3–52, 2002
53. S. Blackmore. *The Meme Machine*. Oxford University Press, Oxford, UK, 1999
54. T. Blickle, L. Thiele. A comparison of selection schemes used in genetic algorithms. Tech. Rep. TIK Report 11, December 1995, Computer Engineering and Communication Networks Lab, Swiss Federal Institute of Technology, 1995
55. E. Bonabeau, M. Dorigo, G. Theraulaz. *Swarm Intelligence: From Natural to Artificial Systems*. Oxford University Press, New York, NY, 1999
56. E. Bonabeau, M. Dorigo, G. Theraulaz. Inspiration for optimization from social insect behaviour. *Nature*, 406 pp.39–42, 2000
57. A. Bonarini, C. Bonacina, M. Matteucci. Fuzzy and crisp representations of real-valued input for learning classifier systems. In: P.L. Lanzi, W. Stolzmann, S.W. Wilson, Eds., *Learning Classifier Systems: From Foundations to Applications*, Vol. 1813 of *LNAI*. Springer, Berlin, Heidelberg, New York, 2000, pp. 107–124
58. L.B. Booker. *Intelligent Behaviour as an adaptation to the task environment*. PhD thesis, University of Michigan, 1982
59. L.B. Booker. Triggered rule discovery in classifier systems. In: Schaffer [333], pp. 265–274
60. P. Bosman, D. Thierens. Linkage information processing in distribution estimation algorithms. In: Banzhaf et al. [37], pp. 60–67
61. M.F. Bramlette. Initialization, mutation and selection methods in genetic algorithms for function optimization. In: Belew, Booker [43], pp. 100–107
62. J. Branke, S. Kirby. *Evolutionary Optimization in Dynamic Environments*. Kluwer Academic Publishers, Boston, 2001
63. J. Branke, H. Schmeck. Designing evolutionary algorithms for dynamic optimization problems. In: Ghosh, Tsutsui [167], pp. 239–262

64. H.J. Bremermann, M. Rogson, S. Salaff. Global properties of evolution processes. In: H.H. Pattee, E.A. Edlsack, L. Fein, A.B. Callahan, Eds., *Natural Automata and Useful Simulations*. Spartan Books, Washington DC, 1966, pp. 3–41

65. L. Bull. *Artificial Symbiology*. PhD thesis, University of the West of England, 1995

66. L. Bull, T.C. Fogarty. Horizontal gene transfer in endosymbiosis. In: C.G. Langton, K.Shimohara, Eds., *Proceedings of the 5th International Workshop on Artificial Life : Synthesis and Simulation of Living Systems (ALIFE-96)*. MIT Press, Cambridge, MA, 1997, pp. 77–84

67. L. Bull, O. Holland, S. Blackmore. On meme–gene coevolution. *Artificial Life*, 6 pp.227–235, 2000

68. L. Bull, J. Hurst. ZCS redux. *Evolutionary Computation*, 10:2, 2002

69. E.K. Burke, J.P. Newall. A multi-stage evolutionary algorithm for the timetable problem. *IEEE Transactions on Evolutionary Computation*, 3:1 pp.63–74, 1999

70. E.K. Burke, J.P. Newall, R.F. Weare. Initialization strategies and diversity in evolutionary timetabling. *Evolutionary Computation*, 6:1 pp.81–103, 1998

71. *1999 Congress on Evolutionary Computation (CEC'1999)*. IEEE Press, Piscataway, NJ, 1999

72. *2000 Congress on Evolutionary Computation (CEC'2000)*. IEEE Press, Piscataway, NJ, 2000

73. *2001 Congress on Evolutionary Computation (CEC'2001)*. IEEE Press, Piscataway, NJ, 2001

74. *2002 Congress on Evolutionary Computation (CEC'2002)*. IEEE Press, Piscataway, NJ, 2002

75. U.K. Chakraborty. An analysis of selection in generational and steady state genetic algorithms. In: *Proceedings of the National Conference on Molecular Electronics*. NERIST (A.P.) India, 1995

76. U.K. Chakraborty, K. Deb, M. Chakraborty. Analysis of selection algorithms: A Markov Chain aproach. *Evolutionary Computation*, 4:2 pp.133–167, 1997

77. P. Cheeseman, B. Kenefsky, W. M. Taylor. Where the really hard problems are. In: *Proceedings of the Twelfth International Joint Conference on Artificial Intelligence, IJCAI-91*, 1991, pp. 331–337

78. K. Chellapilla, D.B. Fogel. Evolving an expert checkers playing program without human expertise. *IEEE Transactions on Evolutionary Computation*, 5:4 pp.422–428, 2001

79. H. Cobb. An investigation into the use of hypermutation as an adaptive operator in a genetic algorithm having continuous, time-dependent nonstationary environments. Memorandum 6760, Naval Research Laboratory, 1990

80. H.G. Cobb, J.J. Grefenstette. Genetic algorithms for tracking changing environments. In: Forrest [158], pp. 523–530

81. C.A. Coello Coello, D.A. Van Veldhuizen, G.B. Lamont. *Evolutionary Algorithms for Solving Multi-Objective Problems*. Kluwer Academic Publishers, Boston, 2002. ISBN 0-3064-6762-3

82. J.P. Cohoon, S.U. Hedge, W.N. Martin, D. Richards. Punctuated equilibria: A parallel genetic algorithm. In: Grefenstette [182], pp. 148–154

83. J.P. Cohoon, W.N. Martin, D.S. Richards. Genetic algorithms and punctuated equilibria in VLSI. In: Schwefel, Männer [343], pp. 134–144

84. D. Corne, M. Dorigo, F. Glover, Eds. *New Ideas in Optimization*. McGraw Hill, London, 1999

85. B.G.W. Craenen, A.E. Eiben, J.I. van Hemert. Comparing evolutionary algorithms on binary constraint satisfaction problems. *IEEE Transactions on Evolutionary Computation*, 2003. in press

86. C. Darwin. *The Origin of Species*. John Murray, 1859

87. R. Das, D. Whitley. The only challenging problems are deceptive: Global search by solving order-1 hyperplanes. In: Belew, Booker [43], pp. 166–173

88. D. Dasgupta, D. Mcgregor. SGA: A structured genetic algorithm. Technical Report IKBS-8-92, University of Strathclyde, 1992

89. Y. Davidor. A naturally occurring niche & species phenomenon: The model and first results. In: Belew, Booker [43], pp. 257–263

90. Y. Davidor, H.-P. Schwefel, R. Männer, Eds. *Proceedings of the 3rd Conference on Parallel Problem Solving from Nature*, No. 866 in Lecture Notes in Computer Science. Springer, Berlin, Heidelberg, New York, 1994

91. L. Davis. Adapting operator probabilities in genetic algorithms. In: Schaffer [333], pp. 61–69

92. L. Davis, Ed. *Handbook of Genetic Algorithms*. Van Nostrand Reinhold, 1991

93. T.E. Davis, J.C. Principe. A Markov chain framework for the simple genetic algorithm. *Evolutionary Computation*, 1:3 pp.269–288, 1993

94. R. Dawkins. *The Selfish Gene*. Oxford University Press, Oxford, UK, 1976

95. R. Dawkins. *The Blind Watchmaker*. Longman Scientific and Technical, 1986

96. L.N. de Castro, J.I. Timmis. *Artificial Immune Systems: A New Computational Intelligence Approach*. Springer, Berlin, Heidelberg, New York, 2002

97. E.D. de Jong, R.A. Watson, J.B. Pollack. Reducing bloat and promoting diversity using multi-objective methods. In: Spector et al. [381], pp. 11–18

98. K.A. De Jong. *An Analysis of the Behaviour of a Class of Genetic Adaptive Systems*. PhD thesis, University of Michigan, 1975

99. K.A. De Jong. Genetic algorithms are NOT function optimizers. In: Whitley [420], pp. 5–18

100. K.A. De Jong, M. Potter, W. Spears. Using problem generators to explore the effects of epistasis. In: Bäck [23], pp. 338–345

101. K.A. De Jong, J. Sarma. Generation gaps revisited. In: Whitley [420], pp. 19–28

102. K.A. De Jong, J. Sarma. On decentralizing selection algoritms. In: Eshelman [137], pp. 17–23

103. K.A. De Jong, W.M. Spears. An analysis of the interacting roles of population size and crossover in genetic algorithms. In: Schwefel, Männer [343], pp. 38–47

104. K.A. De Jong, W.M. Spears. A formal analysis of the role of multi-point crossover in genetic algorithms. *Annals of Mathematics and Artificial Intelligence*, 5:1 pp.1–26, April 1992

105. K. Deb. Genetic algorithms in multimodal function optimization. Master's thesis, University of Alabama, The Clearinghouse for Genetic Algorithms, Tuscaloosa, AL, 1989. TCGA Report No 88002

106. K. Deb. *Multi-objective Optimization using Evolutionary Algorithms*. Wiley, Chichester, UK, 2001

107. K. Deb, S. Agrawal, A. Pratab, T. Meyarivan. A Fast Elitist Non-Dominated Sorting Genetic Algorithm for Multi-Objective Optimization: NSGA-II. In: Schoenauer et al. [337], pp. 849–858

108. K. Deb, D.E. Goldberg. An investigation of niche and species formation in genetic function optimization. In: Schaffer [333], pp. 42–50

278   References

109. J.S. DeBonet, C. Isbell, P. Viola. Mimic: Finding optima by estimating probability densities. *Advances in Neural Information Processing Systems*, 9 pp.424–431, 1997

110. M. Dorigo, E. Sirtori. ALECSYS: A Parallel Laboratory for Learning Classifier Systems. In: Belew, Booker [43], pp. 296–302

111. A.E. Eiben. Multiparent recombination. In: Bäck et al. [27], Chap. 33.7, pp. 289–307

112. A.E. Eiben. Evolutionary algorithms and constraint satisfaction: Definitions, survey, methodology, and research directions. In: Kallel et al. [222], pp. 13–58

113. A.E. Eiben. Multiparent recombination in evolutionary computing. In: Ghosh, Tsutsui [167], pp. 175–192

114. A.E. Eiben, E.H.L. Aarts, K.M. Van Hee. Global convergence of genetic algorithms: a Markov chain analysis. In: Schwefel, Männer [343], pp. 4–12

115. A.E. Eiben, T. Bäck. An empirical investigation of multi-parent recombination operators in evolution strategies. *Evolutionary Computation*, 5:3 pp.347–365, 1997

116. A.E. Eiben, T. Bäck, M. Schoenauer, H.-P. Schwefel, Eds. *Proceedings of the 5th Conference on Parallel Problem Solving from Nature*, No. 1498 in Lecture Notes in Computer Science. Springer, Berlin, Heidelberg, New York, 1998

117. A.E. Eiben, R. Hinterding, Z. Michalewicz. Parameter control in evolutionary algorithms. *IEEE Transactions on Evolutionary Computation*, 3:2 pp.124–141, 1999

118. A.E. Eiben, B. Jansen, Z. Michalewicz, B. Paechter. Solving CSPs using self-adaptive constraint weights: how to prevent EAs from cheating. In: Whitley et al. [416], pp. 128–134

119. A.E. Eiben, M. Jelasity. A critical note on experimental research methodology in EC. In CEC-2002 [74], pp. 582–587

120. A.E. Eiben, Z. Michalewicz, Eds. *Evolutionary Computation*. IOS Press, 1998

121. A.E. Eiben, R. Nabuurs, I. Booij. The Escher evolver: Evolution to the people. In: Bentley, Corne [47], pp. 425–439

122. A.E. Eiben, P.-E. Raué, Z. Ruttkay. Genetic algorithms with multi-parent recombination. In: Davidor et al. [90], pp. 78–87

123. A.E. Eiben, P.-E. Raué, Z. Ruttkay. GA-easy and GA-hard constraint satisfaction problems. In: M. Meyer, Ed., *Proceedings of the ECAI-94 Workshop on Constraint Processing*, No. 923 in LNCS. Springer, Berlin, Heidelberg, New York, 1995, pp. 267–284

124. A.E. Eiben, G. Rudolph. Theory of evolutionary algorithms: a bird's eye view. *Theoretical Computer Science*, 229:1–2 pp.3–9, 1999

125. A.E. Eiben, Z. Ruttkay. Self-adaptivity for constraint satisfaction: Learning penalty functions. In ICEC-96 [212], pp. 258–261

126. A.E. Eiben, Z. Ruttkay. Constraint-satisfaction problems. In: Bäck et al. [28], Chap. 12, pp. 75–86

127. A.E. Eiben, C.A. Schippers. Multi-parent's niche: n-ary crossovers on NK-landscapes. In: Voigt et al. [410], pp. 319–328

128. A.E. Eiben, C.A. Schippers. On evolutionary exploration and exploitation. *Fundamenta Informaticae*, 35:1–4 pp.35–50, 1998

129. A.E. Eiben, I.G. Sprinkhuizen-Kuyper, B.A. Thijssen. Competing crossovers in an adaptive GA framework. In ICEC-98 [214], pp. 787–792

130. A.E. Eiben, J.K. van der Hauw. Solving 3-SAT with adaptive genetic algorithms. In ICEC-97 [213], pp. 81–86

131. A.E. Eiben, J.K. van der Hauw. Graph colouring with adaptive genetic algorithms. *J. Heuristics*, 4:1, 1998
132. A.E. Eiben, J.I. van Hemert. SAW-ing EAs: adapting the fitness function for solving constrained problems. In: Corne et al. [84], Chap. 26, pp. 389–402
133. A.E. Eiben, C.H.M. van Kemenade, J.N. Kok. Orgy in the computer: Multiparent reproduction in genetic algorithms. In: Morán et al. [282], pp. 934–945
134. N. Eldredge, S.J. Gould. *Models of Paleobiology*, Chap. Punctuated Equilibria: an alternative to phyletic gradualism, pp. 82–115. Freeman Cooper, San Francisco, 1972
135. J.M. Epstein, R. Axtell. *Growing Artificial Societies: Social Sciences from Bottom Up.* Brooking Institution Press and The MIT Press, 1996
136. L.J. Eshelman. The CHC adaptive search algorithm: how to have safe search when engaging in non-traditional genetic recombination. In: Rawlins [316], pp. 263–283
137. L.J. Eshelman, Ed. *Proceedings of the 6th International Conference on Genetic Algorithms.* Morgan Kaufmann, San Francisco, 1995
138. L.J. Eshelman, R.A. Caruana, J.D. Schaffer. Biases in the crossover landscape. In: Schaffer [333], pp. 10–19
139. L.J. Eshelman, J.D. Schaffer. Preventing premature convergence in genetic algorithms by preventing incest. In: Belew, Booker [43], pp. 115–122
140. L.J. Eshelman, J.D. Schaffer. Crossover's niche. In: Forrest [158], pp. 9–14
141. L.J. Eshelman, J.D. Schaffer. Productive recombination and propogating and preserving schemata. In: Whitley, Vose [425], pp. 299–313
142. R. Etxeberria, P. Larranaga. Global optimisation using bayesian networks. In: A.O. Rodriguez, M.S. Ortiz, R. Hermida, Eds., *Proceedings of the Second Symposium on Artificial Intelligence (CIMAF-99)*, 1999, pp. 332–339
143. T.C. Fogarty, F. Vavak, P. Cheng. Use of the genetic algorithm for load balancing of sugar beet presses. In: Eshelman [137], pp. 617–624
144. D.B. Fogel. *Evolving Artificial Intelligence.* PhD thesis, University of California, 1992
145. D.B. Fogel. *Evolutionary Computation.* IEEE Press, 1995
146. D.B. Fogel, Ed. *Evolutionary Computation: the Fossil Record.* IEEE Press, Piscataway, NJ, 1998
147. D.B. Fogel. *Blondie24: Playing at the Edge of AI.* Morgan Kaufmann, San Francisco, 2002
148. D.B. Fogel. Better than Samuel: Evolving a nearly expert checkers player. In: Ghosh, Tsutsui [167], pp. 989–1004
149. D.B. Fogel, J.W. Atmar. Comparing genetic operators with Gaussian mutations in simulated evolutionary processes using linear systems. *Biological Cybernetics*, 63:2 pp.111–114, 1990
150. D.B. Fogel, W. Atmar, Eds. *First Annual Conference on Evolutionary Programming*, La Jolla, California, 1992. Evolutionary Programming Society
151. D.B. Fogel, W. Atmar, Eds. *Second Annual Conference on Evolutionary Programming*, La Jolla, California, February 1993. Evolutionary Programming Society
152. D.B. Fogel, L. Fogel, J.W. Atmar. Meta-evolutionary programming. In: R.R. Chen, Ed., *Proceedings of the 25th Asilomar Conference on signals,systms and computers*, 1991, pp. 540–545
153. D.B. Fogel, L.C. Stayton. On the effectiveness of crossover in simulated evolutionary optimization. *BioSystems*, 32:3 pp.171–182, 1994

154. L.J. Fogel, P.J. Angeline, T. Bäck, Eds. *Proceedings of the 5th Annual Conference on Evolutionary Programming.* MIT Press, Cambridge, MA, 1996
155. L.J. Fogel, A.J. Owens, M.J. Walsh. Artificial intelligence through a simulation of evolution. In: A. Callahan, M. Maxfield, L.J. Fogel, Eds., *Biophysics and Cybernetic Systems.* Spartan, Washington DC, 1965, pp. 131–156
156. L.J. Fogel, A.J. Owens, M.J. Walsh. *Artificial Intelligence through Simulated Evolution.* Wiley, Chichester, UK, 1966
157. C.M. Fonseca, P.J. Fleming. Genetic Algorithms for multiobjective optimization: formulation, discussion and generalization. In: Forrest [158], pp. 416–423
158. S. Forrest, Ed. *Proceedings of the 5th International Conference on Genetic Algorithms.* Morgan Kaufmann, San Francisco, 1993
159. S. Forrest, M. Mitchell. Relative building block fitness and the building block hypothesis. In: Whitley [420], pp. 109–126
160. A.A. Freitas. *Data Mining and Knowledge Discovery with Evolutionary Algorithms.* Springer, Berlin, Heidelberg, New York, 2002
161. P.W. Frey, D.J. Slate. Letter Recognition Using Holland-Style Adaptive Classifiers. *Machine Learning,* 6 pp.161–182, 1991
162. B. Friesleben, M. Hartfelder. Optimisation of genetic algorithms by genetic algorithms. In: R.F. Albrecht, C.R. Reeves, N.C. Steele, Eds., *Artifical Neural Networks and Genetic Algorithms.* Springer, Berlin, Heidelberg, New York, 1993, pp. 392–399
163. B. Friesleben, P. Merz. A genetic local search algorithm for solving the symmetric and assymetric travelling salesman problem. In ICEC-96 [212], pp. 616–621
164. C. Gathercole, P. Ross. Dynamic training subset selection for supervised learning in genetic programming. In: Davidor et al. [90], pp. 312–321. Lecture Notes in Computer Science 866
165. D.K. Gehlhaar, D.B. Fogel. Tuning evolutionary programming for conformationally flexible molecular docking. In: Fogel et al. [154], pp. 419–429
166. I. Gent, T. Walsh. Phase transitions from real computational problems. In: *Proceedings of the 8th International Symposium on Artificial Intelligence,* 1995, pp. 356–364
167. A. Ghosh, S. Tsutsui, Eds. *Advances in Evolutionary Computating: Theory and Applications.* Springer, Berlin, Heidelberg, New York, 2003
168. F. Glover. Tabu search: 1. *ORSA Journal on Computing,* 1:3 pp.190–206, Summer 1989
169. F. Glover. Tabu search and adaptive memory programming — advances, applications, and challenges. In: R.S. Barr, R.V. Helgason, J.L. Kennington, Eds., *Interfaces in Computer Science and Operations Research.* Kluwer Academic Publishers, Norwell, MA, 1996, pp. 1–75
170. D.E. Goldberg. Genetic algorithms and Walsh functions: I. A gentle introduction. *Complex Systems,* 3:2 pp.129–152, April 1989
171. D.E. Goldberg. Genetic algorithms and Walsh functions: II. Deception and its analysis. *Complex Systems,* 3:2 pp.153–171, April 1989
172. D.E. Goldberg. *Genetic Algorithms in Search, Optimization and Machine Learning.* Addison-Wesley, 1989
173. D.E. Goldberg, K. Deb. A comparative analysis of selection schemes used in genetic algorithms. In: Rawlins [316], pp. 69–93
174. D.E. Goldberg, B. Korb, K. Deb. Messy genetic algorithms: Motivation, analysis, and first results. *Complex Systems,* 3:5 pp.493–530, October 1989

175. D.E. Goldberg, R. Lingle. Alleles, loci, and the traveling salesman problem. In: Grefenstette [180], pp. 154–159
176. D.E. Goldberg, J. Richardson. Genetic algorithms with sharing for multimodal function optimization. In: Grefenstette [182], pp. 41–49
177. D.E. Goldberg, R.E. Smith. Nonstationary function optimization using genetic algorithms with dominance and diploidy. In: Grefenstette [182], pp. 59–68
178. M. Gorges-Schleuter. ASPARAGOS an asynchronous parallel genetic optimization strategy. In: Schaffer [333], pp. 422–427
179. J. Gottlieb, G.R. Raidl. The effects of locality on the dynamics of decoder-based evolutionary search. In: Whitley et al. [416], pp. 283–290
180. J.J. Grefenstette, Ed. *Proceedings of the 1st International Conference on Genetic Algorithms and Their Applications.* Lawrence Erlbaum, Hillsdale, New Jersey, 1985
181. J.J. Grefenstette. Optimisation of control parameters for genetic algorithms. *IEEE Transaction on Systems, Man and Cybernetics*, 16:1 pp.122–128, 1986
182. J.J. Grefenstette, Ed. *Proceedings of the 2nd International Conference on Genetic Algorithms and Their Applications.* Lawrence Erlbaum, Hillsdale, New Jersey, 1987
183. J.J. Grefenstette. Lamarckian Learning in Multi-Agent Environments. In: Belew, Booker [43], pp. 303–310
184. J.J. Grefenstette. Genetic algorithms for changing environments. In: Männer, Manderick [259], pp. 137–144
185. J.J. Grefenstette. Deception considered harmful. In: Whitley [420], pp. 75–91
186. J.J. Grefenstette, R. Gopal, B. Rosmaita, D. van Guch. Genetic algorithm for the TSP. In: Grefenstette [180], pp. 160–168
187. J.J. Merelo Guervos, P. Adamidis, H.-G. Beyer, J.-L. Fernandez-Villacanas, H.-P. Schwefel, Eds. *Proceedings of the 7th Conference on Parallel Problem Solving from Nature*, No. 2439 in Lecture Notes in Computer Science. Springer, Berlin, Heidelberg, New York, 2002
188. A.B. Hadj-Alouane, J.C. Bean. A genetic algorithm for the multiple-choice integer program. Tech. Rep. 92-50, University of Michigan, 1992
189. P. Hansen, N. Mladenovic̀. An introduction to variable neighborhood search. In: S. Voß, S. Martello, I.H. Osman, C. Roucairol, Eds., *Meta-Heuristics: Advances and Trends in Local Search Paradigms for Optimization. Proceedings of MIC 97 Conference.* Kluwer Academic Publishers, Dordrecht, The Netherlands, 1998
190. G. Harik, D.E. Goldberg. Learning linkage. Tech. Rep. IlliGAL 96006, Illinois Genetic Algorithms Laboratory, Univeristy of Illinois, 1996
191. E. Hart, P. Ross, J. Nelson. Solving a real-world problem using an evolving heuristically driven schedule builder. *Evolutionary Computation*, 6:1 pp.61–81, 1998
192. W.E. Hart. *Adaptive Global Optimization with Local Search.* PhD thesis, University of California, San Diego, 1994
193. M. Herdy. Evolution strategies with subjective selection. In: Voigt et al. [410], pp. 22–31
194. J. Hesser, R. Manner. Towards an optimal mutation probablity in genetic algorithms. In: Schwefel, Männer [343], pp. 23–32
195. M.S. Hillier, F.S. Hillier. Conventional optimization techniques. In: Sarker et al. [331], Chap. 1, pp. 3–25

196. W.D. Hillis. Co-evolving parasites improve simulated evolution as an optimization procedure. In: C.G. Langton, C. Taylor, J.D.. Farmer, S. Rasmussen, Eds., *Proceedings of the Workshop on Artificial Life (ALIFE '90)*, Vol. 5 of *Santa Fe Institute Studies in the Sciences of Complexity*, Redwood City, CA, USA, February 1992. Addison-Wesley, pp. 313–324

197. R. Hinterding, Z. Michalewicz, A.E. Eiben. Adaptation in evolutionary computation: A survey. In ICEC-97 [213]

198. R. Hinterding, Z. Michalewicz, T.C. Peachey. Self-adaptive genetic algorithm for numeric functions. In: Voigt et al. [410], pp. 420–429

199. G.E. Hinton, S.J. Nowlan. How learning can guide evolution. *Complex Systems*, 1 pp.495–502, 1987

200. P.G. Hoel, S.C.Port, C.J. Stone. *Introduction to Stochastic Proceses*. Houghton Mifflin, 1972

201. F. Hoffmeister, T. Bäck. Genetic self-learning. In: Varela, Bourgine [405], pp. 227–235

202. J.H. Holland. Genetic algorithms and the optimal allocation of trials. *SIAM J. of Computing*, 2 pp.88–105, 1973

203. J.H. Holland. Adaptation. In: Rosen, Snell, Eds., *Progress in Theoretical Biology: 4*. Plenum, 1976

204. J.H. Holland. *Adaption in Natural and Artificial Systems*. MIT Press, Cambridge, MA, 1992. 1st edition: 1975, The University of Michigan Press, Ann Arbor

205. W. Hordijk, B. Manderick. The usefulness of recombination. In: Morán et al. [282], pp. 908–919

206. J. Horn, N. Nafpliotis, D.E. Goldberg. A niched Pareto genetic algorithm for multiobjective optimization. In ICEC-94 [210], pp. 82–87

207. C.R. Houck, J.A. Joines, M.G. Kay, J.R. Wilson. Empirical investigation of the benefits of partial Lamarckianism. *Evolutionary Computation*, 5:1 pp.31–60, 1997

208. P. Husbands. Distributed co-evolutionary genetic algorithms for multi-criteria and multi-constraint optimisiation. In: T.C. Fogarty, Ed., *Evolutionary Computing: Proceedings of the AISB workshop*, LNCS 865. Springer, Berlin, Heidelberg, New York, 1994, pp. 150–165

209. H. Iba, H. de Garis, T. Sato. Genetic programming using a minimum description length principle. In: Kinnear [226], pp. 265–284

210. *Proceedings of the First IEEE Conference on Evolutionary Computation*. IEEE Press, Piscataway, NJ, 1994

211. *Proceedings of the 1995 IEEE Conference on Evolutionary Computation*. IEEE Press, Piscataway, NJ, 1995

212. *Proceedings of the 1996 IEEE Conference on Evolutionary Computation*. IEEE Press, Piscataway, NJ, 1996

213. *Proceedings of the 1997 IEEE Conference on Evolutionary Computation*. IEEE Press, Piscataway, NJ, 1997

214. *Proceedings of the 1998 IEEE Conference on Evolutionary Computation*. IEEE Press, Piscataway, NJ, 1998

215. J. Hurst and L. Bull, C. Melhuish. TCS learning classifier system controller on a real robot. In: Guervos et al. [187], pp. 588 –597

216. A. Jain, D.B. Fogel. Case studies in applying fitness distributions in evolutionary algorithms. II. comparing the improvements from crossover and gaussian

mutation on simple neural networks. In: X. Yao, D.B. Fogel, Eds., *Proc. of the 2000 IEEE Symposium on Combinations of Evolutionary Computation and Neural Networks.* IEEE Press, Piscataway, NJ, 2000, pp. 91–97

217. J.A. Joines, C.R. Houck. On the use of non-stationary penalty functions to solve nonlinear constrained optimisation problems with ga's. In ICEC-94 [210], pp. 579–584

218. T. Jones. *Evolutionary Algorithms, Fitness Landscapes and Search.* PhD thesis, The University of New Mexico, Albuquerque, NM, 1995

219. B.A. Julstrom. What have you done for me lately?: Adapting operator probabilities in a steady-state genetic algorithm. In: Eshelman [137], pp. 81–87

220. Y. Kakuza, H. Sakanashi, K. Suzuki. Adaptive search strategy for genetic algorithms with additional genetic algorithms. In: Männer, Manderick [259], pp. 311–320

221. L. Kallel, B. Naudts, C. Reeves. Properties of fitness functions and search landscapes. In: Kallel et al. [222], pp. 175–206

222. L. Kallel, B. Naudts, A. Rogers, Eds. *Theoretical Aspects of Evolutionary Computing.* Springer, Berlin, Heidelberg, New York, 2001

223. H. Kargupta. The gene expression messy genetic algorithm. In ICEC-96 [212], pp. 814–819

224. S.A. Kauffman. *Origins of Order: Self-Organization and Selection in Evolution.* Oxford University Press, New York, NY, 1993

225. A.J. Keane, S.M. Brown. The design of a satellite boom with enhanced vibration performance using genetic algorithm techniques. In: I.C. Parmee, Ed., *Proceedings of the Conference on Adaptive Computing in Engineering Design and Control 96.* P.E.D.C, Plymouth, 1996, pp. 107–113

226. K.E. Kinnear, Ed. *Advances in Genetic Programming.* MIT Press, Cambridge, MA, 1994

227. S. Kirkpatrick, C. Gelatt, M. Vecchi. Optimization by simulated anealing. *Science,* 220 pp.671–680, 1983

228. J.D. Knowles, D.W. Corne. Approximating the nondominated front using the Pareto Archived Evolution Strategy. *Evolutionary Computation,* 8:2 pp.149–172, 2000

229. J.R. Koza. *Genetic Programming.* MIT Press, Cambridge, MA, 1992

230. J.R. Koza. *Genetic Programming II.* MIT Press, Cambridge, MA, 1994

231. J.R. Koza. Scalable learning in genetic programming using automatic function definition. In: Kinnear [226], pp. 99–117

232. J.R. Koza, W. Banzhaf, K. Chellapilla, K. Deb, M. Dorigo, D.B. Fogel, M. Garzon, D.E. Goldberg, H. Iba, R.L. Riolo, Eds. *Proceedings of the 3rd Annual Conference on Genetic Programming.* MIT Press, Cambridge, MA, 1998

233. J.R. Koza, F.H. Bennett. Automatic synthesis, placement,and routing of electrical circuits by means of genetic programming. In: Spector et al. [382], pp. 105–134

234. J.R. Koza, K. Deb, M. Dorigo, D.B. Fogel, M. Garzon, H. Iba, R.L. Riolo, Eds. *Proceedings of the 2nd Annual Conference on Genetic Programming.* MIT Press, Cambridge, MA, 1997

235. J.R. Koza, D.E. Goldberg, D.B. Fogel, R.L. Riolo, Eds. *Proceedings of the 1st Annual Conference on Genetic Programming.* MIT Press, Cambridge, MA, 1996

236. N. Krasnogor. *Studies in the Theory and Design Space of Memetic Algorithms.* PhD thesis, University of the West of England, 2002

237. N. Krasnogor, B.P. Blackburne, E.K. Burke, J.D. Hirst. Multimeme algorithms for protein structure prediction. In: Guervos et al. [187], pp. 769–778

238. N. Krasnogor, S. Gustafson. Toward truly "memetic" memetic algorithms: discussion and proofs of concept. In: D. Corne, G. Fogel, W. Hart, J. Knowles, N. Krasnogor, R. Roy, J. Smith, A. Tiwari, Eds., *Advances in Nature-Inspired Computation: The PPSN VII Workshops*, Reading, UK, 2002. PEDAL (Parallel, Emergent & Distributed Architectures Lab), University of Reading, pp. 9–10

239. N. Krasnogor, J.E. Smith. A memetic algorithm with self-adaptive local search: TSP as a case study. In: Whitley et al. [416], pp. 987–994

240. N. Krasnogor, J.E. Smith. Emergence of profitable search strategies based on a simple inheritance mechanism. In: Spector et al. [381], pp. 432–439

241. M.W.S. Land. *Evolutionary Algorithms with Local Search for Combinatorial Optimization*. PhD thesis, University of California, San Diego, 1998

242. W. B. Langdon, E. Cantú-Paz, K. Mathias, R. Roy, D. Davis, R. Poli, K. Balakrishnan, V. Honavar, G. Rudolph, J. Wegener, L. Bull, M. A. Potter, A. C. Schultz, J. F. Miller, E. Burke, N. Jonoska, Eds. *Proceedings of the Genetic and Evolutionary Computation Conference (GECCO-2002)*. Morgan Kaufmann, San Francisco, 9-13 July 2002

243. W.B. Langdon. *Genetic Programming + Data Structures = Automatic Programming!* Kluwer Academic Publishers, Boston, 1998

244. W.B. Langdon, R. Poli. *Foundations of Genetic Programming*. Springer, Berlin, Heidelberg, New York, 2001

245. W.B. Langdon, T. Soule, R. Poli, J.A. Foster. The evolution of size and shape. In: Spector et al. [382], pp. 163–190

246. C.G. Langton, Ed. *Artificial Life: an Overview*. MIT Press, Cambridge, MA, 1995

247. P.L. Lanzi, W. Stolzmann, S.W. Wilson, Eds. *Advances in Learning Classifier Systems*, Vol. 1996 of *LNAI*. Springer, Berlin, Heidelberg, New York, 2001

248. M. Lee, H. Takagi. Dynamic control of genetic algorithms using fuzzy logic techniques. In: Forrest [158], pp. 76–83

249. S. Lin, B. Kernighan. An effective heuristic algorithm for the Traveling Salesman Problem. *Operations Research*, 21 pp.498–516, 1973

250. J. Lis. Parallel genetic algorithm with dynamic control parameter. In ICEC-96 [212], pp. 324–329

251. J. Lis, M. Lis. Self-adapting parallel genetic algorithm with the dynamic mutation probability, crossover rate, and population size. In: J. Arabas, Ed., *Proceedings of the First Polish Evolutionary Algorithms Conference*. Politechnika Warszawska, Warsaw, 1996, pp. 79–86

252. R. Lohmann. Application of evolution strategy in parallel populations. In: Schwefel, Männer [343], pp. 198–208

253. S. Luke. Genetic programming produced competitive soccer softbot teams for RoboCup97. In: Koza et al. [232], pp. 214–222

254. S. Luke, L. Spector. A comparison of crossover and mutation in genetic programming. In: Koza et al. [234], pp. 240–248

255. W.G. Macready, D.H. Wolpert. Bandit problems and the exploration/exploitation tradeoff. *IEEE Transactions on Evolutionary Computation*, 2:1 pp.2–22, April 1998

256. S.W. Mahfoud. Crowding and preselection revisited. In: Männer, Manderick [259], pp. 27–36

257. S.W. Mahfoud. Boltzmann selection. In: Bäck et al. [26], pp. C2.5:1–4
258. B. Manderick, P. Spiessens. Fine-grained parallel genetic algorithms. In: Schaffer [333], pp. 428–433
259. R. Männer, B. Manderick, Eds. *Proceedings of the 2nd Conference on Parallel Problem Solving from Nature*. North-Holland, Amsterdam, 1992
260. W.N. Martin, J. Lienig, J.P. Cohoon. Island (migration) models: evolutionary algorithms based on punctuated equilibria. In: Bäck et al. [28], Chap. 15, pp. 101–124
261. W.N. Martin, W.M. Spears, Eds. *Foundations of Genetic Algorithms 6*. Morgan Kaufmann, San Francisco, 2001
262. K.E. Mathias, L.D. Whitley. Remapping hyperspace during genetic search: Canonical delta folding. In: Whitley [420], pp. 167–186
263. K.E. Mathias, L.D. Whitley. Changing representations during search: A comparative study of delta coding. *Evolutionary Computation*, 2:3 pp.249–278, 1995
264. G. Mayley. Landscapes, learning costs and genetic assimilation. *Evolutionary Computation*, 4:3 pp.213–234, 1996
265. J. Maynard-Smith. *The Evolution of Sex*. Cambridge University Press, Cambridge, UK, 1978
266. J. Maynard-Smith, E. Száthmary. *The Major transitions in evolution*. W.H.Freeman, 1995
267. J.T. McClave, T. Sincich. *Statistics*. Prentice Hall, 9th edn., 2003
268. J.R. McDonnell, R.G. Reynolds, D.B. Fogel, Eds. *Proceedings of the 4th Annual Conference on Evolutionary Programming*. MIT Press, Cambridge, MA, 1995
269. P. Merz. *Memetic Algorithms for Combinatorial Optimization Problems: Fitness Landscapes and Efective Search Strategies*. PhD thesis, Department of Electrical Engineering and Computer Science, University of Siegen, Germany, 2000
270. P. Merz, B. Freisleben. Fitness landscapes and memetic algorithm design. In: Corne et al. [84], pp. 245–260
271. Z. Michalewicz. *Genetic Algorithms + Data Structures = Evolution Programs*. Springer, Berlin, Heidelberg, New York, 3rd edn., 1996
272. Z. Michalewicz. Decoders. In: Bäck et al. [28], Chap. 8, pp. 49–55
273. Z. Michalewicz, K. Deb, M. Schmidt, T. Stidsen. Test-case generator for nonlinear continuous parameter optimization techniques. *IEEE Transactions on Evolutionary Computation*, 4:3 pp.197–215, 2000
274. Z. Michalewicz, G. Nazhiyath. Genocop III a coevolutionary algorithm for numerical optimisation problems with nonlinear constraintrs. In ICEC-95 [211], pp. 647–651
275. Z. Michalewicz, M. Schmidt. Evolutionary algorithms and constrained optimization. In: Sarker et al. [331], Chap. 3, pp. 57–86
276. Z. Michalewicz, M. Schmidt. TCG-2: A test-case generator for nonlinear parameter optimisation techniques. In: Ghosh, Tsutsui [167], pp. 193–212
277. Z. Michalewicz, M. Schoenauer. Evolutionary algorithms for constrained parameter optimisation problems. *Evolutionary Computation*, 4:1 pp.1–32, 1996
278. J.F. Miller, T. Kalganova, D. Job, N. Lipnitskaya. The genetic algorithm as a discovery engine: Strange circuits and new principles. In: Bentley, Corne [47], pp. 443–466

279. D. Mitchell, B. Selman, H. Levesque. Hard and easy distributions of SAT problems. In: *Proceedings of the Tenth National Conference on Artificial Intelligence.* AAAI Press/MIT Press, Cambridge MA, 1992, pp. 459–465

280. M. Mitchell. *An Introduction to Genetic Algorithms.* MIT Press, Cambridge, MA, 1996

281. D.J. Montana. Strongly typed genetic programming. *Evolutionary Computation,* 3:2 pp.199–230, 1995

282. F. Morán, A. Moreno, J. J. Merelo, P. Chacón, Eds. *Advances in Artificial Life. Third International Conference on Artificial Life,* Vol. 929 of *Lecture Notes in Artificial Intelligence.* Springer, Berlin, Heidelberg, New York, 1995

283. N. Mori, H. Kita, Y. Nishikawa. Adaptation to a changing environment by means of the thermodynamical genetic algorithm. In: Voigt et al. [410], pp. 513–522

284. A. Moroni, J. Manzolli, F. Von Zuben, R. Gudwin. Vox populi: Evolutionary computation for music evolution. In: Bentley, Corne [47], pp. 206–221

285. P. Moscato. Memetic algorithms' home page, visited july 2003: http://www.densis.fee.unicamp.br/~moscato/memetic_home.html

286. P.A. Moscato. On evolution, search, optimization, genetic algorithms and martial arts: Towards memetic algorithms. Tech. Rep. Caltech Concurrent Computation Program Report 826, Caltech, Caltech, Pasadena, California, 1989

287. P.A. Moscato. *Problemas de Otimizacão NP, Aproximabilidade e Computacão Evolutiva:Da Prática à Teoria.* PhD thesis, Universidade Estadual de Campinas,Brasil, 2001

288. H. Mühlenbein. Parallel genetic algorithms, population genetics and combinatorial optimization. In: Schaffer [333], pp. 416–421

289. H. Mühlenbein. The equation for the response to selection and its use for prediction. *Evolutionary Computation,* 5:3 pp.303–346, 1998

290. H. Mühlenbein, G. Paas. From recombination of genes to the estimation of distributions I. binary parameters. In: Voigt et al. [410], pp. 188–197

291. M. Munetomo, D.E. Goldberg. Linkage identification by non-monotonicity detection for overlapping functions. *Evolutionary Computation,* 7:4 pp.377–398, 1999

292. A. Nix, M. Vose. Modelling genetic algorithms with Markov chains. *Annals of Mathematics and Artifical Intelligence,* pp. 79–88, 1992

293. S. Nolfi, D. Floreano. *Evolutionary Robotics: The Biology, Intelligence, and Technology of Self-Organizing Machines.* MIT Press, Cambridge, MA, 2000

294. C.K. Oei, D.E. Goldberg, S.J. Chang. Tournament selection, niching, and the preservation of diversity. Tech. Rep. 91011, University of Illinois Genetic algorithms laboratory, 1991

295. I.M. Oliver, D.J. Smith, J.Holland. A study of permutation crossover operators on the travelling salesman problem. In: Grefenstette [182], pp. 224–230

296. B. Paechter, R.C. Rankin, A. Cumming, T.C. Fogarty. Timetabling the classes of an entire university with an evolutionary algorithm. In: Eiben et al. [116], pp. 865–874

297. J. Paredis. Coevolutionary constraint satisfaction. In: Davidor et al. [90], pp. 46–55

298. J. Paredis. The symbiotic evolution of solutions and their representations. In: Eshelman [137], pp. 359–365

299. J. Paredis. Coevolutionary computation. *Artificial Life,* 2 pp.255–375, 1996

300. J. Paredis. Coevolutionary algorithms. In: Bäck et al. [26]

301. I.C. Parmee. Improving problem definition through interactive evolutionary computing. *Artificial Intelligence for Engineering Design, Analysis and Manufacturing*, 16:3 pp.185–202, 2002

302. M. Pelikan, D.E. Goldberg, E. Cant-Paz. BOA: The Bayesian optimization algorithm. In: Banzhaf et al. [37], pp. 525–532

303. M. Pelikan, D.E. Goldberg, F. Lobo. A survey of optimization by building and using probabilistic models. Tech. rep., Illinois Genetic Algorithms Laboratory, University of Illinois at Urbana-Champaign, 1999

304. M. Pelikan, H. Mühlenbein. The bivariate marginal distribution algorithm. In: R. Roy, T. Furuhashi, P.K. Chawdhry, Eds., *Advances in Soft Computing–Engineering Design and Manufacturing*. Springer, Berlin, Heidelberg, New York, 1999, pp. 521–535

305. C. Pettey. Diffusion (cellular) models. In: Bäck et al. [28], Chap. 16, pp. 125–133

306. C.B. Pettey, M.R. Leuze, J.J. Grefenstette. A parallel genetic algorithm. In: Grefenstette [182], pp. 155–161

307. V.W. Porto, N. Saravanan, D. Waagen, A.E. Eiben, Eds. *Proceedings of the 7th Annual Conference on Evolutionary Programming*, No. 1477 in LNCS. Springer, Berlin, Heidelberg, New York, 1998

308. C. Potta, R. Poli, J. Rowe, K. DeJong, Eds. *Foundations of Genetic Algorithms 7*. Morgan Kaufmann, San Francisco, 2003

309. M.A. Potter, K.A. De Jong. A cooperative coevolutionary approach to function optimisation. In: Davidor et al. [90], pp. 248–257

310. P. Prosser. An empirical study of phase transitions in binary constraint satisfaction problems. *Artificial Intelligence*, 81 pp.81–109, 1996

311. A. Prügel-Bennet, J. Shapiro. An analysis of genetic algorithms using statistical mechanics. *Phys. Review Letters*, 72:9 pp.1305–1309, 1994

312. A. Prügel-Bennett. Modelling evolving populations. *J. Theoretical Biology*, 185:1 pp.81–95, March 1997

313. A. Prügel-Bennett. Modelling finite populations. In: Potta et al. [308]

314. A. Prügel-Bennett, A. Rogers. Modelling genetic algorithm dynamics. In: L. Kallel, B. Naudts, A. Rogers, Eds., *Theoretical Aspects of Evolutionary Computing*. Springer, Berlin, Heidelberg, New York, 2001, pp. 59–85

315. N. Radcliffe. Forma analysis and random respectful recombination. In: Belew, Booker [43], pp. 222–229

316. G. Rawlins, Ed. *Foundations of Genetic Algorithms*. Morgan Kaufmann, San Francisco, 1991

317. I. Rechenberg. *Evolutionstrategie: Optimierung Technisher Systeme nach Prinzipien des Biologischen Evolution*. Fromman-Hozlboog Verlag, Stuttgart, 1973

318. C. Reeves, J. Rowe. *Genetic Algorithms: Principles and Perspectives*. Kluwer, Norwell MA, 2002

319. R.G. Reynolds. Cultural algorithms: Theory and applications. In: Corne et al. [84], Chap. 24, pp. 367–377

320. A. Rogers, A. Prügel-Bennett. Modelling the dynamics of a steady-state genetic algorithm. In: Banzhaf, Reeves [39], pp. 57–68

321. J. Rowe. Population fixed-points for functions of unitation. In: Banzhaf, Reeves [39], pp. 69–84

322. G. Rudolph. Global optimization by means of distributed evolution strategies. In: Schwefel, Männer [343], pp. 209–213

323. G. Rudolph. Convergence properties of canonical genetic algorithms. *IEEE Transactions on Neural Networks*, 5:1 pp.96–101, 1994

324. G. Rudolph. Convergence of evolutionary algorithms in general search spaces. In ICEC-96 [212], pp. 50–54

325. G. Rudolph. Reflections on bandit problems and selection methods in uncertain environments. In: Bäck [23], pp. 166–173

326. G. Rudolph. Takeover times and probabilities of non-generational selection rules. In: Whitley et al. [416], pp. 903–910

327. T. Runnarson, X. Yao. Constrained evolutionary optimization – the penalty function approach. In: Sarker et al. [331], Chap. 4, pp. 87–113

328. A. Salman, K. Mehrota, C. Mohan. Linkage crossover for genetic algorithms. In: Banzhaf et al. [37], pp. 564–571

329. A.L. Samuel. Some studies in machine learning using the game of checkers. *IBM J. Research and Development*, 3 pp.211–229, 1959

330. E. Sanchez, M. Tomassini. *Towards Evolvable Hardware: The Evolutionary Engineering Approach*, Vol. 1062 of *Lecture Notes in Computer Science*. Springer, Berlin, Heidelberg, New York, 1996

331. R. Sarker, M. Mohammadian, X. Yao, Eds. *Evolutionary Optimization*. Kluwer Academic Publishers, Boston, 2002

332. J.D. Schaffer. *Multiple Objective Optimization with Vector Evaluated Genetic Algorithms*. PhD thesis, Vanderbilt University, Tennessee, 1984

333. J.D. Schaffer, Ed. *Proceedings of the 3rd International Conference on Genetic Algorithms*. Morgan Kaufmann, San Francisco, 1989

334. J.D. Schaffer, R.A. Caruana, L.J. Eshelman, R. Das. A study of control parameters affecting online performance of genetic algorithms for function optimisation. In: Schaffer [333], pp. 51–60

335. J.D. Schaffer, L.J. Eshelman. On crossover as an evolutionarily viable strategy. In: Belew, Booker [43], pp. 61–68

336. D. Schlierkamp-Voosen, H. Mühlenbein. Strategy adaptation by competing subpopulations. In: Davidor et al. [90], pp. 199–209

337. M. Schoenauer, K. Deb, G. Rudolph, X. Yao, E. Lutton, J.J. Merelo, H.-P. Schwefel, Eds. *Proceedings of the 6th Conference on Parallel Problem Solving from Nature*, No. 1917 in Lecture Notes in Computer Science. Springer, Berlin, Heidelberg, New York, 2000

338. M. Schoenauer, S. Xanthakis. Constrained GA optimisation. In: Forrest [158], pp. 573–580

339. S. Schulenburg, P. Ross. Strength and money: An LCS approach to increasing returns. In: Lanzi et al. [247], pp. 114–137

340. H.-P. Schwefel. *Numerische Optimierung von Computer-Modellen mittels der Evolutionsstrategie*, Vol. 26 of *ISR*. Birkhaeuser, Basel/Stuttgart, 1977

341. H.-P. Schwefel. *Numerical Optimisation of Computer Models*. Wiley, New York, 1981

342. H.-P. Schwefel. *Evolution and Optimum Seeking*. Wiley, New York, 1995

343. H.-P. Schwefel, R. Männer, Eds. *Proceedings of the 1st Conference on Parallel Problem Solving from Nature*, No. 496 in Lecture Notes in Computer Science. Springer, Berlin, Heidelberg, New York, 1991

344. A.V. Sebald, L.J. Fogel, Eds. *Proceedings of the 3rd Annual Conference on Evolutionary Programming*. World Scientific, 1994

345. J. Shapiro, A. Prügel-Bennet. Maximum entropy analysis of genetic algorithm operators. In: T.C. Fogarty, Ed., *Evolutionary Computing: Proceedings of the 1995 AISB Workshop*. Springer, Berlin, Heidelberg, New York, 1995

346. A.E. Smith, D.W. Coit. Penalty functions. In: Bäck et al. [28], Chap. 7, pp. 41–48

347. A.E. Smith, D.M. Tate. Genetic optimisation using a penalty function. In: Forrest [158], pp. 499–505

348. J.E. Smith. *Self Adaptation in Evolutionary Algorithms*. PhD thesis, University of the West of England, Bristol, UK, 1998

349. J.E. Smith. Modelling GAs with self-adaptive mutation rates. In: Spector et al. [381], pp. 599–606

350. J.E. Smith. The co-evolution of memetic algorithms for protein structure prediction. In: D. Corne, G. Fogel, W. Hart, J. Knowles, N. Krasnogor, . Roy, J. Smith, A. Tiwari, Eds., *Advances in Nature-Inspired Computation: The PPSN VII Workshops*, Reading, UK, 2002. PEDAL (Parallel, Emergent & Distributed Architectures Lab), University of Reading, pp. 14–15

351. J.E. Smith. Co-evolution of memetic algorithms: Initial investigations. In: Guervos et al. [187], pp. 537–548

352. J.E. Smith. Genetic algorithms. In: P.M. Pardalos, H.E. Romeijn, Eds., *Handbook of Global Optimization Volume 2*. Kluwer Academic Publishers, Boston, 2002, pp. 275–362

353. J.E. Smith. On appropriate adaptation levels for the learning of gene linkage. *J. Genetic Programming and Evolvable Machines*, 3:2 pp.129–155, 2002

354. J.E. Smith. Parameter perturbation mechanisms in binary coded gas with self-adaptive mutation. In: Rowe, Poli, DeJong, Cotta, Eds., *Foundations of Genetic Algorithms 7*. Morgan Kaufmann, San Francisco, 2003, pp. 329–346

355. J.E. Smith, M. Bartley, T.C. Fogarty. Microprocessor design verification by two-phase evolution of variable length tests. In ICEC-97 [213], pp. 453–458

356. J.E. Smith, T.C. Fogarty. An adaptive poly-parental recombination strategy. In: T.C. Fogarty, Ed., *Evolutionary Computing 2*. Springer, Berlin, Heidelberg, New York, 1995, pp. 48–61

357. J.E. Smith, T.C. Fogarty. Adaptively parameterised evolutionary systems: Self adaptive recombination and mutation in a genetic algorithm. In: Voigt et al. [410], pp. 441–450

358. J.E. Smith, T.C. Fogarty. Evolving software test data - GAs learn self expression. In: T.C. Fogarty, Ed., *Evolutionary Computing*, No. 1143 in Lecture Notes in Computer Science, 1996, pp. 137–146

359. J.E. Smith, T.C. Fogarty. Recombination strategy adaptation via evolution of gene linkage. In ICEC-96 [212], pp. 826–831

360. J.E. Smith, T.C. Fogarty. Self adaptation of mutation rates in a steady state genetic algorithm. In ICEC-96 [212], pp. 318–323

361. J.E. Smith, T.C. Fogarty. Operator and parameter adaptation in genetic algorithms. *Soft Computing*, 1:2 pp.81–87, 1997

362. J.E. Smith, T.C. Fogarty, I.R. Johnson. Genetic feature selection for clustering and classification. In: *Proceedings of the IEE Colloquium on Genetic Algorithms in Image Processing and Vision*, Vol. IEE Digest 1994/193, 1994

363. J.E. Smith, F. Vavak. Replacement strategies in steady state genetic algorithms: dynamic environments. *J. Computing and Information Technology*, 7:1 pp.49–60, 1999

364. J.E. Smith, F. Vavak. Replacement strategies in steady state genetic algorithms: static environments. In: Banzhaf, Reeves [39], pp. 219–234

365. R.E. Smith, C. Bonacina, P. Kearney, W. Merlat. Embodiment of evolutionary computation in general agents. *Evolutionary Computation*, 8:4 pp.475–493, 2001

366. R.E. Smith, H. Brown Cribbs. Is a Learning Classifier System a Type of Neural Network? *Evolutionary Computation*, 2:1 pp.19–36, 1994

367. R.E. Smith, D.E. Goldberg. Diploidy and dominance in artificial genetic search. *Complex Systems*, 6 pp.251–285, 1992

368. R.E. Smith, J.E. Smith. An examination of tuneable, random search landscapes. In: Banzhaf, Reeves [39], pp. 165–181

369. R.E. Smith, J.E. Smith. New methods for tunable, random landscapes. In: Martin, Spears [261], pp. 47–67

370. R.E. Smith, E. Smuda. Adaptively resizing populations: Algorithm, analysis and first results. *Complex Systems*, 9:1 pp.47–72, 1995

371. C. Soddu. Recognizability of the idea: the evolutionary process of argenia. In: Bentley, Corne [47], pp. 109–127

372. T. Soule, J.A. Foster. Effects of code growth and parsimony pressure on populations in genetic programming. *Evolutionary Computation*, 6:4 pp.293–309, Winter 1998

373. T. Soule, J.A. Foster, J. Dickinson. Code growth in genetic programming. In: Koza et al. [235], pp. 215–223

374. W.M. Spears. Crossover or mutation. In: Whitley [420], pp. 220–237

375. W.M. Spears. Simple subpopulation schemes. In: Sebald, Fogel [344], pp. 296–307

376. W.M. Spears. Adapting crossover in evolutionary algorithms. In: McDonnell et al. [268], pp. 367–384

377. W.M. Spears. *Evolutionary Algorithms: the role of mutation and recombination.* Springer, Berlin, Heidelberg, New York, 2000

378. W.M. Spears, K.A. De Jong. An analysis of multi point crossover. In: Rawlins [316], pp. 301–315

379. W.M. Spears, K.A. De Jong. On the virtues of parameterized uniform crossover. In: Belew, Booker [43], pp. 230–237

380. W.M. Spears, K.A. De Jong. Dining with GAs: Operator lunch theorems. In: Banzhaf, Reeves [39], pp. 85–101

381. L. Spector, E. Goodman, A. Wu, W.B. Langdon, H.-M. Voigt, M. Gen, S. Sen, M. Dorigo, S. Pezeshk, M. Garzon, E. Burke, Eds. *Proceedings of the Genetic and Evolutionary Computation Conference (GECCO-2001)*. Morgan Kaufmann, San Francisco, 2001

382. L. Spector, W.B. Langdon, U.-M. O'Reilly, P.J. Angeline, Eds. *Advances in Genetic Programming 3*. MIT Press, Cambridge, MA, 1999

383. N. Srinivas, K. Deb. Multiobjective optimization using nondominated sorting in genetic algorithms. *Evolutionary Computation*, 2:3 pp.221–248, Fall 1994

384. C.R. Stephens, I. Garcia Olmedo, J. Moro Vargas, H. Waelbroeck. Self-adaptation in evolving systems. *Artificial life*, 4 pp.183–201, 1998

385. C.R. Stephens, H. Waelbroeck. Schemata evolution and building blocks. *Evolutionary Computation*, 7:2 pp.109–124, 1999

386. C. Stone, L. Bull. For real! XCS with continuous-valued inputs. *Evolutionary Computation*, p. in press, 2003

387. J.C.W. Sullivan. *An Evolutionary Computing Approach to Motor Learning with an Application to Robot Manipulators.* PhD thesis, University of the West of England, 2001
388. P. Surry, N. Radcliffe. Innoculation to initialise evolutionary search. In: T.C.Fogarty, Ed., *Evolutionary Computing: Proceedings of the 1996 AISB Workshop.* Springer, Berlin, Heidelberg, New York, 1996, pp. 269–285
389. G. Syswerda. Uniform crossover in genetic algorithms. In: Schaffer [333], pp. 2–9
390. G. Syswerda. Schedule optimisation using genetic algorithms. In: Davis [92], pp. 332–349
391. G. Syswerda. A study of reproduction in generational and steady state genetic algorithms. In: Rawlins [316], pp. 94–101
392. R. Tanese. Parallel genetic algorithm for a hypercube. In: Grefenstette [182], pp. 177–183
393. D.M. Tate, A.E. Smith. Unequal area facility layout using genetic search. *IIE transactions*, 27 pp.465–472, 1995
394. A. Teller. The evolution of mental models. In: Kinnear [226], pp. 199–219
395. L. Tesfatsion. Preferential partner selection in evolutionary labor markets: A study in agent-based computational economics. In: Porto et al. [307], pp. 15–24
396. L. Tesfatsion. Guest editorial: Agent-based modeling of evolutionary economic systems. *IEEE Transactions on Evolutionary Computing*, 5 pp.437–441, October 2001
397. S.R. Thangiah, R. Vinayagamoorty, A.V. Gubbi. Vehicle routing and time deadlines using genetic and local algorithms. In: Forrest [158], pp. 506–515
398. D. Thierens, D.E. Goldberg. Mixing in genetic algorithms. In: Forrest [158], pp. 38–45
399. S. Tsutsui. Multi-parent recombination in genetic algorithms with search space boundary extension by mirroring. In: Eiben et al. [116], pp. 428–437
400. P.D. Turney. How to shift bias: lessons from the Baldwin effect. *Evolutionary Computation*, 4:3 pp.271–295, 1996
401. R. Unger, J. Moult. A genetic algorithm for 3D protein folding simulations. In: Forrest [158], pp. 581–588
402. J.I. van Hemert, A.E. Eiben. Mondriaan art by evolution. In: E. Postma, M. Gyssens, Eds., *Proceedings of the Eleventh Belgium/Netherlands Conference on Artificial Intelligence (BNAIC'99)*, 1999, pp. 291–292
403. C.H.M. van Kemenade. Explicit filtering of building blocks for genetic algorithms. In: Voigt et al. [410], pp. 494–503
404. E. van Nimwegen, J.P. Crutchfield, M. Mitchell. Statistical dynamics of the Royal Road genetic algorithm. *Theoretical Computer Science*, 229 pp.41–102, 1999
405. F.J. Varela, P. Bourgine, Eds. *Toward a Practice of Autonomous Systems: Proceedings of the 1st European Conference on Artificial Life.* MIT Press, Cambridge, MA, 1992
406. F. Vavak, T.C. Fogarty. A comparative study of steady state and generational genetic algorithms for use in nonstationary environments. In: T.C. Fogarty, Ed., *Evolutionary Computing.* Springer, Berlin, Heidelberg, New York, 1996, pp. 297–304
407. F. Vavak, T.C. Fogarty. Comparison of steady state and generational genetic algorithms for use in nonstationary environments. In ICEC-96 [212], pp. 192–195

408. F. Vavak, T.C. Fogarty, K. Jukes. A genetic algorithm with variable range of local search for tracking changing environments. In: Voigt et al. [410], pp. 376–385

409. F. Vavak, K. Jukes, T.C. Fogarty. Adaptive combustion balancing in multiple burner boiler using a genetic algorithm with variable range of local search. In: Bäck [23], pp. 719–726

410. H.-M. Voigt, W. Ebeling, I. Rechenberg, H.-P. Schwefel, Eds. *Proceedings of the 4th Conference on Parallel Problem Solving from Nature*, No. 1141 in Lecture Notes in Computer Science. Springer, Berlin, Heidelberg, New York, 1996

411. M.D. Vose. *The Simple Genetic Algorithm*. MIT Press, Cambridge, MA, 1999

412. M.D. Vose, G.E. Liepins. Punctuated equilibria in genetic search. *Complex Systems*, 5:1 pp.31, 1991

413. C. Watkins. *Learning from delayed rewards*. PhD thesis, University of Cambridge, 1989

414. P.M. White, C.C. Pettey. Double selection vs. single selection in diffusion model GAs. In: Bäck [23], pp. 174–180

415. D. Whitley. Permutations. In: Bäck et al. [27], Chap. 33.3, pp. 274–284

416. D. Whitley, D. Goldberg, E. Cantu-Paz, L. Spector, I. Parmee, H.-G. Beyer, Eds. *Proceedings of the Genetic and Evolutionary Computation Conference (GECCO-2000)*. Morgan Kaufmann, San Francisco, 2000

417. D. Whitley, K. Mathias, S. Rana, J. Dzubera. Building better test functions. In: Eshelman [137], pp. 239–246

418. L.D. Whitley. Fundamental principles of deception in genetic search. In: Rawlins [316], pp. 221–241

419. L.D. Whitley. Cellular genetic algorithms. In: Forrest [158], pp. 658–658

420. L.D. Whitley, Ed. *Foundations of Genetic Algorithms - 2*. Morgan Kaufmann, San Francisco, 1993

421. L.D. Whitley, S. Gordon, K.E. Mathias. Lamarkian evolution, the Baldwin effect, and function optimisation. In: Davidor et al. [90], pp. 6–15

422. L.D. Whitley, F. Gruau. Adding learning to the cellular development of neural networks: evolution and the Baldwin effect. *Evolutionary Computation*, 1 pp.213–233, 1993

423. L.D. Whitley, J. Kauth. Genitor: A different genetic algorithm. In: *Proceedings of the Rocky Mountain Conference on Artificial Intelligence*, 1988, pp. 118–130

424. L.D. Whitley, K.E. Mathias, P. Fitzhorn. Delta coding: An iterative search strategy for genetic algorithms,. In: Belew, Booker [43], pp. 77–84

425. L.D. Whitley, M.D. Vose, Eds. *Foundations of Genetic Algorithms 3*. Morgan Kaufmann, San Francisco, 1995

426. S.W. Wilson. ZCS: A zeroth level classifier system. *Evolutionary Computation*, 2:1 pp.1–18, 1994

427. S.W. Wilson. Classifier fitness based on accuracy. *Evolutionary Computation*, 3:2 pp.149–175, 1995

428. S.W. Wilson. Generalization in the XCS classifier system. In: Koza et al. [232], pp. 665–674

429. S.W. Wilson. Get Real! XCS with Continuous-Valued Inputs. In: P.L. Lanzi, W. Stolzmann, S.W. Wilson, Eds., *Learning Classifier Systems. From Foundations to Applications*, Vol. 1813 of *LNAI*. Springer, Berlin, Heidelberg, New York, 2000, pp. 209–219

430. D.H. Wolpert, W.G. Macready. No Free Lunch theorems for optimisation. *IEEE Transactions on Evolutionary Computation*, 1:1 pp.67–82, 1997

431. S. Wright. The roles of mutation, inbreeding, crossbreeding, and selection in evolution. In: *Proc. of 6th Int. Congr. on Genetics*, Vol. 1. Ithaca, NY, 1932, pp. 356–366

432. X. Yao. Evolving artificial neural networks. *Proceedings of the IEEE*, 87:9 pp.1423–1447, 1999

433. X. Yao. Evolutionary computation: A gentle introduction. In: Sarker et al. [331], Chap. 2, pp. 27–53

434. X. Yao, Y. Liu. Fast evolutionary programming. In: Fogel et al. [154]

435. X. Yao, Y. Liu, K.-H. Liang, G. Lin. Fast evolutionary algorithms. In: Ghosh, Tsutsui [167], pp. 45–94

436. X. Yao, Y. Liu, G. Lin. Evolutionary programming made faster. *IEEE Transactions on Evolutionary Computing*, 3:2 pp.82–102, 1999

437. J. Zar. *Biostatistical Analysis*. Prentice Hall, 4th edn., 1999

438. B. Zhang, H. Mühlenbeim. Balancing accuracy and parsimony in genetic programming. *Evolutionary Computing*, 3:3 pp.17–38, 1995

439. E. Zitzler, M. Laumanns, L. Thiele. SPEA2: Improving the strength pareto evolutionary algorithm for multiobjective optimization. In: K.C. Giannakoglou, D.T.. Tsahalis, J. Périaux, K.D. Papailiou, T.C. Fogarty, Eds., *Evolutionary Methods for Design Optimization and Control with Applications to Industrial Problems*, Athens, Greece, 2001. International Center for Numerical Methods in Engineering (Cmine), pp. 95–100

Index

Natural Computing Series

W.M. Spears: Evolutionary Algorithms. The Role of Mutation and Recombination. XIV, 222 pages, 55 figs., 23 tables. 2000

H.-G. Beyer: The Theory of Evolution Strategies. XIX, 380 pages, 52 figs., 9 tables. 2001

L. Kallel, B. Naudts, A. Rogers (Eds.): Theoretical Aspects of Evolutionary Computing. X, 497 pages. 2001

M. Hirvensalo: Quantum Computing. 2nd ed., XI, 190 pages. 2004 (first edition published in the series)

G. Păun: Membrane Computing. An Introduction. XI, 429 pages, 37 figs., 5 tables. 2002

A.A. Freitas: Data Mining and Knowledge Discovery with Evolutionary Algorithms. XIV, 264 pages, 74 figs., 10 tables. 2002

H.-P. Schwefel, I. Wegener, K. Weinert (Eds.): Advances in Computational Intelligence. VIII, 325 pages. 2003

A. Ghosh, S. Tsutsui (Eds.): Advances in Evolutionary Computing. XVI, 1006 pages. 2003

L.F. Landweber, E. Winfree (Eds.): Evolution as Computation. DIMACS Workshop, Princeton, January 1999. XV, 332 pages. 2002

M. Amos: Theoretical and Experimental DNA Computation. Approx. 200 pages. 2004

A.E. Eiben, J.E. Smith: Introduction to Evolutionary Computing. XV, 299 pages. 2003

G. Ciobanu (Ed.): Modelling in Molecular Biology. Approx. 300 pages. 2004

A. Ehrenfeucht, T. Harju, I. Petre, D.M. Prescott, G. Rozenberg: Computation in Living Cells. Approx. 175 pages. 2004

R. Paton, H. Bolouri, M. Holcombe, J. H. Parish, R. Tateson (Eds.): Computation in Cells and Tissues. Approx. 350 pages. 2004

L. Sekanina: From Theory to Hardware Implementations. XVI, 194 pages. 2004

Printing: Saladruck Berlin
Binding: Stürtz AG, Würzburg